Teach Yourself
VISUALLY™
Digital Video

by Jinjer and Richard Simon

Visual

From

maranGraphics®

&

Wiley Publishing, Inc.

Teach Yourself VISUALLY™ Digital Video

Published by
Wiley Publishing, Inc.
909 Third Avenue
New York, NY 10022
Published simultaneously in Canada

maranGraphics, Inc.
5755 Coopers Avenue
Mississauga, Ontario, Canada
L4Z 1R9

Library of Congress Control Number: 2002108090

ISBN: 0-7645-3688-5

Manufactured in the United States of America

10 9 8 7 6 5 4 3 2 1

1K/RZ/QY/QS/IN

Trademark Acknowledgments

Important Numbers

For U.S. corporate orders, please call maranGraphics at 800-469-6616 or fax 905-890-9434.

For general information on our other products and services or to obtain technical support please contact our Customer Care Department within the U.S. at 800-762-2974, outside the U.S. at 317-572-3993 or fax 317-572-4002.

Permissions

Wiley Publishing, Inc. is a trademark of Wiley Publishing, Inc.

U.S. Corporate Sales	U.S. Trade Sales
Contact maranGraphics at (800) 469-6616 or Fax (905) 890-9434.	Contact Wiley at (800) 762-2974 or Fax (317) 572-4002.

Some comments from our readers...

"I have to praise you and your company on the fine products you turn out. I have twelve of the *Teach Yourself VISUALLY* and *Simplified* books in my house. They were instrumental in helping me pass a difficult computer course. Thank you for creating books that are easy to follow."

—*Gordon Justin (Brielle, NJ)*

"I commend your efforts and your success. I teach in an outreach program for the Dr. Eugene Clark Library in Lockhart, TX. Your *Teach Yourself VISUALLY* books are incredible and I use them in my computer classes. All my students love them!"

—*Michele Schalin (Lockhart, TX)*

"Thank you so much for helping people like me learn about computers. The Maran family is just what the doctor ordered. Thank you, thank you, thank you."

—*Carol Moten (New Kensington, PA)*

"I would like to take this time to compliment maranGraphics on creating such great books. Thank you for making it clear. Keep up the good work."

—*Kirk Santoro (Burbank, CA)*

"I write to extend my thanks and appreciation for your books. They are clear, easy to follow, and straight to the point. Keep up the good work!"

—*Seward Kollie (Dakar, Senegal)*

"What fantastic teaching books you have produced! Congratulations to you and your staff. You deserve the Nobel prize in Education in the Software category. Thanks for helping me to understand computers."

—*Bruno Tonon (Melbourne, Australia)*

"Over time, I have bought a number of your 'Read Less-Learn More' books. For me, they are THE way to learn anything easily."

—*José A. Mazón (Cuba, NY)*

"I was introduced to maranGraphics about four years ago and YOU ARE THE GREATEST THING THAT EVER HAPPENED TO INTRODUCTORY COMPUTER BOOKS!"

—*Glenn Nettleton (Huntsville, AL)*

"Compliments To The Chef!! Your books are extraordinary! Or, simply put, Extra-Ordinary, meaning way above the rest! THANK YOU THANK YOU THANK YOU! for creating these."

—*Christine J. Manfrin (Castle Rock, CO)*

"I'm a grandma who was pushed by an 11-year-old grandson to join the computer age. I found myself hopelessly confused and frustrated until I discovered the Visual series. I'm no expert by any means now, but I'm a lot further along than I would have been otherwise. Thank you!"

—*Carol Louthain (Logansport, IN)*

"Thank you, thank you, thank you....for making it so easy for me to break into this high-tech world. I now own four of your books. I recommend them to anyone who is a beginner like myself. Now....if you could just do one for programming VCR's, it would make my day!"

—*Gay O'Donnell (Calgary, Alberta, Canada)*

"You're marvelous! I am greatly in your debt."

—*Patrick Baird (Lacey, WA)*

**maranGraphics is a family-run business
located near Toronto, Canada.**

At **maranGraphics**, we believe in producing great computer books — one book at a time.

maranGraphics has been producing high-technology products for over 25 years, which enables us to offer the computer book community a unique communication process.

Our computer books use an integrated communication process, which is very different from the approach used in other computer books. Each spread is, in essence, a flow chart — the text and screen shots are totally incorporated into the layout of the spread.

Introductory text and helpful tips complete the learning experience.

maranGraphics' approach encourages the left and right sides of the brain to work together — resulting in faster orientation and greater memory retention.

Above all, we are very proud of the handcrafted nature of our books. Our carefully-chosen writers are experts in their fields, and spend countless hours researching and organizing the content for each topic. Our artists rebuild every screen shot to provide the best clarity possible, making our

screen shots the most precise and easiest to read in the industry. We strive for perfection, and believe that the time spent handcrafting each element results in the best computer books money can buy.

Thank you for purchasing this book. We hope you enjoy it!

Sincerely,

Robert Maran
President
maranGraphics
Rob@maran.com
www.maran.com

CREDITS

Acquisitions, Editorial, and Media Development

Project Editor
Maureen Spears

Acquisitions Editor
Jen Dorsey

Product Development Supervisor
Lindsay Sandman

Copy Editor
Jill Mazurczyk

Technical Editor
Dennis Short

Editorial Manager
Rev Mengle

Permissions Editor
Laura Moss

Manufacturing
Allan Conley, Linda Cook,
Paul Gilchrist, Jennifer Guynn

Special Help
Sherry Kinkoph

Production

Book Design
maranGraphics®

Production Coordinator
Nancee Reeves

Layout
Melanie DesJardins, LeAndra Johnson,
Kristin McMullan

Screen Artists
Mark Harris, Jill A. Proll

Illustrators
Ronda David-Burroughs, David E. Gregory,
Sean Johannesen, Russ Marini, Steven Schaerer

Proofreader
Laura L. Bowman

Quality Control
Laura Albert, John Bitter, Susan Moritz

Indexer
Infodex Indexing Services, Inc.

ACKNOWLEDGMENTS

General and Administrative

Wiley Technology Publishing Group: Richard Swadley, Vice President and Executive Group Publisher; Bob Ipsen, Vice President and Executive Publisher; Barry Pruett, Vice President and Publisher; Joseph Wikert, Vice President and Publisher; Mary Bednarek, Editorial Director; Mary C. Corder, Editorial Director; Andy Cummings, Editorial Director.

Wiley Production for Branded Press: Debbie Stailey, Production Director

ABOUT THE AUTHORS

Jinjer Simon has been actively involved in the computer industry for the past 17 years. Her involvement includes programming, providing software technical support, training end-users, developing written and online user documentation, creating software tutorials, and developing Web sites. She is the author of several computer books, including *Windows CE For Dummies*, *Windows CE 2 For Dummies*, and *Excel Programming: Your visual blueprint for creating interactive spreadsheets*. She currently works as a consultant for MillenniSoft, Inc., providing Web site development, writing online documentation, and creating video productions for distribution both over the Internet and on DVD.

Richard Simon has been a pioneer in new technology since 1985 when he started a consulting company to develop PC solutions for businesses. As an early Windows developer, Richard has been on the leading edge of new technologies, including client/server, Internet, and .NET. Richard is a former CTO of over eight years for a software development company that developed and marketed applications to Fortune 100 companies. He currently is the Co-Founder and CEO of MillenniSoft, Inc., which provides consulting services ranging from computer programming to video production. He is also an accomplished author of several Windows programming books, including *Windows 98 Programming For Dummies* and *Windows 2000 Programming For Dummies*. Richard is an avid photographer and videographer.

Jinjer and Richard live in Coppell, Texas with their two children, and two active Jack Russell Terriers.

AUTHORS' ACKNOWLEDGMENTS

Upon completion of a book, authors are given the challenge of acknowledging the efforts of all those involved in the project. Although as authors we have the task of providing the appropriate text, screen shots, and images for the book, there is an enormous amount of work that must be completed by the production team at Wiley Publishing to make sure the book elements all come together, especially with this type of book. Unfortunately, it is nearly impossible to recognize everyone's efforts individually. Therefore, we want to acknowledge the efforts of all individuals involved in the completion of the book.

We want to thank Jen Dorsey, the acquisitions editor, for getting this project going and dealing with all the scheduling and permission issues along the way. This book would not have been completed without the dedicated efforts of Maureen Spears, the project editor.

Her efforts to make sure the book conveyed the information in the best format for the reader did not go unnoticed. We appreciate her patience and hard work on this project. Working with Maureen, the copy editor, Jill Mazurczyk, did a fantastic job of making sure the text was accurate. The technical editor, Dennis Short, provided some excellent input on the book. His knowledge of the industry provided an invaluable resource for the development of this book. Thanks to Sherry Kinkoph for her efforts to help us refine the flow of some chapters.

A project of this type requires a special thank you to the graphics and production staff at Wiley Publishing for their effort to lay out the book and develop the necessary graphic images. The graphics developed for the book are excellent.

We would like to thank the many individuals that provided information and use of different video equipment. Specifically, Cooter's Village Camera in Highland Park, and Tweeter Home Entertainment for allowing us to take photos of different video camera equipment.

Finally we want to thank our agent Neil Salkind at Studio B for his help with the contract issues related to this project.

TABLE OF CONTENTS

Chapter 1

INTRODUCING DIGITAL VIDEO

Chapter 2

EXPLORING DIGITAL VIDEO EQUIPMENT

Chapter 3

WORKING WITH LIGHTING

Chapter 4

WORKING WITH SOUND

Chapter 5

PLAN YOUR VIDEO

Chapter 6

SHOOTING DIGITAL VIDEO

TABLE OF CONTENTS

EDITING SOLUTIONS AND EQUIPMENT

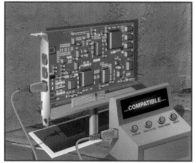

TRANSFERRING FOOTAGE TO A COMPUTER

TIMELINE TASKS

Chapter 10 ADDING AND SYNCHRONIZING SOUND

TABLE OF CONTENTS

Chapter 11 — ADDING TRANSITIONS

Chapter 12 — ADDING SPECIAL EFFECTS

Chapter 13

Chapter 14

Chapter 15

HOW TO USE THIS TEACH YOURSELF VISUALLY BOOK

Teach Yourself VISUALLY Digital Video contains straightforward sections, which you can use to learn the basics of shooting, editing, and storing your digital video. This book is designed to help a reader receive quick access to any area of question. You can simply look up a subject within the Table of Contents or Index and go immediately to the section of concern. A *section* is a self-contained task that walks you through a computer operation step-by-step. That is, with rare exception, all the information you need regarding an area of interest is contained within a section.

The General Organization of This Book

The first six chapters of this book contain fully illustrated narratives that tell you how to sucessfully film your digital video.

The second nine chapters contain sections that help you learn how to edit and publish your video using four different editing programs: Adobe Premiere, Apple Final Cut Pro, Apple iMovie, and Windows Movie Maker. Each section contains an introduction, a set of screen shots, and, if the task goes beyond 1 page, a set of tips. The introduction tells why you want to perform the task, the advantages and disadvantages of performing the task, and references to other related tasks in the book. The screens, located on the bottom half of each page, show a series of steps that you must complete to perform a given section. The tip portion of the section gives you an opportunity to further understand the task at hand, to learn about related tasks in other areas of the book, or to apply alternative methods.

The Organization of Each Chapter

Teach Yourself VISUALLY Digital Video has 15 chapters. Chapter 1 explains all the practical things you can do with digital video. Chapter 2 discusses the essential features you need to consider when purchasing a camera. Chapters 3 and 4 discuss the various properties of light and sound and explain how to use them to your advantage when filming your video. In Chapter 5, you learn how to organize yourself before you shoot by designing a storyboard. You learn how to shoot this storyboard, edit what you shoot, and transfer your footage to a computer in Chapters 6, 7, and 8. You learn how to work with the timelines in the various editing packages in Chapter 9, while 10 shows you how to use these packages to edit and enhance the existing sound on your video. Chapters 11, 12, and 13 illustrate how to add special effects, transitions, titles, and animation to your footage. Chapters 14 and 15 discuss what to do with your final footage, including how to publish it and store it on a Video Disc.

Who This Book Is For

This book is highly recommended for the visual learner who wants to learn the basics of Digital Video, and who may or may not have prior experience with a computer.

What You Need to Use This Book

To perform the tasks in this book, you need a computer installed with one of the following:

- Adobe Premiere
- Final Cut Pro
- iMovie
- Windows Movie Maker

Final Cut Pro and iMovie require the installment of OS X. Windows Movie Maker requires the installation of Windows XP. Although this book illustrates the use of Adobe Premiere with Windows XP, Adobe also provides a version for use on OS X.

Mac Requirements

- PowerPC® processor: G3, G4, or G4 dual
- Mac OS system software version 9.1, 9.2, or Mac OS X version 10.1

Windows Requirements

- Intel® Pentium® II, III, or 4 processor Microsoft® Windows® 98, Windows 98 Special Edition, Windows Millennium Edition, Windows

2000 with Service Pack 2, or Windows XP (recommended upgrade procedure)

- 128MB of RAM
- 180MB of available hard-disk space
- For Adobe® PostScript® printers: Adobe PostScript Level 2 or Adobe PostScript 3™

Conventions When Using the Mouse

This book uses the following conventions to describe the actions you perform when using the mouse:

Click

Press and release the left mouse button. You use a click to select an item on the screen.

Double-click

Quickly press and release the left mouse button twice. You double-click to open a document or start a program.

Right-click

Press and release the right mouse button. You use a right-click to display a shortcut menu, a list of commands specifically related to the selected item.

Click and Drag, and Release the Mouse

Position the mouse pointer over an item on the screen and then press and hold down the left mouse button. Still holding down the button, move the mouse to where you want to place the item and then release the button. Click and dragging makes it easy to move an item to a new location.

The Conventions in This Book

A number of typographic and layout styles have been used throughout Microsoft Office XP to distinguish different types of information.

Bold

Indicates text, or text buttons, that you must click in a menu or dialog box to complete a task.

Italics

Indicates a new term being introduced.

Numbered Steps

Indicate that you must perform these steps in order to successfully perform the task.

Bulleted Steps

Give you alternative methods, explain various options, or present what a program will do in response to the numbered steps.

Notes

Give you additional information to help you complete a task. The purpose of a note, which appears in italics, is threefold: It can explain special conditions that may occur during the course of the task, warn you of potentially dangerous situations, or refer you to tasks in the same, or a different, chapter. References to tasks within the chapter are indicated by the phrase "*See the section...*" followed by the name of the section. References to other chapters are indicated by "*See Chapter...*" followed by the chapter number.

Icons

Icons in the steps indicate a button that you must click to execute a command.

Operating System Difference

If you are using a Mac, this book assumes that you have OS X installed on your computer. If you have a PC, this book assumes that you have Windows XP installed on your computer. Other OS and Windows versions may give different results than those presented in this book.

Also, although Adobe Premiere is available for use on both the Mac and PC, this book only illustrates its use on a PC. If you are using Adobe Premiere on a Mac, you will find the same features discussed in this book, however to access a specific feature, you may find slight variations in the commands.

CHAPTER 1

Introducing Digital Video

Are you curious about digital video? This chapter provides some basic information that introduces you to the world of digital video.

LUNDERSTANDING DIGITAL VIDEO

Fast becoming a popular technology, you can use digital video to create your own video productions. You can transfer the digitally recorded data to your office or home computer and edit the footage using digital editing software. You can also save the finished project to a variety of user-friendly formats so that others can view your videos.

My Summer Vacation 2002

What Is Digital Video?

Digital video is video you record with a digital camcorder or video you capture into a computer. Until recently, video was recorded mainly in analog format. With improvements to computer chip technologies, users can now record high-quality video in digital format. Both analog and digital video capture and store images and audio, but they store the information in one of two different formats.

Analog Video Recording

Prior to digital video, all camcorders recorded video in analog format onto tape storage media. Traditional analog video stores a recording of light and sound fluctuations. Analog video equipment records even the slightest changes in light, color, and sound as fluctuations in electronic signals. The process closely resembles the method your own eyes and ears use to process information. When you hear a sound, your ears process it as a change in the volume. Your eyes process images as changes in color and light.

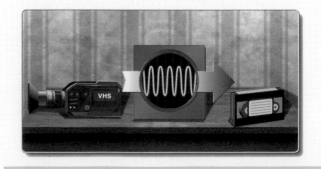

Analog Video Disadvantages

Fluctuations in analog signals greatly influence analog recordings. When copying analog video, the recording equipment *re-samples* the signal. Re-sampling is the process in which the equipment plays the original footage and captures a copy of the fluctuations in light and sound. Each recorded copy is potentially changed by the slightest variation in the equipment or storage media, resulting in a less than exact reproduction of the original. In addition, tape storage media can stretch, warp, and deteriorate over time.

Digital Video Advantages

A primary advantage of digital video stems from the binary format, which you can copy multiple times without loss of quality. When you copy digital video, you create an exact copy of the original binary image no matter how many times you copy or re-play the footage. The binary format also allows for *compression*. Compression is the process in which a program reduces your footage in size, allowing you to store more images in the same space. Digital video has many different compression schemes including the DV format, which video cameras use to store footage.

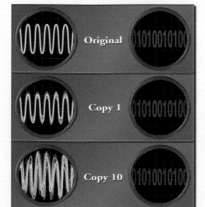

Digital Video Recording

Digital video stores all images in a *binary format*, which uses a series of 1's and 0's to represent each image and associated sounds. When a digital video camera receives sound and video images, it creates an exact record of the data in binary format. This process occurs for each frame of footage with each frame capturing a complete replication of the sound and image and storing it on the digital media. Digital video's high-quality images make it the most popular option in consumer-end video cameras today.

Video Formats and the Computer

The ability to view and edit digital video on the computer is one reason the technology is so popular. To edit video on your computer using video editing software, you must *digitize* the video. When you digitize your footage, you convert it to a binary format. Because computers read binary formats, you can easily transfer digital video to a home or office computer. To edit analog video, you must use a capture card to digitize the analog signals into binary format. For more about transferring video footage to your computer, see Chapters 7 and 8.

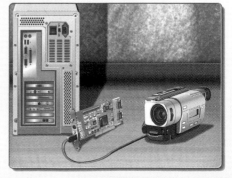

FORMATS AND USES OF DIGITAL VIDEO

As you begin to work with digital video, you should familiarize yourself with its many file types and uses. Digital video types vary based upon the source of the digital video. Digital video cameras typically only support one of two formats: DV or MPEG. When you use a computer, you encounter many different types of digital video.

Some formats allow you to *stream* your video — a process in which you transfer a continuous flow of data, which your computer can play as it downloads.

DIGITAL VIDEO FORMATS

Format	Use
Digital Video (DV)	A generic term that describes digital rather than analog format and the video data stored in a DV camcorder. You record data as a stream of digital information, which contains the video picture and sound.
Motion Pictures Expert Group (MPEG)	A format for smaller consumer cameras where space is a premium. You use MPEG for recording, editing, and transferring files. You use MPEG for creating DVD and Video CDs.
Audio Video Interleave (AVI)	A Microsoft multimedia file format, similar to MPEG and QuickTime, you use this for transferring and editing files. AVI provides several different compression and playback options that you can select to match the needs of your project.
Quicktime (MOV)	With this format, you can transfer, edit, and view files on a computer, both Mac and PC, or Web site. You can stream large digital video files with this format.
RealMedia (RM)	High compression, low-quality format; for viewing footage on a computer or Web site. Provided by Real Networks, this format allows you to *stream*, or play audio and video content in real-time as you download it from a Web site.
Windows Media Format (WMV)	High compression, low quality format; for viewing footage on a computer or Web site. You can stream digital video with this format.

DIGITAL VIDEO USES

You can use Digital Video in a wide variety of end products. The possibilities are endless.

Visual Media

Digital video cameras provide the ability to play back and review all of your digital video footage. Many cameras feature small LCD monitors for displaying the video, but you can also view the footage through the viewfinder. In addition, you can view video by copying it from the camera to a computer or playing it back on a television.

Web sites

You can spruce up a Web site by adding digital video. In a business environment, you can use digital video for items such as product demos, training courses, and how-to lessons. On a personal Web site, you can place footage for friends and relatives of special events such as vacations or holidays. You can also advertise with digital video using animated graphic images and live footage. Once created, you can distribute your digital advertising via the Internet either as e-mail messages or by placing ads on Web sites.

Video CDs and DVDs

Video CDs and DVDs provide great mediums for storing video footage, or for distributing your product. For example, you can create a digital video business card and distribute it to interested clients. Video CDs work well for videos that do not require high-quality. You can play video CDs on computers and most modern DVD players. DVDs, on the other hand, are a higher capacity medium that allows for the production of high-quality digital video. You may find that DVD creation more difficult than Video CDs in that it requires more expensive hardware; although, consumer-end products are becoming more readily available.

Presentations

You can use digital video to create personal or professional presentations for display on computer screens, overhead projectors, or televisions. You can also distribute presentations via the Internet or place them on video CDs or DVDs.

UNDERSTANDING DIGITAL VIDEO PRODUCTION

You can use the same elements of video production employed by film studios and production houses to create and produce your own video projects. If you are new to digital video, take a moment and familiarize yourself with the various aspects of video production.

Understanding Digital Video Equipment

Before you collect any digital footage, you need the right camera. You have many different options to consider when purchasing a digital video camera. The key is to select a camera in a preferred size with the features you desire. To select a digital video camera, see Chapter 2. By

using sound and lighting effectively, you can improve the quality of your digital video footage. See Chapter 3 for details on lighting and lighting equipment, and Chapter 4 for capturing sound effectively.

Create Digital Video Footage

After you select the appropriate equipment for recording the digital video and have a plan in place, you can start recording your footage. You want good, quality footage, especially if you plan to edit it into a finished format. Being mindful of issues such as locating your camera properly and controlling your camera's movement gives you more with which to work in later stages of your project. See Chapter 6 for pointers on recording your digital video footage.

Create a Storyboard

No matter what you record, you need to create a plan before you start capturing your footage. By *storyboarding*, before you record, you preplan the events, people, and places that you want to capture in your footage. See Chapter 5 for details about planning your video.

Wedding Storyboard

Scene 1 Scene 2

Scene 3 Scene 4

Editing Your Digital Video

You can copy your digital video footage to your computer and use one of the available software products to add special effects. You can also use recording hardware to edit your footage, although you may find this more difficult to handle than using a computer. See Chapter 7 for information about editing solutions for your digital video, and Chapter 8 for information on transferring the footage to your computer.

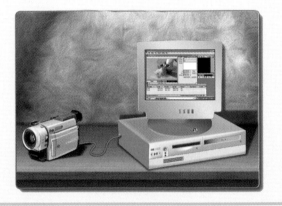

Refine Your Video's Sound

Sound plays an important role in the quality of your final video. Not only can you use the sound recorded in your footage, you can also add additional sounds and music to enhance your video. See Chapter 10 for details about incorporating sounds into your video.

Customize Your Video with Effects

Digital video software packages provide a multitude of different transitions and special effects that you can incorporate into your video. See Chapters 11 and 12 for details about transitions and special effects. You can also enhance your video with titles and animations. See Chapter 13 for details about adding titles and animation.

Finalize and Distribute Your Video

Once you complete your video, you can place it in a desired format. You can share the video over the Internet or store it on media for distribution. See Chapter 14 for details on distributing your video. See Chapter 15 for information on creation of Video discs.

CHAPTER 2

Exploring Digital Video Equipment

Do you plan to buy a new digital video camcorder? Or do you just want to know why some are more expensive than others? This chapter explores different types of digital video equipment and the features they provide.

DISTINGUISHING CAMERAS FROM CAMCORDERS

Although professionals use the terms *digital video camera* and *digital video camcorder* interchangeably, a definite distinction exists between the two. Before you begin shopping, make sure you understand the differences.

Digital Video Cameras

A *digital video camera* consists of a lens, an image chip that converts captured images to electrical signals, and circuits that allow the camera to display the electrical signals on a screen as well as circuits that convert the signals into digital format. Not to be confused with digital cameras, which capture still image photos, manufacturers design digital video cameras to capture video, although most digital video cameras also provide the ability to capture still images.

Web Cameras

Digital video cameras connect directly to your computer through a cable. The most popular form of digital video camera is a *Web camera*, a device you connect to your computer to send video over the Internet. You can use this device for videoconferencing or to chat face-to-face with family. You can also use this type of camera to capture video that you want to edit.

Web Camera Disadvantages

When you use a Web camera with the Internet, you may notice that the video appears more like a bunch of still images. This has to do with the lags in the transfer of data over the Internet. The higher the resolution, the slower and more choppy the video appears.

Digital Video Camcorders

A *digital video camcorder* is a digital video camera that includes a built-in video recorder. The recorder allows you to record footage and store it on a tape cassette or other storage media. Because the camcorder allows for immediate storage of whatever you record, you can take the camcorder anywhere. Digital video camcorders come in several sizes.

Digital-8

MiniDV

Types of Digital Video Camcorders

You have two main types of digital video camcorders available for your use today: MiniDV and Digital-8. Each type utilizes a different format for storing recorded video footage. You can learn more about these formats in the next section, "Digital Video Formats." Regardless of which format you choose, each camcorder type records footage and creates digital video you can view and edit on a computer.

DIGITAL VIDEO FORMATS

You can find many different makes and models of digital video camcorders on the market today. Before you begin shopping, make sure you understand the differences between the available storage formats. Different camcorders use different types of storage media for saving recorded video footage.

Camcorder Formats

The two most common types of digital video camcorders are MiniDV and Digital-8. MiniDV use DV format, the standard consumer digital format. MiniDV camcorders store recorded video onto mini tape cassettes. Digital-8 camcorders store recorded video on Hi8 tapes. Some camcorders also use memory cards and sticks, much like digital cameras, for storing still photos or small video clips.

Upcoming Formats

Just arriving in the marketplace, some exciting new types of digital video camcorders utilize built-in CD-RW, or Compact Disc-Rewritable, drives and DVD-RAM discs to store footage. You can also find some camcorders that store footage on MicroMV tape, an even smaller format than DV tape cassettes. Until the newer formats catch on, most digital video camcorders available use the DV or Digital-8 formats, also called *consumer formats*.

DV Format

A worldwide standard, DV, or *digital video*, uses a small cassette tape to record audio and video signals. The standard ensures that you can exchange the video signals between different digital equipment. DV cassette tapes can record 60 minutes of video recording in SP, standard play, mode and 90 minutes in LP, long play, mode.

Digital-8 Format

The Digital-8 format, developed by Sony, is a variation of the DV format that records video and audio signals on Hi8 analog cassette tapes. This allows you to use recorded video on equipment that plays 8mm and Hi8 tapes as well as copy footage from 8mm and Hi8 tapes into a digital format you can edit on the computer. Cheaper than the tapes that DV camcorders use, the digital video you record to Hi8 tapes consumes much more space than analog video. Hi8 tapes can hold 60 minutes of digital video or 120 minutes of analog video.

Sorting Digital from Analog

You can find numerous digital camcorders on the market, but be careful not to confuse digital video camcorders with analog camcorders. Analog camcorders include VHS, S-VHS, VHS-C, 8mm, and Hi8. Each uses a different tape cassette storage, also called *legacy formats*. To edit video recorded with an analog camcorder, you must first digitize the video into binary format the computer can read. You can do this if your computer has a capture board installed. See Chapter 7 to learn more.

SHOPPING FOR A DIGITAL VIDEO CAMCORDER

Digital video camcorders range in price, features, and sizes. To determine which camera is for you, start by determining what price range you can afford. Secondly, take time to think about the ways in which you want to use the device.

Prices

As the technology grows in popularity, prices for digital video camcorders continue to drop. You can find a good digital video camcorder for well under $1,000, or you can spend over $2,000 for a professional-quality camcorder. The video camcorder industry has coined a new phrase, *prosumer*, which classifies a camcorder as marketable to both professionals and consumers. You can find plenty of prosumer camcorders within the $2,000– $5,000 price range.

Analyze Your Uses

Before you do pick a camcorder, first consider how you want to use the device. If you plan on shooting vacation footage or family videos to share with the relatives, an inexpensive model may suit your needs. If you intend to hire yourself out to shoot wedding videos, or plan to make your own amateur movies, consider investing in a higher-end model. The Sony DCR-VX2000 and the Cannon GL1 are two good examples of prosumer camcorders.

Professional Uses

If you want television-quality video output, you should invest in a professional-level camcorder. If you select a camcorder for work, consider the output quality you want for your videos and how you intend to use them. A higher-end model gives you better output quality and features than a less expensive model. The Canon XL1S is a good example of a professional-level camcorder.

Weight

Another thing to consider when choosing a digital video camcorder is weight. Camcorders weigh as little as 1 1/2 pounds to over 6 pounds. If you intend to shoot footage over a long period of time, you may consider a camcorder's heavier weight a problem. If this is the case, you may need to invest in a good tripod. For more on tripods, see the section "Camcorder Accessories."

Size

How you grip and hold a camcorder can also become a factor in your selection. The most popular size sold today, palm-sized camcorders allow you to grip the main body of the camcorder in the palm of your hand. You may find larger sizes more cumbersome, but they also offer a greater array of features.

Features

Features vary from one camcorder to the next, and the more features you want, the more you can expect to pay. Make a list of what features you must have in a camera. At the very minimum, a good digital video camcorder includes the items on the table. The remaining sections in this chapter go into more detail about these and other features available among camcorders.

Minimum Digital Video Camcorder Requirements

Feature	Purpose
Lens	The optical component that collects and focuses incoming images much as the human eye does
Viewfinder	Shows your footage in black and white, or color
CCD chip or chips	Converts the images into a digital format
Input and output connectors	Connect the camcorder to a computer or television
Built-in microphone	Picks up your narrative during shooting
Power supply	Powers your camcorder
Video recorder transport	The controls for playing the footage like a VCR

PARTS OF A DIGITAL VIDEO CAMCORDER

As you shop and use a digital video camcorder, you must learn to identify the key parts of the device.

Viewfinder

All camcorders come with a *viewfinder*, much like a regular still image camera, that allows you to see what you are recording. The viewfinder is an eyepiece with a tiny video screen that shows the images in black and white, or color.

Power Supply

Most camcorders include a *battery* or *battery pack* as well as an *external power supply*. The battery clips into the camcorder and allows you to record footage when you do not have access to a power source. The power supply allows you to plug into a nearby power source without the need of a battery pack. Many camcorders come with a separate battery charger.

Input and Output Connectors

Camcorders include extra jacks for plugging in external devices, such as stereo headphones, or connecting the device to a VCR. To edit recorded digital footage, the camcorder must have a *FireWire port*, also called an I-Link or IEEE 1394 port. For more on transferring your footage from your camera to your computer, see Chapter 8.

Operating Controls

The *operating controls* allow you to turn the camcorder on and off, start and stop recording, change modes and settings, and more. The number and placement of controls vary from one model to the next, but most are in easy reach as you hold the device.

Different makes and models of digital video camcorders vary in features and location of controls.

Lens

Essential to any camera, the camcorder *lens* is the eye that views the images you want to capture on video. Most lenses are built-in and include two types of magnification or zoom: optical and digital. Learn more about these in the section "Lenses."

LCD Screen

In addition to viewing what you are shooting through the camcorder's viewfinder, many camcorders include a pop-out LCD screen. The *LCD screen* is a flat video screen, often in color, that allows you to see a larger version of the viewfinder images.

Microphone

Most camcorders include a built-in stereo microphone, typically located near the front of the camcorder, to record audio along with the video images. This type of microphone works well for most situations, but if you need better audio sound and control, consider purchasing additional microphones. For more on controlling and editing the sound in your video, see Chapters 4 and 10.

Video Recorder Transport

The Video Recorder Transport operates like a built-in VCR in your camcorder. Use the controls to play, pause, rewind, and fast forward the recorded footage.

POWER SUPPLY

You can power a digital video camcorder using rechargeable battery packs or by plugging it in to an electrical outlet. If you plan to record a lot of indoor video, make sure the camcorder you purchase includes an external power source that allows you to operate the camcorder without a battery. To film outdoor footage, the camcorder needs a battery.

Batteries Included

Most camcorders include a battery and recharger. Rechargeable battery packs, which attach to a battery slot on the camcorder, come in different sizes, with larger battery packs powering your camcorder longer. Video camcorders accept specific types of battery packs, so check the requirements before purchasing one.

Consider carrying a spare battery pack to ensure you do not run out of battery power while recording. Using features other than the viewfinder, such as the LCD monitor or a camera light, make the battery run down faster.

Types of Batteries

Rechargeable battery packs come in three types: Nickel Cadmium (NiCad), Nickel-Metal Hydride (HiMH), and Lithium Ion (Li-Ion). You can damage NiCad batteries if you partially charge them before fully discharging all of their power. Because of their lightness and durability, most companies sell new camcorders with Li-Ion batteries, which means you can recharge them even if they still carry a partial charge.

Battery Size and Quantity

Typically, the battery pack that comes with the camera only lasts about one hour before you need to recharge it. Just remember that different features on the camcorder, such as the LCD screen, use up more battery power. If you want to purchase a larger capacity battery, this means carrying a larger battery, something you may want to avoid with a compact video camera. For compact cameras, consider purchasing multiple smaller batteries.

Determine Battery Life

To provide a method for monitoring your battery life, cameras displays an icon in the viewfinder or the LCD monitor to show the amount of life left in the battery. You need to monitor this icon to ensure that you do not run out of power in the middle of your desired footage.

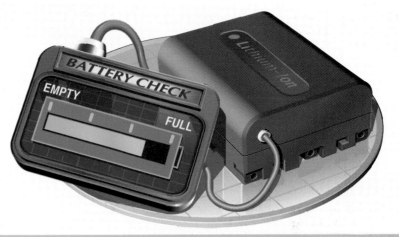

Recharging a Battery Pack

You can recharge your battery pack in one of two methods. Some require you to directly plug the camera into an electrical outlet to charge the attached battery pack. Others require that you place the battery pack into a separate battery charger. A separate battery charger gives you the advantage of plugging in one battery charger while using a second one on your camera. If your camera does not come with a separate battery charger, you can purchase one. You can also purchase battery chargers that plug into a cigarette lighter if you want to charge your battery in your car.

LENSES

The *lens*, or eye of your digital video camcorder, captures the images you want to record. Every camcorder comes with a built-in lens, and most allow you to attain several levels of magnification. A few makes and models even allow you to change lenses to create different views of your subject matter.

Lens Sizes

When you shop for a digital video camcorder you may notice that lens sizes vary. Typically, the more compact the video camcorder, the smaller the lens. A lens captures each image by concentrating the light behind the lens representing the image. The larger the lens, the more light it captures, which means higher quality footage. Video camcorder manufacturers use either plastic or glass lenses. Although lighter, footage that you shoot with a plastic lens may not seem as sharp as a glass lens. Also, plastic lens tend to scratch more than glass.

Optical Zoom

The *optical zoom* feature increases the image size when you zoom in by adjusting the optical lens to change the focal length. Because you reduce the area of view when you zoom in, you give the appearance of being closer to your subject. Although the area of view reduces, the same amount of light enters the camera causing no change in resolution.

Optical Zoom

Digital Zoom

When you use the digital zoom feature, the camera zooms in on and expands the center of the image by digitally adding more pixels to the image. This process, called *interpolation*, results in a lower image quality than one in which you optically zoom in on the subject. Digital zoom does affect the video resolution. When shooting casual video footage, this may not become an issue, but with professional-level recordings, the quality of the resolution may become important.

Digital Zoom

Reading the Zoom Specification

As you shop for a digital video camcorder, you may notice the zoom feature advertised as a selling point on the box. For example, the specification *10x optical/120x digital zoom* indicates the lens can magnify the subject up to 10 times and up to 120 times digitally. Of the two specifications, the optical zoom is the most important. If you plan to shoot a lot of close ups, your camcorder needs to have a greater optical zoom. The digital zoom, though impressive, loses video quality beyond the optical zoom setting.

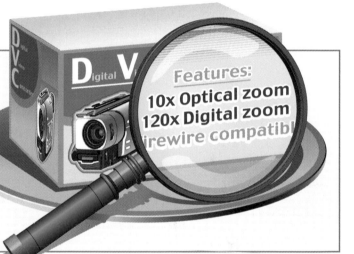

Additional Lens Converters

Some camcorders allow you to change lenses or add converters. For example, to film a wider area than your built-in lens allows, consider using a wide-angle converter. To magnify a close image, you can attach a close-up converter to the end of your lens. You may find these lens converters especially useful when you film in a confined space. Not all camcorders allow you to add attachments, so if you find this type of video important, look for one that allows for lens converters.

UNDERSTANDING CCDS

Digital video camera lenses capture images in the form of light and concentrate the light on the CCD, or *Charged Couple Device*, chips within the camera. Take a moment to understand how the number, size, and resolution of the CCDs within your digital video camcorder affect the quality of your video footage.

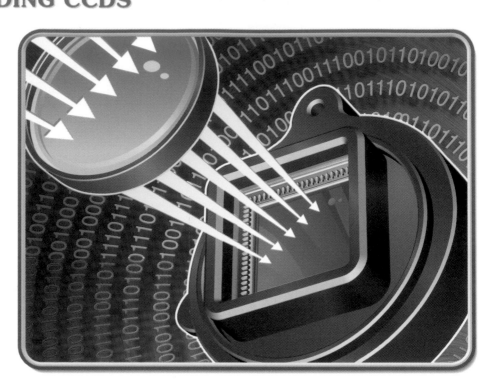

CCD Anatomy

Every digital video camcorder has either one or three CCDs that capture the image from the lens. A semiconductor chip with light sensitive sensors, CCDs convert the light from the lens into *binary format*, a series of 1's and 0's, which represent each image and associated sound. Digital video uses binary format to store all images. For more digital video definitions, see Chapter 1.

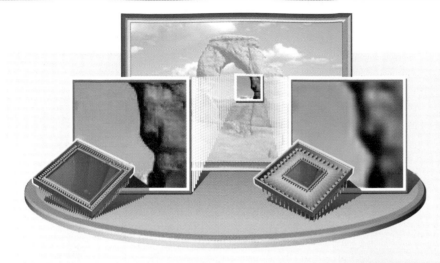

CCD Size

CCDs vary in size, with larger CCDs containing more light sensors than smaller ones. Each light sensor on the CCD represents a pixel of resolution in the digital image. This means that having a larger CCD and higher resolution generally provides a better digital image.

Multiple CCDs

The CCDs detect light in red, green, and blue components. A single CCD must convert all three colors simultaneously. Some high-end digital video camcorders offer 3 CCDs with each separate CCD responsible for capturing an individual color: red, green, and blue. Using a lens with 3 CCDs results in better video color clarity.

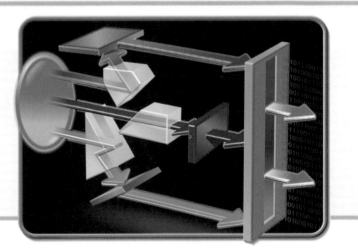

Light Sensitivity

CCDs measure the range of light sensitivity in the metric unit *lux*. The lower the lux, the better the camera can record in low-light settings. Similar to night vision equipment, some CCDs are sensitive to infrared light, which allows you to shoot video in almost total darkness.

INPUT AND OUTPUT OPTIONS

All digital video camcorders include additional jacks, which you can use to plug in external devices, such as stereo headphones or microphones, or to connect the camcorder to another device, such as your computer. This section gives you an overview of common input and output jacks you can expect to find on most camcorders. To transfer digital and analog footage to your computer, *see* Chapter 8.

Input Connectors

Input connectors allow you to hook up external equipment to your camcorder. For example, you may want to connect your camcorder to a VCR or another camcorder. The better camcorders include more jacks, such as color-coded jacks for audio channels and S-Video jacks for higher quality video input.

Dual Function Jacks

Some camcorders utilize one set of jacks that serve dual functions so that you can switch to input or output, while others may include jacks for inputting and outputting analog video. If you plan to transfer recorded footage to analog devices, look for a camcorder that includes analog video in and out. This enables you to copy VHS tapes to digital video or vice versa.

What Is a FireWire?

To transfer and edit video footage on your computer, your camcorder must have a FireWire jack or port. Developed by Apple, FireWire is common on Macs, but goes by other monikers for PCs. FireWire ports are also called I-Link (Sony) or IEEE 1394. Regardless of the name, the function remains the same — it enables you to transfer up to 400 million bits of digital data per second from your camcorder to your computer. For more on transferring footage, see Chapter 8.

Preparing Your Computer for Camcorder Output

For your computer to receive digital video data from your camcorder, it must also have a FireWire port. Most Macs include a FireWire port, but not all PCs have one. You can easily add a FireWire adapter card, also referred to as an I-Link or IEEE 1394 card, to your system for less than $100. Some digital editing software also comes with a FireWire card. You also need a FireWire cable to connect the computer and the camcorder. Cables run anywhere from $30–$50.

Output Connectors

Some camcorders feature dedicated output jacks, the most common of which is the headphone jack. You might use headphones to better hear the audio you record along with the video footage.

EXPLORE OTHER CAMCORDER FEATURES

When shopping for a digital video camcorder, not all of the features you need to know about are visible on the camcorder itself. Many features work behind the scenes inside the camcorder as you shoot video footage. This section explores some of the unseen, but equally important, camcorder features you should know about.

Most camcorders allow you to access and change options and setup features through a menu system that appears on the video screen in the viewfinder or on the LCD screen.

Image Stabilization

Stabilization is an important feature to consider in a camcorder. Without stabilization, a slight hand movement becomes very apparent in your video recording. You can compensate for your movement while shooting video footage with either optical or digital image stabilization, available on most digital video camcorders. *Optical stabilization* uses a series of lenses to reduce camera movement, while *digital image stabilization* uses digital technology to correct camera movements. However, image stabilization can only reduce a small amount of movement and you may want to use a tripod or similar support to help keep your camera stable.

Shooting Modes

Digital video camcorders have different shooting modes for recording your video footage. Each camcorder has an automatic, or easy, mode where the camera selects the appropriate settings automatically depending on the lighting conditions. In this mode, the camcorder automatically sets the shutter speed, aperture, gain, and white balance for you. You can use other shooting modes to customize the settings and improve the quality of your video footage. For example, when you place your camcorder in full manual mode, you adjust all settings manually.

Close-ups | Fluorescent Lighting | Dominant Color

WHITE BALANCE

MANUAL — AUTO

White Balance

You can use the White Balance option to control how your camcorder interprets colors in different types of lighting. If available, adjust the white balance manually for close-ups, rapidly changing lighting, when you have fluorescent or mercury vapor lighting, or when you have a subject in one dominant color, such as a person in a blue outfit against an ocean. If your video camcorder does not allow you to manually adjust white balance, you can adjust for Indoor or Outdoor lighting — another form of white balance.

Zebra Stripe Indicator

You can use the Zebra option on your digital video camcorder to determine if you have adjusted the brightness properly. When you turn this setting on, the camcorder displays diagonal stripes in the viewfinder or LCD screen, indicating areas of overexposure. You can often improve the exposure simply by changing the camera angle, but it may require other steps, such as closing a curtain to reduce the sunlight. The zebra stripe lines do not record on the tape.

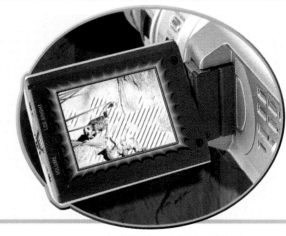

Aperture

The aperture, also called the *iris*, controls how much light the camcorder passes through the lens by changing the size of the lens opening. The camcorder's programmed auto exposure (program A/E) controls the aperture automatically, unless you override the control. For example, you may want to change the aperture to improve the lighting of your subject. You adjust the size of the opening by setting the camera's *f-stop*. The lower the f-stop number, the more light passes through the lens. For example, an aperture setting of f16 allows only a small amount of light to enter through the very center of the lens, but f1.6 allows light to enter through nearly the entire lens. For more on adjusting your camera for different lighting situations, see Chapter 3.

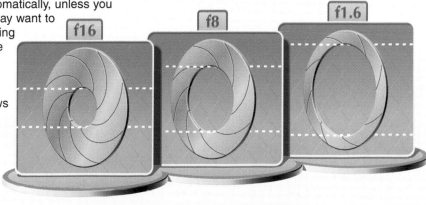

f16   f8   f1.6

CAMCORDER ACCESSORIES

Digital video camcorders have several different accessories that you can use to improve the ease of recording your footage. Remember that some accessories, such as remotes, are specific to your camera.

Remote Control

Remote controls allow you to start and stop shooting from a distance. For example, you can set up your camera to record events within a particular area of your house and then turn the camera recording off and on with the remote.

Lights

You can purchase additional lighting equipment to help you illuminate the scenes you want to record on video. Most camcorders include a connector port for attaching an additional light source. For best results, purchase lighting equipment designed specifically for your type of camcorder. If you plan to shoot footage for weddings or more professional projects, you might also purchase additional separate light sources, such as spot and scoop lights, to place around the scene you intend to film.

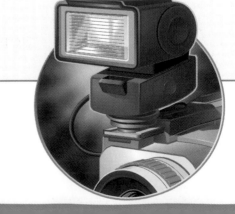

Tripod

Because they limit the movement of your camera, tripods improve the quality of your video footage by eliminating blurriness and shakiness. Because tripods come in all different sizes, you need to find a size sturdy enough for your camera, but also easy to transport. You should also consider a tripod with a fluid-head, which provides a fluid-like, smooth motion when you move the camera on the tripod.

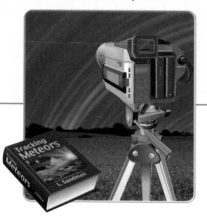

Lens Filters

You can use a *filter* — a piece of glass you attach to the end of the lens — to change the appearance of the light before it hits the lens, to create special effects. Besides the built-in filters available in some cameras, you can add a wide variety of external filters, such as polarization and neutral density filters. For example, UV filters shield your camera lens from UV, or ultra-violet, rays and clarify your picture. Inexpensive and easy to replace, UV filters also serve to protect your camera lens from dust and scratches.

Waterproofing

If you want to shoot outdoors in all types of weather, consider investing in a rain cover for your digital video camera. A rain cover protects your camera from the elements, but still allows you to film the desired footage. If shooting underwater video is one of your goals, make sure a housing exists for your digital video camera before purchasing that camera.

Bluetooth™ Technology

Some digital video cameras include wireless communication capabilities called Bluetooth. If you have a Bluetooth-enabled camera, you can send e-mail with video attachments wirelessly through the aid of the Bluetooth adaptor. To use Bluetooth to access the Internet from your video camera, you must have a Bluetooth adaptor connected to a phone line or network. The adaptor receives the signal from the video camera and transmits it over the network.

CHAPTER 3

Working with Lighting

Because light contributes greatly to the quality of your video, this chapter provides information on how to use it to your advantage when shooting your video footage.

CHARACTERISTICS OF LIGHT

To achieve the desired effects with your video, you need to have the right amount and type of lighting. Whether you film in daylight, fluorescent lighting, or even candlelight, take the time to learn about the characteristics of lighting and how they can enhance or detract from your video recordings.

Light Intensity

Light intensity is the brightness of the existing lighting. For example, sunlight produces a dramatically brighter light than candlelight, therefore, a greater light intensity. Your video camcorder's CCD chip requires a minimum amount of light intensity to record an image. You regulate the light intensity by adjusting the *aperture setting*. The *aperture* is the diameter of the opening in your camera's lens that allows light in. The larger the aperture number is, the smaller the diameter of the opening. For example, a setting of f22 lets in less light than f8. In darker settings, you can improve the amount of light that the CCD receives by decreasing the aperture setting — and thus increasing the amount of light — on your video camcorder. In brighter settings, you can decrease the light intensity by increasing the aperture setting — thus decreasing the amount of light — on your video camcorder, or by using filters. See Chapter 2 to learn more about CCD chips.

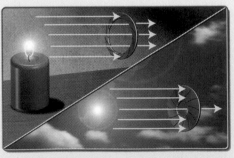

Quality of Light

You have two types of lighting, *direct* and *indirect*. Sunlight, the best example of direct lighting, makes images easy to capture and produces clear and sharp shadows from objects. You can reproduce direct lighting indoors with spotlights and other lights that shine directly on your subject. Direct lighting produces a much harsher video picture.

You see indirect, or diffuse, lighting on an overcast day. More evenly distributed, indirect light creates less shadowing, making it ideal for shooting footage. You create indirect lighting indoors by bouncing the light off of another source, such as a white wall or ceiling, or by using specialized lighting equipment called *reflectors*. See the section "Lighting Equipment" for information on reflectors.

Light Contrast

Light contrast refers to the relationship between the darkest and lightest areas in your scene. If you place your subject in front of a brightly lit background, the subject appears too dark on your video. You need to balance the high contrast between images by either adjusting your lighting or by moving the location of your camcorder.

Light Direction

Light direction, which is relative to the position from which you shoot, affects the appearance of the subject. For example, shooting directly into light creates contrast problems, and direct sunlight can create glares off of your camera lens. For best results, place your light source either behind you or to one side, depending on the effect you want to achieve. If you cannot adjust the lighting direction by moving the light source, move the camcorder to obtain the desired direction.

9500°K	Clear Blue Sky
7000°K	Overcast Sky
5500°K	Sun at Noon
3750°K	Cool Fluorescent
3000°K	Halogen
2700°K	100W Incandescent
2250°K	40W Incandescent/ Warm Fluorescent
1500°K	Candle Light

Light Color Temperature

Light from different sources produces different coloring of your subject. For example, shooting by candlelight produces an orange/yellow cast on the subject matter, while shooting under fluorescent lights produces bluer color tones. You measure differences in coloring, referred to as *color temperature*, in degrees Kelvin. Light color temperature ranges from a red to blue cast. You correct light coloring temperature effects with filters, which come in a variety of types for specific lighting situations. You can also adjust lighting by adding additional lights to the scene, or by placing *gels*, colored sheets of plastic film, in front of lights. For example, if you add a standard photographic light with a Kelvin rating of 3200, you can reproduce daylight lighting. You can also use the White Balance feature on your video camera to control the color temperature. See Chapter 2 for more information about White Balance.

LIGHTING EQUIPMENT

When natural or indoor lighting does not create the lighting effect you want, you can use lighting equipment to illuminate your subject matter. For example, you can employ equipment to brighten or soften the existing light for a scene. You can also utilize equipment to assist in lighting placement.

Although you can use any form of lighting, you achieve the best results with lighting equipment specifically designed for video recording.

Types of Lighting

When shopping for lighting equipment, consider the main ways in which you plan to light the scenes in your video. The typical lighting setup consists of a combination of three different lights: a *key light*, a *fill light*, and a *backlight*. Key lighting is the principal light source, while fill lighting fills in areas of your scene not lit by key lighting. You use key lighting, also called *hard lighting*, to create a direct light source on your subject matter. You use fill lighting, also called *soft lighting*, to fill in glaring shadows and to create a wash of light for your scene. A backlight is anything that gives the subject matter more dimension, and separates the subject from the background.

Attachable Camera Lights

Video camera lights, the most convenient form of additional lighting, allow you to easily carry a portable light source with you. You use the lights by attaching them to the top of your video camcorder. Some video camera lights draw their power from the battery attached to your camcorder, while others run off of a separate rechargeable battery. These lights typically range from 2 watts to 20 watts in power. Attached camera lights act as key lighting for your subject matter.

Video Lights

To increase the lighting of your scene, you can use additional video lights, which you place on stands. The various types of video lights you can purchase include spotlights, scoops, and fresnels. A *spotlight* aims light at a specific area. A *scoop* light fills in shadows and lights backgrounds. A *fresnel*, which is a spotlight with spherical reflectors, directs light to a specific area. Video lights come in a wide range of wattages.

Light Stands

If you purchase additional lighting equipment, also consider purchasing stands to hold each of your video lights, and clamps to attach the lights to the stands. You not only use light stands to hold different video lights, but also to hold filters and reflectors for the lights. You can easily fold light stands, which typically consist of a pole and base, and transport them.

Filters and Reflectors

You can use *filters* and *reflectors* to soften the light that a video light produces. When you use a reflector, the light shines onto the reflector and bounces back at the subject of the video, creating a softer effect. Filters provide a similar effect by diffusing the light source. You can learn more about filter types in the section "Gels and Filters."

GELS AND FILTERS

You can use filters and gels to alter the appearance of your light. Both gels and filters control light captured by your video camera, but they accomplish this in different ways.

Filters

You generally attach a *filter* to your camera lens to change the appearance of light as it enters your camcorder. A *filter* is simply a piece of glass or plastic lens. Interference filters reflect unwanted portions of the color spectrum away and only allow the appropriate color to pass through the lens. Because they are made of glass, these filters are more expensive and easier to break.

Gels

You can place *gels* between a light source or a fill light and your subject. This reduces the effects of harsh lighting, or changes the light temperature before it hits the subject. A *gel*, simply a colored sheet of plastic film, acts as an absorption filter. You place a gel in front of a light source to block specific portions of the color spectrum to create the desired color temperature. Gels come in various colors to absorb the appropriate colors. Gels also come as opaque sheets designed to filter harsh light sources.

Filters for Cameras and Light Sources

You can add a filter to the camcorder lens itself to create a different lighting effect. Besides the built-in filters available in some cameras, you can add a wide variety of external filters to create the lighting effect you want in your video.

Another way to use a filter to control light intensity, quality, and color is by attaching a gel filter directly to the light source. For example, if you need to make the lighting of your subject appear warmer, you might attach a gel filter to your light source to change its color.

UV Haze Filter

An important filter you should definitely add to your list of camcorder accessories is the *UV lens filter*. UV lens filters shield your camcorder lens from UV, or ultra-violet, rays and clarify your picture. Because these filters are inexpensive and easy to replace, they also serve to protect your camcorder lens from dust and scratches.

Specialty Lens Filters

You can apply many different types of lens filters to your digital video camcorder, depending upon the effects you want to achieve.

Filter	Use
Polarization	Saturates the colors to provide better contrast between the subject and background. You use this filter to film surfaces where light rays become polarized, such as water or glass.
Neutral Density	You use ND filters to reduce the amount of light reaching the CCDs in your video camcorder and to prevent your footage from appearing overexposed, or washed-out. Some camcorders include built-in ND filters.
Center	Prevents the video footage edges from darkening in wide-angle shots.
Color Compensating	Compensates for color loss in different lighting conditions, such as fluorescent lighting. Filters come in primary colors of red, green, and blue, and secondary colors of cyan, magenta, and yellow.
Contrast	Reduces the high-contrast portions of the image without darkening the rest of the image.
Fog	Creates the effect of a light fog by making lights glow and flare, and by reducing the contrast and sharpness of images.
Intensifier	Enhances a specific color in your image without affecting the other colors. For example, you can use a blue intensifier to enhance a blue sky.
Skylight	A pink-tinted filter that reduces the blue cast of daylight.
Spot	Focuses on a circular section of the image while blurring the surrounding images.
Star	Creates a multi-beam star effect for light sources.

LIGHTING ON A BUDGET

You may find that accumulating the various items you need to create an effective lighting system is a costly proposition. To cut the cost of professional quality lights, consider visiting your local home improvement store, where you can find or build the different elements for an effective do-it-yourself lighting set.

When creating your own lighting, be mindful of power requirements for the selected lights and use the appropriate extension cords.

One disadvantage of creating your own lighting set is that you may not find it as compact and portable as professional-grade lights.

Everyday Lights

You can purchase a set of shop lights at your local hardware store. Shop lights put out a lot of light, can come with their own light stand, and have a color temperature of about 3200 K, which creates a yellow light — optimal for a video camcorder in an indoor setting. When using indoor lighting, set the White Balance on your camcorder to indoors to adjust for the yellow lighting. Learn more about White Balance in Chapter 2.

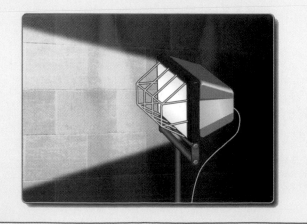

Limit the Use of Fluorescent Lamps

Because video camcorders work optimally in either common 3200 K household lighting or 5600 K outdoor lighting, consider limiting use of household fluorescent lamps, which have a green cast and a color temperature of 4000 K. Extensive use of fluorescent lighting can creating a green cast in your video. If you use a fluorescent lamp, consider either purchasing a filter for your camcorder to compensate for the light, or using gels over the light to remove the green cast. Learn more about filters in the section "Gels and Filters."

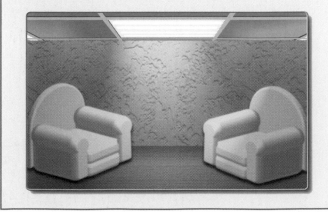

Create Reflectors

You can use tin foil to make a good reflector. Cover a piece of foam board with tin foil so that you expose the shinny side of the foil. Shinier surfaces, such as tin foil, make good reflectors, while bright white surfaces, such as white poster board or even foam board, make good diffusers, creating a softer light than reflected light.

Clamp Lights

Hardware stores sell an abundance of different clamps and clips that you can use to attach your lights and reflectors to the light stands. Even common clothes-pins work well for attaching a reflector or diffuser to the outside of a light. Just take care not to allow the reflector or diffuser sheet to touch the light bulb, or the sheet may melt.

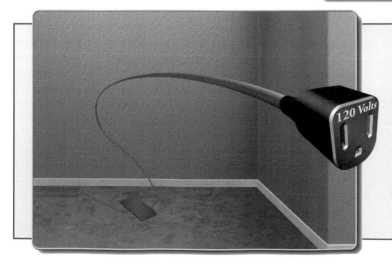

Extension Cords

When hooking up your lighting, you need to make sure you use extension cords with the appropriate voltage rating. Each light you use requires a specific amount of power. Make sure the extension cords you use are rated to produce the amount of power your lights require.

Also, make sure you secure the extension cords to avoid anyone tripping over them. Use tape to secure the cord to the ground. Try to run the cords out of the main traffic path, such as along a wall or behind furniture.

OUTDOOR LIGHTING TECHNIQUES

Shooting footage outdoors presents several challenges, particularly if you film on a sunny day. Although sunlight makes for a wonderful free light source, you cannot control its direction or movement. Follow these tips to help improve your outdoor lighting problems.

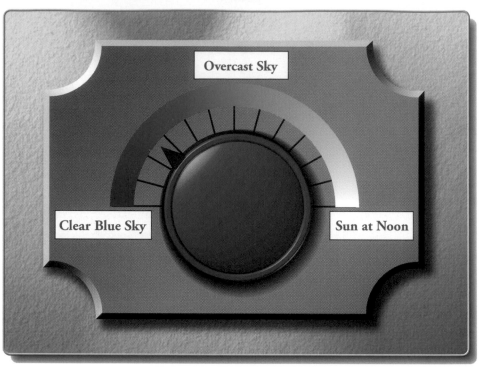

Overcast Sky

Clear Blue Sky

Sun at Noon

Film in Sunlight

When you shoot outside, be mindful of the brightness of the sun. Too much sunlight, such as noonday sun, can make a scene appear washed out, creating a flat appearance. Ideally, you should avoid outdoor filming on a bright, sunny afternoon. For best coloring, film near dawn or dusk, during what film makers call the "magic hour." Also consider the useful technique of filming on an overcast day, or in a shady area where you block or filter the direct sun.

Camcorder Placement in Sunlight

If you must film in sunlight, never aim your camcorder directly towards the sun. This causes glare on your lens. Position your camcorder so that you have the sun to the side or behind you. Also be mindful of lighting changes that occur as the sun moves in and out of clouds. If your camera has a small viewfinder, you should always avoid placing it in direct sunlight. Sunlight can enter and easily damage or destroy the viewfinder LCD.

Using a Reflector

Reflectors compensate for uneven daylight when you film outdoors. By using a reflector, you can reflect light back onto your subject, creating an indirect light source. You can accomplish this by pointing your light at the reflector and then reflecting the light onto your subject. You may find this effect more desirable than direct lighting. Reflectors can include a commercial reflector purchased from a camera shop, a white painted wall, a white poster board, or a foam-core board.

Eliminate Extreme Shadows

Subjects in direct sunlight cast heavy shadows. For example, a person sitting in the sun may have unflattering shadows cast on their face. If at all possible, have your subject move into a more shaded area, such as under a tree, where soft shadows can add contrast and depth to your video. Softer shadows are more flattering when filming people. If you cannot move your subject, use a diffuser or reflector to reduce the effects of the direct sunlight.

Move from Outdoors to Indoors

If you move from outdoors to indoors while filming, automatic camcorder settings can cause either underexposure or overexposure footage because your camcorder does not quickly adjust to drastic changes in lighting. If it is available on your camcorder, use the White Balance feature. When you turn on this feature, the camcorder automatically adjusts for light color differences that occur when filming. Typically, the camcorder knows how to adjust for daylight conditions and interior light conditions. If your camcorder does not offer White Balance controls, you may need to manually set the exposure to maintain focus on the subject as your lighting changes. See Chapter 2 for more information about White Balance.

INDOOR LIGHTING TECHNIQUES

You can employ numerous techniques for lighting indoor scenes. However, almost all involve the use of extra lighting sources, whether additional video lights or other lighting equipment you use to illuminate the setting. The techniques and tips in this section can help you get the most out of your indoor lighting endeavors.

See the section "Lighting Equipment" to learn more about additional video lights you can purchase.

About Three-Point Lighting

The ideal setup for indoor shooting is the *three-point lighting* technique, which combines a key light, a fill light, and a backlight. You can also accomplish three-point lighting by using a key light and two fill lights. This technique produces consistent lighting of your subject. See the section "Lighting Equipment" to learn more about types of key and fill lights.

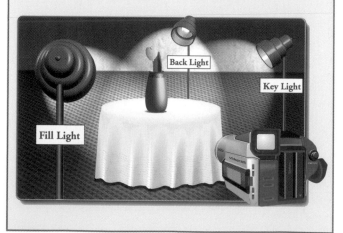

Three-Point Light Positioning

Use a key light as the main lighting for your subject with the three-point lighting technique. You should place the key light in front of your subject, but offset it so that your subject can avoid looking directly at the light if they look at the camcorder. Fill lights eliminate shadows and illuminate the contrast of the subject. Fill lighting can consist of one or two lights typically positioned off to the side of the subject. You can also use reflectors as fill lights. Use a backlight behind the subject to help add depth to the subject and illuminate the background.

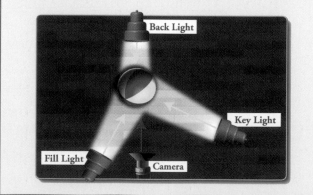

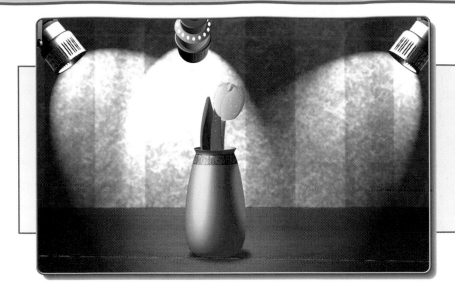

Light Height

Avoid placing lighting at the same height as your subject. Place each light — the key, fill, and back lights — above your subject at a 45 degree angle. You can also try placing your fill lights below the center plane to reduce the shadowing effects on the subject.

Close Windows

Windows can create an undesirable effect on your video by introducing an uncontrollable amount of light. If at all possible, cover windows and use your own artificial light sources to light your scene. You may find that you can produce the desired lighting by simply closing a window shade to reduce the direct light source. For uncovered windows, avoid filming with the camcorder pointed directly toward a window.

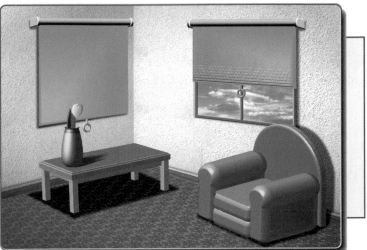

Bounce Light

Bouncing light occurs when you reflect the light off of some source back onto your subject. Bounced light provides a softer light source, which gives your indoor video footage a less grainy appearance. You can bounce lights off of many different materials, including a piece of white poster board or foam-core board. You can use a reflector source as a fill light that catches the light from the key light or another fill light and bounces it back on the subject. When using bounced light, watch out for unintended bounces.

ADJUST SHUTTER FOR LOW LIGHT

You may not always find it feasible, or even desirable, to add more lighting to the scene you want to film. Most camcorders allow you to manually change the shutter settings to adjust for low lighting. In low light settings, you need to have a slower shutter to allow your camcorder to capture more light.

Light Regulation

The shutter controls the amount of light that enters the lens of the camcorder. The *shutter speed* indicates the amount of time required to capture one image of digital video. The longer the shutter remains open, the more light can enter the lens. The shutter speeds on your digital video camcorder are measured in fractions of a second. For example, 1/125 means that it takes 1/125 of a second to capture a single image.

Reduce Shutter Speed

When working in low light situations, you want to reduce the shutter speed to allow the shutter to remain open longer and to allow the lens to capture more light. For example, if your camcorder has shutter speeds from 1/60 to 1/15000, you want to select the 1/60 setting for dark settings.

SPECIAL LIGHTING FEATURES

You do not need to accomplish all lighting effects with external lights. Some digital video camcorders provide unique features that you can use to enhance your video footage. Because special lighting features are typically specific to certain manufacturers, you need to make sure your camcorder includes these features before purchasing it, especially if you find a particular effect important to your situation.

NightShot®

Sony provides the NightShot Infrared System on some of its digital video camcorders. This technology allows you to capture images up to 10 feet away in total darkness using the infrared technology built into the video camcorder. You can increase this distance to 100 feet away by incorporating special infrared lighting. If you plan to do a lot of night filming, make sure you purchase a camcorder that can handle this task.

Sand and Snow

Canon provides a Sand and Snow exposure setting on some of their digital video camcorders. You want to use this setting when recording scenes with bright colored backgrounds, such as children building a snowman on a bright snowy day, or creating a sandcastle on a sunny beach. When you use this setting, the camcorder adjusts the exposure so that your subject does not appear overexposed.

Spotlight

Canon provides a spotlight exposure setting to capture subjects with a dark background, such as a performer on a stage. When you use this setting, the camcorder adjusts the exposure for the center of the frame to achieve the proper exposure level. You should also try this setting when filming nighttime sporting events. It helps to reduce the glare of the bright lights.

CHAPTER 4

Working with Sound

Sound quality is an important part of video recording. This chapter teaches you the ins and outs of capturing sound along with your video footage.

USING SOUND IN VIDEOS

Sound plays just as important a role in your video recording as the images you shoot. You can use sound in numerous ways to enhance, inform, and create just the right effect for your video production. This section introduces you to the various ways you can use sound.

Dialogue

Conversation is a primary element of most videos. Dialogue can consist of just one person talking, two or more people talking, or an off-camera interviewer asking questions of an on-camera interviewee. Dialogue happens quite naturally when filming events such as birthday parties, wedding receptions, and other informal family gatherings. For more formal productions, such as a corporate presentation, you may need to plan dialogue, called *scripting*, or allow the people appearing in your video to prepare and rehearse their lines in advance. If you intend to make dialogue an important part of your video, be sure to use the necessary sound equipment to capture all the talking in the scenes you film.

Narration

You hear narration, or *voiceover* sound, while viewing other images in your video. You use narration when you find natural dialogue impossible. For example, if you shoot your video in an extremely noisy location, such as a factory or football game, you might add voiceover dialogue later to better explain the action you recorded. You can record narration separately and add it to the video footage during the editing process.

Background Sounds

You use background sound, or *ambient* sound, to give a scene more realism. For example, if you film outdoors, background sound might include birds singing in the distance, leaves blowing in the trees, or rain falling on a roof. You may require additional sound equipment to record background sounds.

Sound Effects

Sound effects can enhance your visual footage. For example, the sounds of a squeaky door, footsteps, and thunder create a sense of suspense. You can record many types of sound effects and add them to your video later. For a fee, you can utilize *sound effects libraries*, which are vast collections of sound effects recorded and licensed for commercial use.

Music

You can also use music in your video. Typically, you add musical soundtracks in post-production as you edit your video. Music can create a mood, help tell a story, and enhance the effectiveness of your message. You can buy stock music to use in your video productions, or create your own music. Be warned, however, that using music from a commercial recording, such as a CD, is a violation of copyrights, particularly if you intend to sell and distribute your video.

UNDERSTANDING SOUND PROPERTIES

Before you begin recording sound, you need to understand the various properties of sound. Sound properties can affect the quality of your recordings and the way in which you choose to record.

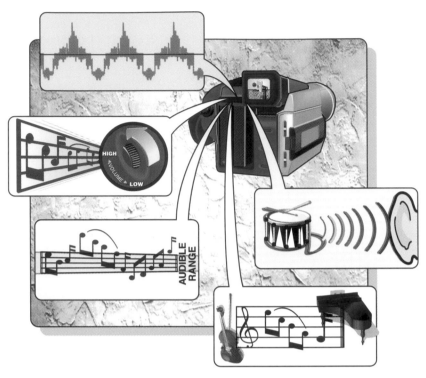

Sound Waves

All sound exists in the form of waves. Sounds transmit primarily through the air, although they can also transmit through more solid objects, such as a musical instrument. Each sound has different *amplitudes* that indicate the strengths of the sound wave. *Frequencies* indicate the rates that the sound waves vibrate. The various amplitudes and frequencies create the sound wave.

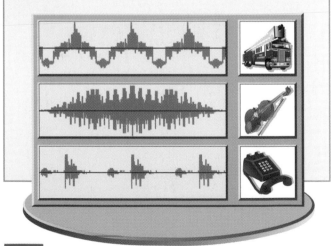

Amplitude

In simple terms, the amplitude of a sound wave represents the volume level with higher amplitudes indicating louder sounds. You measure amplitudes of sounds in decibels (db). For example, a jet taking off has an amplitude of 125 db.

When recording, make sure that the audience can distinguish the sound you want to capture from the background sounds. This may require you to place an external microphone somewhere in your scene to capture only the sound you want.

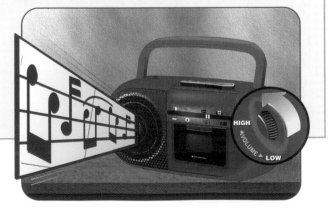

Frequency

Frequency indicates the pitch, or how high or low the sound is. You measure frequency in hertz (Hz). The human ear can hear sounds in the range of 20 to 20,000 Hz, with 20 Hz being the lowest pitch and 20,000 Hz being a very high pitch.

Timbre

Timbre describes the entire makeup, or personality of a sound. Typically a single sound consists of various frequencies, both primary and secondary. A timbre consists of multiple tones called *harmonics*. The timbre allows you to differentiate between two sounds. For example, the timbre of a piano and your voice differ, even when you sing the same notes as those that someone plays on the piano.

Amplitude and Frequency Relationship

Human ears capture sounds better at speech frequencies. You typically need to increase the amplitude of sounds outside that range for your ears to recognize them. Microphones do not process frequencies equally either.

The beauty of digital video is that once you capture your audio and video, you can adjust the amplitude of different sounds through the process of editing to make them more apparent.

TYPES OF SOUND EQUIPMENT

The quality of your sound equipment determines the quality of the sound you record when shooting video footage. Most video camcorders come with a built-in microphone, which you may not find sufficient for the sounds you intend to record along with your footage. You can use additional sound equipment to help you capture just the right sounds.

Camcorder Microphones

The built-in microphone you find on most camcorders captures stereo sound in either 12-bit or 16-bit mode. To learn more about these modes, see the section "Control Camcorder Sound Levels." Camcorders include an automatic setting for controlling the sound level for the microphone. If you plan to use your camcorder for more than just casual videotaping, such as shooting weddings or more professional video productions, look for a camcorder that allows you to manually adjust sound levels.

Microphone Attachments

Most of the higher-end digital video camcorders accept wind sock attachments on the microphone. These attachments help to improve the quality of the sound that the attached microphone records by blocking the wind noise — up to 40 mph — before it reaches your microphone. By blocking the wind noise, these attachments improve the quality of the sound that the microphone captures.

External Microphones

The main drawback with using a built-in microphone stems from the fact that you have them away from your subject, which makes it more difficult to capture all of the desired sounds. To remedy the situation, consider purchasing additional microphones. External microphones come in several different types and cost as little as $29. You plug the microphone into the video camcorder and then place it in a location where you can better capture the sounds from your subject. External microphones include handheld microphones, lavalieres that clip to a person's clothing, and wireless microphones. Before you purchase extra microphones, make sure your camcorder has the necessary external jacks to accommodate them.

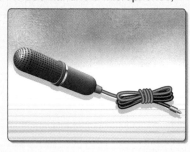

Microphone Mount

When placing an external microphone in a scene, you should have a microphone stand or mount to hold it in place. When you secure the microphone in a mount, not only does it maintain its position, but you can also angle it to capture the best sound. If you do not want to see a microphone in the scene, use a long-range or boom microphone that hovers over the person speaking. You mount boom microphones to a long pole.

Headphones

Essential to any serious recording, headphones connect to your video camcorder and allow you to monitor the sound that comes from the microphone. You can find inexpensive headphones or earphones to fit most camcorders.

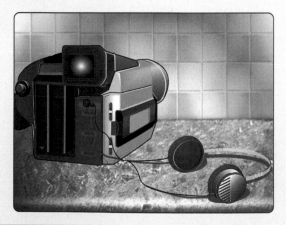

Audio Mixer

If you want even more control over the sound from an external microphone, you can add an audio mixer, which adjusts the amount of sound that the camcorder receives. With a mixer, you can capture the sound from multiple microphones and adjust the audio level from each microphone. You can even mute a specific microphone from the mixer. Mixers use audiometers to show you sound amplitude.

UNDERSTANDING HOW MICROPHONES WORK

You can use several different types of microphones, depending on your specific needs. You classify microphones using two methods: By their transducer type or by their directional pickup pattern.

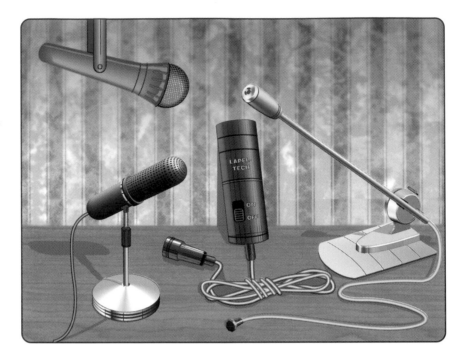

TRANSDUCER TYPES

Dynamic Microphones

Dynamic microphones require no external power to capture sound, making them the most inexpensive and widely used type of microphone. A *dynamic microphone* consists of a diaphragm, attached to a fine wire that suspends in the magnetic field of a magnet. When the sound wave hits the diaphragm, the coil moves and creates an electrical current, which represents the sound. Dynamic microphones produce a high-quality sound and you can use them for more rugged shooting environments.

Condenser Microphones

Condenser microphones require power to capture sound, either with batteries or an external power source. More sensitive than, but not as rugged as, dynamic microphones, *condenser microphones* consist of a very thin metal diaphragm stretched over a piece of metal or ceramic. The power causes a constant charge on the two elements. When sound waves hit the diaphragm, fluctuations occur in the electrical charge representing the sound. Condenser microphones range from costly studio microphones to inexpensive amateur microphones.

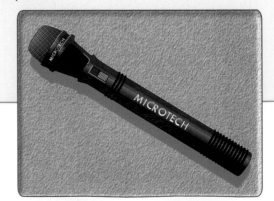

DIRECTIONAL PATTERNS

Omnidirectional Microphones

An omnidirectional microphone captures sound from all directions. Use this type of microphone to capture sound from multiple directions, such as recording a musical performance, or a sporting event. Because they are the least sensitive to wind noise, you typically have omnidirectional microphones built-in to your camcorder. Omnidirectional microphones generally start at $30 and up.

Unidirectional Microphones

A unidirectional microphone captures sound from one primary direction. Use this type of microphone for recording interview footage. You should place these microphones close enough to capture the sound from the subject. If you do a lot of interviewing, you may want to consider personal microphones, such as lavalieres, that you attach to the subject. These range in price from $30 on up.

Long-Range Microphones

Long-range microphones, also called shotgun microphones, capture sound from a specific point in your scene. You generally use long-range microphones when you do not want to see an actual microphone in the scene. Frequently used in television and film production, a sound person off to the side of the set holds a shotgun microphone over the person. Because the microphone picks up only the sound of the object at which you aim it, it requires a steady hand and good aim to operate a shotgun microphone. Such microphones range in price from $40 to well over $1,000.

MICROPHONE PLACEMENT TECHNIQUES

Where you place a microphone in the scene is every bit as important as the type of microphone you select. Ultimately, the distance you select for a microphone depends on the sensitivity of the equipment and the type of sound you want to capture. If you have an audio mixer, you can use different types of microphones to achieve a fuller sound.

Your placement may determine what kind of microphone you use. For more on the different types of microphones, see the section "Understanding How Microphones Work."

Close Microphone

Use a close microphone when shooting interview footage, or when you want to capture sound from a specific location in a scene. Typically, you place a close microphone within the range of 1 inch to 3 feet from the subject. However, if you place the microphone closely, you can capture noises such as breathing or clothes rustling from the subject. If you place the microphone too far from the subject, you run the risk of recording too much background noise. Take time to experiment with the placement of a close microphone to ensure the quality of the sound before you start recording.

You can use either unidirectional or omnidirectional microphones for close microphones depending upon the sound you want to capture. For example, an interview would work best with a unidirectional microphone.

Distant Microphone

You place distant microphones, commonly called *Shotgun* microphones, 3 feet or more from the subject. You want to use this type of microphone positioning when recording multiple subjects, such as an orchestra. You need to experiment with your microphone location to find a spot where you evenly capture the sound from all the subjects in the scene, but keep the background sounds at a minimum. You can also use a distant microphone to record ambient sound, such as the sound of a waterfall or birds singing. Typically, you want to use an omnidirectional microphone as your distant microphone.

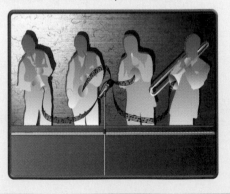

Accent Microphone

You can use an accent microphone with a distant or close microphone to balance the sound. For example, if you want to capture a soloist in an orchestra with a close microphone, you can place an accent microphone at a more distant range to capture a fuller sound. If you use an accent microphone, you need to also use an audio mixer to adequately adjust the amplitude of the sound so it does not overpower the primary microphone.

Three-to-One Rule

When you use two microphones for recording stereo sound, the sound should arrive at both microphones simultaneously. Use the three-to-one rule to determine where to position the microphones. For one subject, place the two microphones an equal distance from the subject, three times the distance apart as they are from the subject. For example, if the microphones are 3 feet from the subject, you need to place them 9 feet apart.

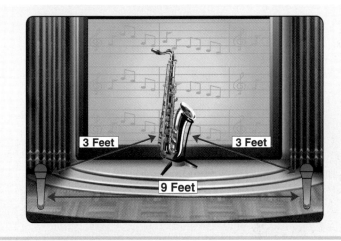

X-Y Technique

Another technique you can use to capture stereo sound involves placing two microphones together with the capsules of the microphone crossing to form an X pattern.

You should only use this technique in situations where you find the three-to-one technique unfeasible due to the space restraints of your recording area. This technique provides stereo sound, but it does not provide the quality that the three-to-one technique does.

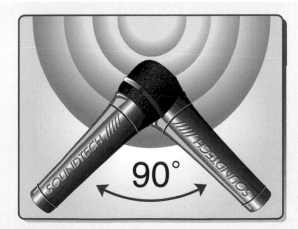

CONTROL CAMCORDER SOUND LEVELS

You need to control the level of the sound that your video camcorder receives to ensure you achieve the desired end result. Just because you can hear a sound does not mean your camcorder can detect it. You also need to monitor the sound level to prevent distorted or high-pitched sounds.

Automatic Sound Level

All digital video camcorders have an automatic setting for controlling the sound level, also called *gain*. The camcorder automatically adjusts these levels based on the sound you record. You need to monitor the sound to check that the camcorder makes the appropriate adjustments to capture the desired sound. Headphones can help you with this task. If you do not receive the anticipated results, you probably need to move your microphone.

Manually Adjust Sound Levels

Higher-end camcorders provide the ability to manually adjust the sound levels. In manual mode, you can override the automatic settings and adjust for unexpected sound levels that may occur. If recording quality sound is important to you, consider looking for a camcorder that includes manual audio level controls. Manual controls give you greater flexibility for controlling sound levels as you record.

Recording Stereo Sound

Nearly all digital video camcorders allow you to record stereo sound. On most camcorders, you can select from two different modes: 16-bit and 12-bit. You select a specific mode depending on whether you want to edit the sound later from your video camcorder.

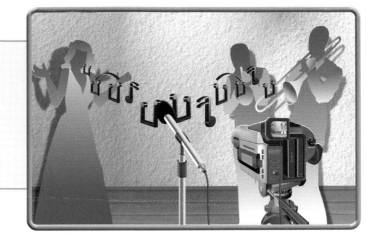

16-Bit Sound

You select 16-bit sound if you want to record the highest quality of sound with your video camcorder. When you record in this mode, the camera records two 16-bit stereo channels. The only method you can use to alter sound for 16-bit video is with a computer or other video editing hardware. You use this mode as your default for recording all sound because it provides the highest sound quality.

12-Bit Sound

If you intend to alter sound on your video camera before transferring it to a computer, you need to record 12-bit sound. This mode allows you to insert pre-recorded audio and voiceover narration after recording the video. If you intend to add voiceover audio, record the video in *standard-play*, or SP, mode.

SOUND RECORDING TIPS

Sounds come from many different sources and can hurt or help your video footage. For example, sounds that you do not notice during filming, such as a plane flying overhead, may become the dominant sounds you hear in your video playback. Although you can remove excess noise while editing your video footage, you can save yourself some work by not introducing them when you record.

Avoid Power Cords

Power cords can create a hum or buzz sound that your microphone may pick up. Avoid placing the microphone near power cords or other devices.

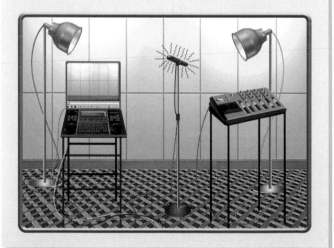

Turn off Appliances

Common household appliances such as refrigerators, freezers, and air conditioners can create unwanted noise in your video. You may not notice the noise while recording, but a sensitive microphone picks up the noise. Avoid placing microphones near these devices. If you find this impossible, turn them off temporarily while recording.

Correct Empty Room Echos

When you record in a room with solid walls or uncarpeted floors, sound reverberates off the walls creating a hollow sound. These types of sounds are called *hot* sounds because they create an audio signal that an audio mixer's meter considers too hot or high to read. You can correct hot sounds by placing blankets, couch cushions, and pillows around the room to trap the sound.

Keep Your Set Quiet

Be careful not to position your microphone near other people. Microphones pick up the closest sounds. Therefore, noises from other people, especially those standing off camera but near the camcorder or other microphone source, may sound louder than your subject. This especially holds true for built-in microphones on the camcorder. Sensitive attached microphones can pick up the sounds of the camcorder operator, including breathing, coughing, and talking.

Weather

Wind, rain, and thunder are all weather-related noises that can affect your sound. Although it may not seem too loud, the microphone captures the wind noise, the biggest culprit in recording, making it seem louder than you subject noise.

To help correct weather-related noises, most digital video camcorders offer a Wind Screen option that filters out the wind noise from the built-in microphone. If your camcorder provides this option, make sure you turn it on when filming outside, even on days you do not think of as particularly windy. The slightest breeze can affect the sound quality. You can also use a wind sock. For more information, see the section "Types of Sound Equipment."

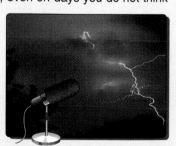

Sound Check

You may not recognize all of the sounds that you capture on your video. To avoid any surprise sounds, record your scene in advance without the subjects. This allows you to listen to the video and hear and eliminate any unwanted sounds. Adjust your microphones to compensate for those sounds before recording your actual video.

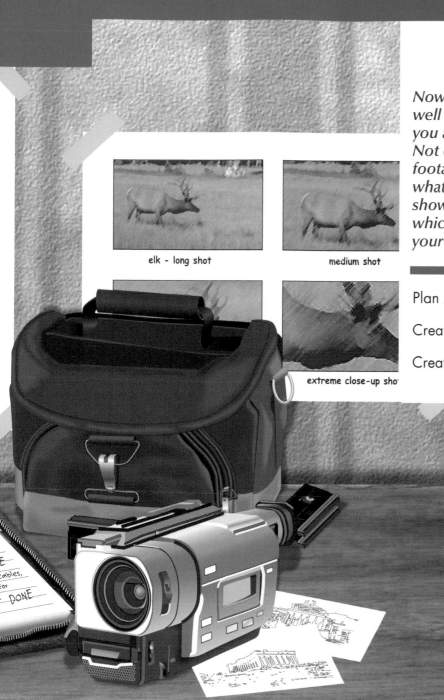

elk - long shot

medium shot

extreme close-up shot

Plan Your Video

Now that you have a camcorder, as well as lighting and sound equipment, you are ready to start shooting, right? Not quite. You need to plan your video footage beforehand to determine what you want to film. This chapter shows you some important ways in which you can prepare for shooting your digital video.

PLAN AHEAD

Planning ahead can help you shoot the footage you need. Even if you plan on shooting footage for a casual event, such as a family outing or birthday party, pre-planning can make the whole process much easier. If you plan ahead, you can anticipate any issues up front and determine the type of equipment or personnel you need to produce the desired footage.

Start with a Storyboard

A *storyboard* is a visual layout, or list, of the shots and scenes you anticipate in the video. You use a storyboard to help you plan the amount and type of footage you need to record. Commonly associated with professional productions, such as television and film, storyboards can also help you prepare to shoot anything from a trip to the zoo to a wedding or anniversary party. You can learn more about how to use storyboards in the next section, "Create a Storyboard."

Determine a Location

Whether you plan to record a family event or a corporate presentation, decide up front where you want to actually film. Do you want to shoot outside? What time of day? What kind of lighting do you have available? Do you need to bring along extra lighting or sound equipment? Your equipment list depends on your location. For example, multiple locations may require two sets of gear.

Some locations require prior permission before you can shoot video footage on the premises. Make sure you contact the appropriate personnel in advance.

Anticipate Weather

If you plan to shoot outdoor footage, anticipate the weather conditions you may face once you reach your destination. For example, an overcast day may require the use of additional lighting equipment, or a windy day may require microphone attachments for blocking out the noise of the wind. Also be prepared for changing weather conditions, such as rain. Be sure to bring along materials for protecting your camcorder and other equipment, such as plastic covering and lens cloths for cleaning the camcorder lens. Because they can damage your camcorder, avoid the extreme temperature ranges that may result from going from indoors to outdoors.

Bring Extra Supplies

When planning ahead, be sure to include all the extra items you may need for the shoot, such as costumes, props, and backup equipment. For example, you need to have an adequate supply of cassette tapes on which to record and adequate power for your camcorder. If you plan to use battery power to record your video footage, bring along extra batteries. Because you may want to record more footage than anticipated, extra tapes and batteries are handy to have around.

Coordinate Cast

Determine your video's subjects as well as their availability. For example, if you want to shoot a corporate presentation about a new product, make sure all the key people you want to capture on video can meet when you plan to record footage. If your video includes a full cast, anticipate any costume and prop requirements. Also, make sure your subjects have signed any necessary permission forms before you start filming. Once you have your cast together, you may want to have everyone rehearse their parts before you start shooting.

Coordinate Crew

For elaborate shoots, particularly those that are more professional in nature such as a presentation, clearly define the roles of the people participating. Regardless of whether you have a crew of three or thirty, decide who does what and who is in charge. Follow the example of the broadcast world, assigning jobs such as director, producer, and so on. For example, someone takes the role of director and oversees the shoot and makes sure the overall vision is carried out. Another person acts as the producer, carrying out pre-planning and completing the project. Other roles may involve technical consultants to oversee subject matter, videographer/photographer to run the camcorder, sound technicians, and so on. Have your crew members practice their roles during your cast's rehearsal.

CREATE A STORYBOARD

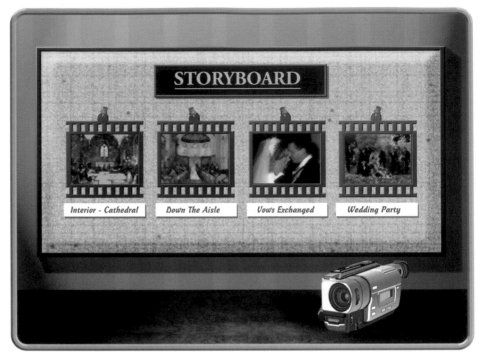

You can use a storyboard to help you organize and shoot a video. A *storyboard,* a visual outline or layout of the footage you want to record, lists the order in which the scenes of your final video appear. Storyboards are helpful to the novice videographer as well as the professional.

Simple Storyboards

You can create a storyboard, which typically resembles a comic strip with a different scene in each box, on paper or using your computer. Storyboards start from the beginning, including the intro or title text you want to include, and end with the credits. You can make the storyboard visuals as simple as stick figures or as elaborate as full-blown color sketches. Regardless of the visual style, all storyboards result in an outline you can follow when you actually start filming the footage, and they allow you to communicate to your crew the entire plan for the video.

Storyboard Software

If you intend to do a lot of video recording of different events, you may want to consider purchasing a storyboarding software package, such as E-Story or StoryBoard Quick. These software packages simplify the process by providing different graphics that you can insert as video scenes.

Identify Key Scenes

The first step in creating a storyboard involves identifying the *key scenes* in your video. Proper identification of scenes in the planning stage results in a better organized shooting schedule. Draw a box to illustrate each key scene on your storyboard paper, or consider creating scenes on separate cards so that you can re-order them as needed. Try to anticipate the different scenes you want to capture. It also helps to draw the scene from the angles that you want to film.

Order Scenes Chronologically

Once you identify your key scenes, you need to determine their chronological order in your final video. If you draw your ideas on cards, you can organize individual cards in the order in which you want to record, and then tape them into place on your storyboard. If you storyboard your video on paper, you can draw lines between storyboard boxes indicating the scene order.

Add Descriptive Notes

Consider adding *descriptive notes* to your storyboard to better identify the type of scene you want to capture. Descriptive notes help provide a goal or purpose for each scene. For example, when shooting at the zoo, instead of just drawing a picture of monkeys, add notes reminding you to shoot footage of a monkey eating a banana or swinging from a tree. If your video includes narration, be sure to add narration notes as well. You can also include notes about the type of music or sound effects you want to add later in the editing process to accompany the scene.

Specify Types of Shots

You can use different camera angles to capture the same footage. For example, if you film an interview, you may want to include footage of the interviewer as well as the interviewee. Camera angles include shots such as close-ups, extreme close-ups, long shots, medium shots, knee shots, and more. Take time to indicate on your storyboard whether you want to capture a certain shot or shots of the scene or subject matter. You can learn more about camera shots in Chapter 6.

CREATE A SHOOTING SCRIPT

Similar to a storyboard, a shooting script consists of a sequential list of shots you want to record. You can build this list based upon the key scenes that you specified in your storyboard. Because you do not shoot all video productions in chronological order, a shooting script helps you determine a logical order in which to shoot your video.

List Shots

From your storyboard, create a list of each of the shots you need to capture. Provide a short description of the shot you want to capture including the type of shot, such as a close-up, or wide angle.

Place Shots in Order

Next, reorder the shots in your list in the best order for capturing. For example, if one of the locations you plan to use is only available on a certain day, you may need to schedule all the shots for that location first. You often order your list depending on the availability of cast and crew, your locations, and weather you anticipate. You may also base the list so that you alternate the difficult and easy shots. Or you may want to order your shots to do the hardest shots first. You should order your list of shots on when you can capture them, not how you want them to appear in the final video. You may find this order completely different from the way you ordered your storyboard.

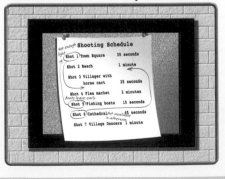

Specify Shot Length

When creating a shooting script, you should also include information about the length, measured in time, of each shot on the list. You need to make sure you capture plenty of footage for each scene. You can always delete footage, but once you record a scene, you cannot easily add more footage later. If you want your final video to contain 10 seconds of footage, you should plan on shooting at least 20 seconds to make sure you have plenty of good footage.

Anticipate Event Timelines

When filming some events, you must plan your shots around a specific timeline. For example, if you plan to shoot a wedding, you know you must capture certain shots based on the order of the ceremony. If you intend to create a vacation video of your cruise, you may need a list that duplicates your trip itinerary. You need to determine what order events will occur so you can ensure that you are ready to capture shots at the appropriate time.

Include Shots for Introduction and Credits

Be sure to include the shots you require for the introduction and ending of your video project. If you have specific shots in mind, such as footage to act as a background to scrolling credits or titles, be sure your shooting list includes the necessary shots and time lengths.

CHAPTER 6

Shooting Digital Video

Ready to start shooting your video footage? This chapter explains various shooting techniques and camera angles to help you make the most of your recording time.

TYPES OF CAMERA SHOTS

You can use a variety of camera shots to enhance your video. A *camera shot* is simply a size or range, such as a close-up or wide angle shot. Camera shots typically require you to change the camcorder zoom or the distance of the camcorder from the subject matter. Each shot type is based upon how much of the subject and the amount of background you capture in the video frame.

Be careful not to overuse any one shot. A variety of camera shots can make a casual video appear more professional and polished.

Extreme Long Shot

You use *extreme long shots* to show the relationship of your subject to the surrounding background. Extreme long shots, also called *wide shots* (WS), are good for showing a big-picture view of the scene or establishing a location before going into close-ups of the subject matter. You can also use extreme long shots to give a grand view of the scenery.

Long Shot

Long shots (LS) give a closer image of your subject, but still show a complete image of the subject and their surroundings. Use long shots when filming people moving around the scene.

Medium Long Shot

Use a *medium long shot*, also called a knee shot, to show a portion of the subject, for example, from the knee up. Short-range shots can help establish the relationship between two or more people in a scene.

Medium Shot

Use a *medium shot* to show the top half of the subject. If you are filming a person, you would film from the waist up. You can interchange this shot with the medium close-up for filming interviews.

Medium Close-up Shot

You use a *medium close-up*, or MCU, shot to zoom in closer on the desired portion of you subject. Also called a *bust shot*, this type of shot typically includes the person's chest on up to the head. This is a good shot for an interview because it shows the person's shoulder and head. Many newscasts mix both the medium close-up with the knee shot.

Close-up Shot

A *close-up shot*, or CU, zooms in to include the subject from the shoulders to the top of the head. Typically used to film people, use close-up shots for dramatic emphasis. Overuse of the close-up makes the viewer uncomfortable. A variation of the close-up is the *big close-up* (BCU) — a full-head shot.

Extreme Close-up

Use an *extreme close-up* (ECU), also called a macro shot, when you need to get an extremely detailed view of the subject. When filming people, you zoom in on the subject and keep the shot very tight, so that you can see the person's face, or even facial details, such as the eyes or mouth. Use this type of shot for rare dramatic emphasis. When filming subject matter other than people, you may find the extreme close-up shot great for targeting things like small animals, insects, and small objects.

SET CAMERA HEIGHT

You can vary camera height, or vertical angle, for your camera shots to add visual interest or change the viewer's perception.

Eye-Level

You shoot most camera shots at eye-level, which means the camcorder lens records the footage at a neutral camera height, usually the average height of a person. Because they view the subject head on, professionals consider eye-level shots objective. Typically, you want to use this type of shot when filming people.

Above Eye-Level

Use this type of shot if you want to give the appearance of looking down on your subject. This type of shot works well for providing the layout of the scene, for example when you film from the top of a pyramid to show the layout of the surrounding ruins. Be careful when using this type of shot when you film people because it may make the subject appear weak or inferior.

Below Eye-Level

This type of shot looks up at the subject matter. When filming objects, this shot illustrates the height of a particular object, such as a large building or pyramid. When filming people, this type of shot makes the person seem dominant.

ADD VIDEO DEPTH

You can create the appearance of depth in your video so that the images do not appear flat. The *z-axis* refers to the depth of an object. For example, you do not want a subject, such as a picture on a piece of paper, to appear one-dimensional. Rather you want to capture the depth of the object by showing that the object has a front and back.

Avoid Lining Up Subjects

Lining up objects, especially horizontally, and shooting them straight on creates a flat appearance. You want objects to appear staggered within your image to give the images depth.

Show Shadows

Shadows help to create the appearance of depth. When filming images, position your camcorder to capture the natural shadows that form on the image, or, if needed, add shadows by using extra lighting equipment. See Chapter 3 to learn more about lighting.

Contrast Foreground and Background

Avoid situations where you have very little contrast between a foreground object and the background. For example, filming a man in a black coat against a dark background may make the image look one-dimensional, but filming him against a lighter background gives the image depth. Try to create contrast between the subject colors when possible.

UNDERSTANDING CAMERA MOVEMENTS

You can use camera movements to add action to your video footage. Rather than aim and shoot, employ camera movements to change the way in which the viewer perceives the subject matter. Use a tripod to stabilize the camcorder. Most tripods include rudimentary controls for turning and swiveling the camcorder, and locking it into place.

Keep in mind that changing the position of your camera also changes your lighting conditions. See Chapter 3 for more on what to do for changing lighting conditions.

Pan

A pan is a horizontal movement of the camcorder. To pan a shot, use the handle on the tripod to slowly move the camcorder from right to left or left to right, keeping the camcorder and tripod in a fixed position. You can use pan movements to shoot footage of a moving subject, such as a person walking, a horse running, or a car driving by.

Types of Pans

You can use a *following pan* to track a cast member from one area of the scene to another, or to trail an object as it enters the frame until it exits. For example, if you shoot a video of a car driving by, set up the camcorder to capture the car as it enters the scene, then pan with the direction of the car and stop panning when the car exits the scene. You can use a *surveying pan* to enter a scene and locate a specific subject or object. For example, if you shoot footage in a crowded arena, you might perform a surveying pan to scan across the crowd and stop on a particular person.

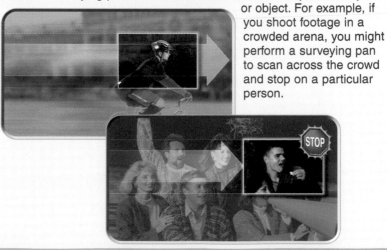

Tilt

Tilting involves moving the camcorder up and down while the camcorder and tripod remain in a fixed position, similar to nodding your head. Use tilting movements to follow actions or establish height or depth. For example, if you shoot footage of a tall building, you might start shooting the base of the building, then tilt slowly up to reveal the full height of the building.

Dolly

Dollying, moving the camcorder forward or backward, is a filming technique that movie studios use. This technique is difficult to accomplish with most tripods because they do not have wheels. You can accomplish a similar effect by placing your tripod on any dolly device, such as a wheeled office chair, and slowly rolling it forward. Dollying shots differ from zoom shots in that they follow action by mimicking the subject's movement, creating a relationship with the subject as it moves in the scene. You might use a dolly shot to follow someone into a building, for example. Repositioning the camcorder with a dolly shot may involve changes in the scene's lighting. For more information on lighting, see Chapter 3.

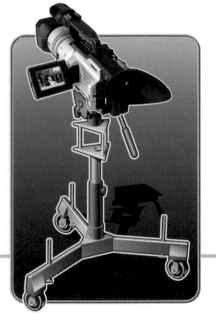

Truck

A *truck* shot provides an actual 360-degree movement around an object. Truck shots differ from pan shots in that the entire camcorder moves position, thus changing relationship to the subject matter. For example, a truck shot may start with a side view of a person, but swing around to view the front of the person. Like the dolly shot, you cannot possibly take a truck shot with a standard tripod. You can mount the tripod onto a dolly device, such as a platform with wheels. If you cannot figure out a way to mount your tripod on wheels, you can slowly walk around your subject to create a truck shot. Keep in mind that repositioning the camcorder may involve changes in the scene's lighting.

UNDERSTANDING FRAME COMPOSITION

When you frame your shot, you control the placement of subject matter within the scene. *Composition*, also called *framing*, involves arranging the subject matter within the areas inside a frame.

Apply Rule of Thirds

A common technique for composing subject matter in a video frame is the *rule of thirds*. Imagine a tic-tac-toe grid placed on your camcorder's viewfinder forming three horizontal areas and three vertical areas across the image. For good composition, try to align horizontal subjects with one of the three horizontal areas of the grid, or align vertical subjects with one of the three vertical areas of the grid. If you shoot footage of a city skyline, for example, line up the image on one of the horizontal lines of the imaginary grid.

Target Composition Zones

You call the squares in the *rule of thirds* grid *composition zones*. By placing your subject matter on one of the four intersecting lines in the grid, you can ensure the image uses a balanced composition. You can use composition zones to help give your subject matter added visual appeal. For example, if you shoot a subject sitting in the grass, frame the subject so you do not have it centered in the viewfinder. Rather, center the subject over a vertical line in the imaginary grid.

Avoid Centering

Most people naturally want to center subject matter in the middle of photograph, and the same thing happens to people using camcorders. Although centering the subject works well for an interview, too much centering detracts from the image and bores viewers.

Watch for Headroom

Another common mistake users make when composing their video images is not achieving proper headroom for people shots. If you show too much space between the subject's head and the top edge of the video frame, your subject may look too small or off-center against its background. Too little space cuts off the top of the person's head. Try to find a balance when filming people.

Safety Margins

Computer monitors can display the entire video frame during playback, but television monitors typically crop off the outer edges of the frame. For this reason, make sure you show important subject matter within the video *safe zones*, also called *safety margins*. Many camcorders today include one or two rectangles, which appear in the viewfinder, to help you place your subject matter within the safety margins while filming. You can consider anything appearing inside the inner rectangle safe. The camera crops off anything outside the rectangle when you play your footage.

CAMERA-HOLDING TECHNIQUES

One of the keys to good digital video filming involves learning how to hold your camcorder properly. Unwanted camera movement can ruin good footage fast. The smaller the camcorder, the easier it is for you to move it unintentionally while filming. Built-in image stabilization features of the camcorder help to correct some movement, but other techniques also help to improve the quality of your footage.

Image Stabilization

When shooting video in situations where you need to hold your video camcorder, make sure you turn on the image stabilization feature, if the camcorder includes this feature. Image stabilization controls the small jitters that occur while holding a video camcorder.

When to Turn Off Image Stabilization

Although image stabilization can greatly improve your video by compensating for small movements, you may want to avoid using the feature if you intend to shoot in low light or if you use the digital zoom. Image stabilization can introduce obvious digital artifacts, in the form of small pixels, into your video in these situations.

Tripods

The best method for stabilizing your video camcorder during filming involves placing it on a tripod. The tripod holds the camcorder stable so you can move it from side to side or up and down without excess movement. See Chapter 2 to learn more about camcorder equipment.

Monopods

Similar to a tripod, monopods have one leg instead of three. Because you can fold up monopods, and because they are smaller and lighter than tripods, you can easily carry them with you on the go. A monopod allows you to stabilize the camcorder in one spot, but you must hold onto the monopod at all times.

Stabilize Yourself

If you do not have access to a tripod or monopod, you can find other ways to stabilize yourself to reduce movement of the camcorder. You can lean against stable objects, such as walls, trees, or poles while filming. When you do not have a stable object nearby, you can stabilize yourself by holding the camcorder in one hand and using the other hand to brace the arm holding the camcorder. You can also kneel and hold the camcorder on your knee.

Move Slowly

Another way to prevent too much shakiness during filming involves moving very slowly as you work with the camcorder. Abrupt movements do not look good in your video footage.

ZOOMING TECHNIQUES

You can adjust the zoom feature on your camcorder to show a closer image of your subject. All camcorders come with different zoom capabilities. Do not rely solely upon zooming when positioning for a shot. Ideally you need to position yourself as closely as possible to the subject and then adjust zooming to show features.

Zoom Button

All digital video camcorders come with at least one zoom button. Typically located on the right side of your camcorder within easy reach of your fingers, this button works like a toggle switch that zooms in on your subject when you press it forward and zooms back out when you press it backward. Because these buttons are quite sensitive, you can control the speed of the zoom by the amount of pressure you place on the button.

Avoid Zooming When You Film

You rarely want to zoom while you actually film a shot. The video that you shoot during the zoom is uninteresting and not something you want in the final video. If you want to zoom in, stop the recording, zoom to the desired shot, and start filming again.

Optical Zoom Only

Most video camcorders have both an optical and a digital zoom. Of the two, the optical zoom is more important. When you use the digital zoom feature, the camera zooms in on and expands the subject by digitally adding more pixels to the image, which effects the video resolution. When shooting casual video footage, you may not find this an issue, but with professional-level recordings, extra pixels may affect the quality of the resolution. The optical zoom provides a much sharper image because it uses the lens to zoom in on the subject. See Chapter 2 for more information on the Optical Zoom.

Zoom Slowly

If you decide to include a zooming action as part of your video footage, be sure to zoom slowly and smoothly. Quick, jerky zooms do not create attractive footage. A slow, steady zoom requires some practice.

UNDERSTANDING DEPTH OF FIELD

You need to determine the desired *depth of field*, also called focus depth, which is the amount of scene in focus in front of or behind your subject. You establish this based upon the amount of zoom and the aperture setting on your camcorder. Depending on your setting, you either isolate your subject or keep the background in focus for an overall shot.

MORE DEPTH

Zoom Out

Zooming out creates a broader depth of field for your shot. Typically, the more you zoom out, the more you make the entire shot in focus, especially at your camcorder's widest-angle setting. You can create even more depth by adding a wide-angle lens adaptor to your camcorder. See Chapter 2 to learn more about additional lenses.

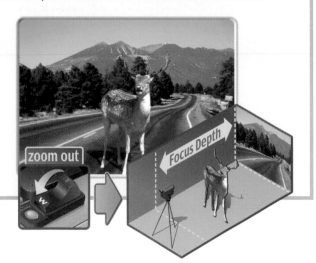

Close Aperture

If you use manual mode to reduce the aperture setting on your camcorder, you increase the depth of field. Basically, as less light enters the lens, more of the shot is in focus.

LESS DEPTH

Zoom In

You can use the optical zoom on your camera to decrease the field of depth. The more you zoom in on an object, the more the background appears blurred and out of focus. Keep in mind that this occurs when you use the digital zoom.

Open Aperture

You can reduce focus depth with the aperture settings by making manual adjustments. When you open the aperture, you allow more light to hit the lens, and the depth of field reduces around your subject.

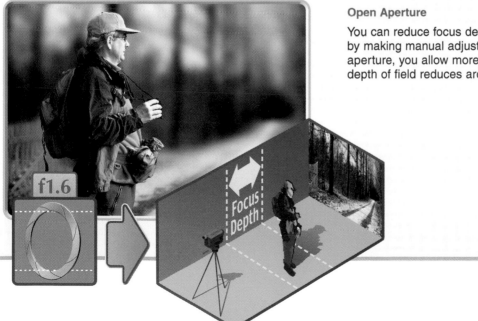

SHOOTING TECHNIQUES FOR DIFFERENT SUBJECT TYPES

You can employ different shooting techniques to capture different types of subject matter for your footage. For example, shooting digital video of animated subjects, such as people or animals, requires different techniques than shooting still subjects, such as landscape or architecture. This section gives you some tips for shooting different types of subject matter.

People

When you record images of people, you need to determine what type of footage you want. Do you want to capture the mood of the person or the actions? People display their moods based upon facial expressions and gestures. Capturing the mood typically requires close-up shots. When filming people, you want to position the camera at their eye level. Avoid the appearance of the people posing for your video footage.

Animals

Shooting footage of animals often requires a lot of patience, especially wild animals. Before attempting to shoot footage, gather information about the animal and its habits. Knowing what an animal eats allows you to better position yourself for the ideal footage; if you stay near the food source, you can wait for the animal to come to you rather than blindly search for it.

If possible, allow an animal to get used to your presence before you start filming. You can capture more natural footage if you do not startle the animal with your presence.

Sporting Events

When you shoot footage of a sporting event, you need to do some pre-planning. You want to position yourself in a location to capture the events without changing positions. Moving from one end of the court to another can create confusion in your video footage. Try to include shots such as fan reaction, players getting ready, and close-up shots of individual players. When filming action shots, you should increase the shutter speed of your camcorder. Keep in mind that moving in and out of the bright lights can cause overexposure in your video footage.

Landscape

When you record footage of a natural landscape, you capture footage with very little movement. You want to keep your camera still, so a tripod is definitely a must. Decide what proportion of the sky to the ground you want to include in the footage. For example, if you capture a tree during a storm, include a portion of the stormy sky as part of the footage. Include people and animals in the shot to help illustrate the size and characteristics of the landscape.

Moving Objects

When you have moving objects in your footage, your camcorder typically needs to move to keep up with the movement.

Your camcorder can move while you remain stationary, *panning*, or you can move along with your camcorder, *tracking*. With panning, do not immediately pan when you start filming. You need to give the viewer a chance to visualize the starting position. When you reach the stop, continue filming in that position for a few seconds.

If you decide to track along with the moving object, set the shot size before you start filming. Maintain the same shot size while you track the subject. Zooming and tracking do not mix well in the same footage. For more on panning and tracking, see the section "Understanding Camera Movements." For more on zooming, see the section "Understanding Depth of Field."

Creating Motion Blur

You can use a *motion blur*, blurring the background of a moving object, to enhance the movement of an object. With a motion blur effect, you enhance the movement of the object because you blur all stationary objects behind the subject. Motion blurs only work when filming objects moving horizontally across the horizon, not toward or away from you. Use a slow shutter speed, such as 1/60, and manually set the focus so that your subject appears focused in the center portion of the frame. After you start filming, pan slowly to keep the subject in the center of your frame.

SHOOT CHROMA KEYS

You can use chroma keys to add special effects to your footage later. *Chroma keys* are essentially a technique of shooting a blue screen image that you can later overlay with other images. Your local television newscast uses blue-screen techniques to film newscasts, particularly the weather report.

Although the weatherman appears to stand in front of a map, he is actually standing in front of a blue screen. The production staff overlays the map on the blue screen to make both images appear together.

Select Your Backdrop

To create footage for use as a chroma key, you must use a solid color backdrop. The best colors are green and blue, hence the name *blue screen*. No matter what color you pick, you should make it a different color than the other images in the video.

Although you typically perform your chroma key against a background, you can use any solid color object as a chroma key effect. For example, a cast member might hold up a solid colored object or poster board behind your subject. Later, you can replace the object or poster board with another video image.

Position Subjects

Next, you arrange the person or objects you want to include in the shot against the chosen background.

Light Evenly

Make sure you light your backdrop evenly so no shadows or highlights show up. If you place people or objects in front of the backdrop, make sure they do not cast shadows on the backdrop. Also, avoid having the color background reflect on your subject. This reflection, referred to as *spill*, is difficult to remove when creating your chroma-keyed image.

Overlay Video

You can only really overlay video on your backdrop by editing the video on a computer. See Chapter 12 for details on overlaying the video with the chroma-keyed shot.

CAPTURE STILL PHOTOS

Nearly all video camcorders allow you to capture still shot digital images, which you can use like any other digital photograph.

Keep in mind, you can capture a still shot image of any digital video shot when you place the footage on your computer.

Picture Quality

Although video camcorders can capture still shots, they do not produce the same high quality images as a digital still camera. Good digital cameras create pictures with images that have two to three times the number of pixels as those produced by digital video camcorders. You find the image quality difference most noticeable when you attempt to enlarge the images.

Picture Storage

Each digital video camcorder provides a different method for storing still photographs. Most video camcorders store the photographs on the same storage medium you use for the video footage. Other manufacturer's video camcorders, such as Sony, store photographs using a separate storage medium.

Picture Button

Digital video camcorders that allow you to take photographs each have a photo button that you click when you want to capture a still image. You typically find this button near the video record button. On some video camcorders, you can snap a photograph while simultaneously recording video.

Picture Use

You can use digital photographs for a wide variety of purposes. After you store them on your digital medium, you can download them to your computer so that you can print them, e-mail them, or even add them to your video presentation.

CHAPTER 7

Editing Solutions and Equipment

After you record video, you can edit the footage using your computer. Editing digital video requires additional hardware and software products. This chapter gives you a look at the equipment and software you need to effectively edit digital video.

EXPLORE SYSTEM REQUIREMENTS

You can transfer your digital video footage to your computer and edit it into a final video project. To do so, your computer must meet a few system requirements. Working with digital video requires a powerful computer with adequate hardware options. Although your computer works well for word processing options, you may not find it powerful enough to handle loading and editing digital video files.

CPU

Most video editing software packages, such as Adobe Premiere or Apple iMovie, require a high-speed processor to function properly. The *central processing unit*, or CPU, acts as the brains of your computer, processing all instructions, calculations, and events. In the case of digital video editing, the faster your CPU, the faster you can process video frames and effects. The speed of the processor dictates the speed of your computer, measured in megahertz (MHz) or gigahertz (GHz). For PC users, you need at least a 300 MHz or higher processor for successful video editing, and for Mac users, a PowerPC processor.

RAM

Most video editing programs use a great deal of RAM for performance and stability. RAM, short for *random access memory*, specifies the amount of temporary storage available to your computer. The computer uses RAM to temporarily store open files and programs, such as video clips. Measured in megabytes (MB), the more RAM you have available on your computer, the better the performance. Your system typically needs a minimum of 128MB of RAM to handle editing digital video. If your computer does not have much RAM, you can upgrade the amount by adding additional memory chips.

Hard Drive Storage

When using a computer to edit video, you need plenty of hard drive space. Your computer's hard drive stores operating system, program, and data files. You measure hard drive storage in megabytes (MB) or gigabytes (GB). You need about 2GB of hard drive space for every 10 minutes of digital video footage. This means you need about 12GB for footage from a one-hour MiniDV tape cassette. If you plan to do a lot of video editing, buy a large-capacity hard drive.

Video and Sound Cards

To get the most out of your video editing, your system should also include a good color video card, also called a *display adapter*, and a high resolution monitor display to allow adequate space for different video editing options. A video card transforms video data into the display you see on your computer monitor. Video cards also have their own memory for storing graphic images; the higher the memory, the better the image quality. Video cards come in several sizes: 16MB, 32MB, 64MB, and 128MB. To properly hear the video's sound, you may also find a good sound card and quality speakers a necessity.

CD and DVD Drives

You need a CD-ROM drive to install most video editing software. For real productivity with your video editing, however, you need a CD-RW (read/write) drive. This type of drive allows you to store digital video footage onto CDs. If your computer includes a DVD drive that allows you to burn, or write, DVDs, you can also store videos onto DVDs. CDs can only store about 650MB on one disc, while a DVD can store 4.7GB. You can purchase drives that allow you to read and write both CDs and DVDs. See Chapter 15 for more information on storing video on DVDs and CDs.

Video Capture Port

To connect your digital video camcorder to your computer for video footage transfer, your computer needs a FireWire or iLink connection port, also called an IEEE 1394 port. Your camcorder must also have such a port. You can learn more about FireWire ports in the section, "Install a Firewire Capture Card." For more on transferring your footage, see Chapter 8.

If you plan to capture analog video footage, you must install an analog capture board, or card, on your computer. An analog capture card digitizes your analog footage so that you can edit it on your computer. Analog capture cards allow you to hook up analog camcorders to transfer footage. You can find analog capture cards for less than $200.

INSTALL A FIREWIRE CAPTURE CARD

To edit digital video, your computer must include a FireWire port, also called an IEEE 1394 port. If you use Sony products, the port is called an iLink. Regardless of the name, the function remains the same. FireWire ports, or cards, provide a high-speed connection of up to 400 megabits per second, making it ideal for transferring digital video from camcorder to computer and back.

For more on transferring your footage from your camera to your computer, see Chapter 8.

Add a FireWire Port

Few multimedia computer systems include an installed FireWire port. If your system does not, you can add one by purchasing a FireWire card at any computer store. FireWire cards are relatively inexpensive, ranging from $30 and up. Some video editing software manufacturers bundle such cards with their programs, so you get both the card and the editing software in one fell swoop. Some cards also allow you to capture analog footage as well as digital footage using separate connectors. You must purchase an *Open Host Controller Interface* — OHCI — compliant card and make sure the card meets your computer's system requirements before attempting to install the card. For example, most cards require a 233 MHz processor or faster.

Software Compatibility

Be sure to purchase a FireWire card that is compatible with the video editing software you intend to use. For example, if you intend to use Adobe Premiere as your video editing program, make sure that the manufacturer certifies the FireWire card to work with Premiere. For example, Windows Movie Maker, for PC users, supports all OHCI-compliant IEEE 1394 cards, Intel, and Philips USB — Universal Serial Bus — capture devices. iMovie, for Mac users, supports all Mac FireWire ports. You can also check the software manufacturers' Web site to find out which cards they support.

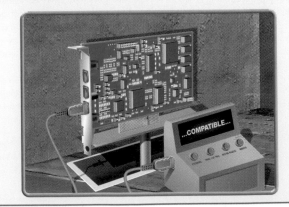

Install a FireWire Card

You need to open the computer and install the card in one of the PCI — or Peripheral Component Interconnect — slots on the computer's motherboard. PCI slots are typically white or ivory color. The FireWire connectors on the card display on the back of the computer, allowing you to hook up a FireWire cable to connect the camcorder to the computer. Be sure to follow the installation instructions included with the card. If you have never installed an internal component before, be sure to seek technical help.

FireWire Cable

You connect you video camcorder to the computer using a FireWire cable. You attach one end of the cable to your computer and the other end to the video camcorder. Before purchasing a FireWire cable, check the size of the connection on your video camcorder. Because the ends of the FireWire cables come in different sizes, you need to make sure you use a cable that matches your camcorder connection.

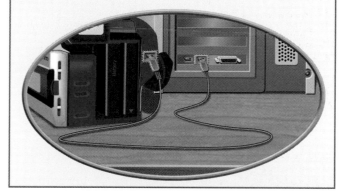

Camera DV Codec

All DV capture cards have built in CODECs for managing the compression and decompression of the video during transfer. Codec is short for compression/decompression. Compressing your video makes the video transfer from the camcorder much smoother. Also, some editing packages require you to connect the camcorder to the computer to edit your video. With a DV capture card, you do not need to connect the camcorder to the computer when you edit footage.

Plug and Play

All devices connected to a FireWire port are *Plug and Play*. This means that your computer immediately recognizes the video camcorder and that your camera automatically sets up to work with the computer. You can also connect and remove your video camcorder from the computer. The computer automatically recognizes it when you connect it.

UNDERSTANDING ANALOG CAPTURE CARDS

You can use an analog capture card, also called a *board*, to transfer analog video footage to your computer for editing. Analog capture cards work a bit differently than FireWire cards. For starters, they digitize the footage from analog format to digital format so that you can work with the footage on your computer. If you use an analog camcorder, such as a VHS or Hi8 camcorder, you need to install a compatible analog capture card on your computer.

Analog Camcorders

Until recently, analog video footage was the norm for capturing video. If you have an analog camcorder — such as VHS, VHS-C, S-VHS, 8mm, and Hi8 — you probably also have plenty of analog videotapes of family events and other recordings in your videotape library. You can turn the footage into digital video with the help of an analog capture card. Before you begin looking for an analog capture card, first identify your analog camcorder. VHS-type camcorders can connect directly to a VCR. VHS camcorders use standard size VHS tape cassettes, while VHS-C and S-VHS camcorders use a compact tape cassette and an adapter to connect to a VCR. 8mm and Hi8 camcorders connect directly to a television for viewing playback.

Shopping for an Analog Capture Card

You can purchase an analog capture card at any computer store. Analog cards are relatively inexpensive, from $40 on up, and you can find good bargains bundled with the video editing software. For example, for around $149.99, you can purchase Dazzle Multimedia's Digital Video Creator that includes both a capture card and software. Make sure the card meets your computer's system requirements before attempting to install the card. Like FireWire cards, most analog cards require a 233 MHz processor or faster.

Types of Analog Connections

Analog capture cards use input/output connections that allow you to hook up an analog camcorder to transfer footage. Footage digitizes as it goes through the card. Analog capture cards include both regular composite video and S-video inputs and outputs. VHS and 8mm camcorders use composite vidoo jacks, which combine both luminance (brightness) and chrominance (color) signals into one analog signal stream. Composite jacks look like RCS stereo jacks. Hi8 and S-VHS camcorders use S-video jacks, which split luminance and chrominance into two wires. To ensure the best quality video, select high-quality cables that are only as long as you need to make the connection. Longer cables mean you have more of a chance of video signal degradation.

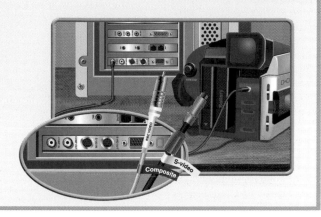

Install an Analog Capture Card

You need to open the computer and install the card in one of the *Peripheral Component Interconnect* — PCI — slots on the computer's motherboard. The connectors on the card appear on the back of the computer allowing you to hook up a camcorder to the computer. Be sure to follow the installation instructions included with the card. For example, you may need to set a few switches on the card before closing the computer's case. If you have never installed an internal component before, be sure to seek technical help.

Software

Your analog capture card requires software to make it work with your computer and your camcorder. After installing the card, install the necessary software that came with the card, being careful to follow the manufacturer's directions. After you install the software, you can hook up the camcorder and test the connection.

UNDERSTANDING VIDEO EDITING SOFTWARE

You can use digital video editing software to edit your video footage. You can find numerous video editing programs on the market today, or your computer may already come with a program you can use. For example, both Microsoft Windows XP and Mac OS X come with a basic video-editing package to capture video footage to the computer, add simple transitions, and output a final video. Before choosing a program, first familiarize yourself with the function and features you can expect to find.

Traditional Video Editing

Until recently, video editing was a chore best accomplished through professional video equipment. Linear in nature, traditional video production starts by transferring video elements to a master videocassette tape in the order in which the editor wants them to appear in the final video. Time-consuming, this process, called *linear editing*, involves shifting back and forth between tapes to find the desired footage. If the editor needs a new scene, he or she must go back and redo all subsequent scenes to make room for the new scene.

Non-Linear Editing Today

Today's video editing software is considered *non-linear*. Instead of assembling a video using numerous tape players, monitors, and expensive editing equipment, you assemble your video on the computer. You assemble clips on a *timeline*, a graphical representation of the entire video project. The program immediately inserts any changes you make to the sequence of your video elements, and subsequent clips shift over to make room for the new footage. Much like you can edit words in a word processing program, you can edit clips in a video editing program.

Types of Video Editing Software

When deciding which video editing software to use, first determine exactly what types of things you want to do with your footage. Do you want to create simple home videos to share with family and friends, or do you want to create professional-level video productions with specialized transitions, titles, and effects? Windows Movie Maker for PCs, included with Windows XP, and iMovie for Macs, included with Mac OS X, are both good beginner-level programs for simple video editing tasks. For greater editing options, consider a program like Pinnacle Studio DV or MGI Videowave. Both retail for under $100. If you want to pursue professional-quality editing features, try a program like Adobe Premiere, MediaStudio Pro, or Apple Final Cut Pro. The higher-end programs cost a lot more, starting at $450 on up.

Capture Video

A primary function of any video editing program is allowing you to transfer the footage to your computer. This transfer process, called *capturing*, enables you to copy portions of your recorded footage, called *clips*, and store them on your computer's hard drive. Most video editing software allows you to specify start and stop points for the footage you want to capture. Some of the more sophisticated programs, such as Adobe Premiere, can even help you batch groups of clips and capture them all at once. In addition to video, most programs allow you to import audio files to use with the video footage, such as music. For more on capturing and batching your video, see Chapter 8.

Arrange Your Clips

After you capture clips into the program, you can arrange the clips in the order in which you want them to appear. Most video editing software uses a timeline feature to visually show where each clip starts and stops. You specify the order of the clips in your video by selecting a clip from the list and dragging it onto the timeline. The beauty of non-linear editing is that it allows you to easily move clips around without having to reassemble the video from scratch. For more on working with timelines, see Chapter 9.

Add Transitions, Titles, and Effects

Most video editing software offers a feature for adding simple transitions. A transition is how one clip moves into the next. Transitions can range from simple cuts, where one clip ends and another starts, or more sophisticated effects, such as fading out one clip and fading in the next. You can also find titling features in most video editing programs that allow you to create title text for your video, such as opening credits or presentation text. Some programs also offer features for creating special effects, such as masks and keys. For more on transitions, special effects, and adding titles, see Chapters 11, 12 and 13, respectively.

TOUR OF WINDOWS MOVIE MAKER

If you use a PC, you can create simple video presentations by combining clips and music using Windows Movie Maker. Movie Maker is a standard Windows XP product that comes as part of the operating system.

Toolbars

Contains all of the options available within Windows Movie Maker.

Monitor Window

Plays individual clips or the entire project.

Collections Area

Lists all of the video collections — containers for organizing clips. Each collection is a separate Movie Maker project.

Clips List

Displays all of the clips, audio and video, within the collection.

Record Narration Button

Click this button to record narration to add to your video.

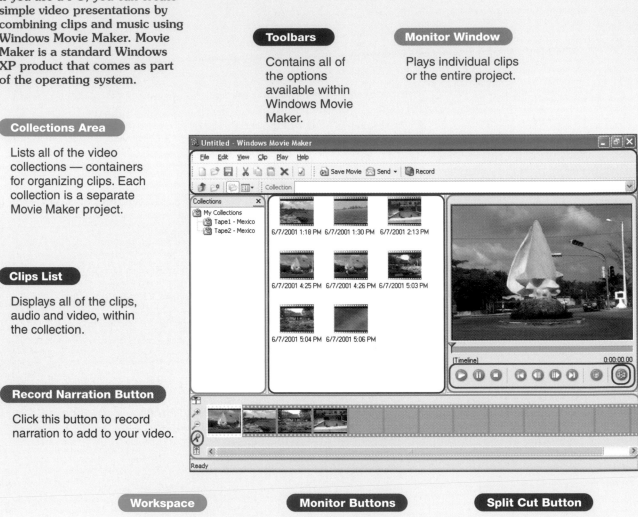

Workspace

Displays the video project either in storyboard or timeline view.

Monitor Buttons

Click the appropriate button to play, stop, fast forward, backup, or pause the video clip.

Split Cut Button

Splits the video clip at the current location.

If you have a Mac, you can create simple video presentations by combining clips and music with iMovie. Apple iMovie 2.0 comes standard with the Mac OS X operating system.

Scrubber Bar

As you play video, the scrubber bar, which represents a timeline, indicates the location of the playhead within that clip or clips.

Menu

Contains all of the options available within iMovie.

Playhead

Displays above the timeline and the scrubber bar, and indicates the position of the current video frame within the entire video.

Design Panels

Lists all available options you can add to your video, when you click one of five buttons: **Clips**, **Transitions**, **Titles**, **Effects**, and **Audio**. The Clips Panel is also referred to as the *Shelf*.

Monitor Window

Plays individual clips or the entire project.

Monitor Buttons

Click the appropriate button to play, stop, fast forward, rewind, or to pause the video clip.

Clip/Timeline Viewer

When you select the Clip viewer, the clips display in the order they appear in the video. When you select the Timeline viewer, the video and audio tracks display for the video.

Clips Button

Displays a list of available video clips.

Transitions Button

Displays a list of available transitions. You can preview the transition in the window.

Titles Button

Allows you to add titles to a specific location in your video. You can select different effects for displaying the title text.

Effects Button

Allows you to change the look of a video clip.

Audio Button

Displays a list of audio you can add, or you can import your own audio.

TOUR OF ADOBE PREMIERE

Adobe Premiere is one of the most popular packages for working with digital video. The software runs on both Microsoft Windows XP and Mac OS X. Adobe Premiere often comes bundled with different video capture cards. Adobe Premiere works well with all of the other Adobe graphic products.

Toolbars

Contains shortcut tools for working with clips and effects.

Monitor Window

Shows both the source and program view of the video clips.

Timeline Window

Organizes your clips sequentially showing the duration and location of each clip in the project.

Project Window

Lists all clips (audio, video, still images, and sequence) in the open video project.

Floating Palettes

Provides options for selecting, editing, and viewing clips.

Playback Controls

Buttons for playing, forwarding, rewinding, stopping, and looping through video clips.

Apple Final Cut Pro is a popular video editing package available for the Mac OS X operating system. This product provides many advanced video editing features not available with iMovie.

Displays the source video so you can select the clips you want.

Menu

Contains all of the options available within Final Cut Pro.

Canvas Window

Displays the edited sequence of video clips.

Transport Controls

Click the appropriate button to play, stop, fast forward, or rewind the video clip.

Editing and Marking Controls

Click the appropriate button to mark the beginning and end of a clip.

Browser Window

You select elements of your video from this window by clicking on the desired video clip or transition, and dragging it to the desired location in the Timeline window.

Effects Tab

Provides access to Final Cut Pro's audio and video effects, filters, and generators.

Timeline Window

Lists the sequences in the selected project in chronological order. You have a separate sequence for each audio and video track.

Audio Meters

Display audio output levels for your project.

Tool Palette

Provides buttons for editing, zooming, cropping, and distorting timeline clips.

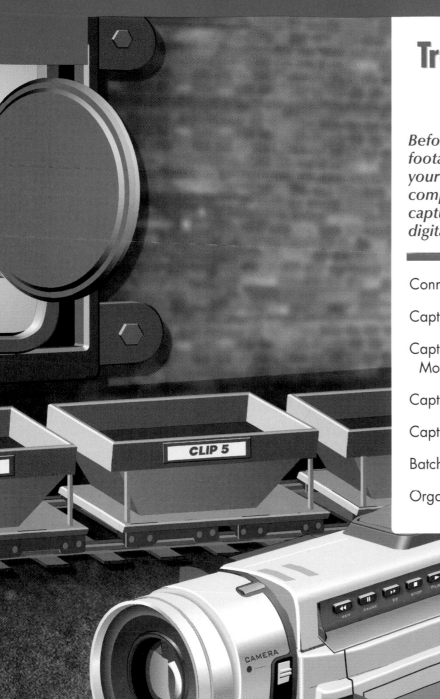

CHAPTER 8

Transferring Footage to a Computer

Before you can edit your video footage, you must transfer it from your digital video camera to the computer. This chapter looks at capturing digital video using different digital video software programs.

CONNECT A VIDEO SOURCE

To start transferring your footage, you must connect your video source to a computer. Your video footage can come from a digital video camera, a recording deck, or even an analog video source. The source of your video determines the method you use to connect to the computer. You follow a three-step procedure for digital cameras. With analog cameras, you have different ways to capture and edit on your computer. Select the method that works best for your computer and video camera setup.

DIGITAL SOURCE

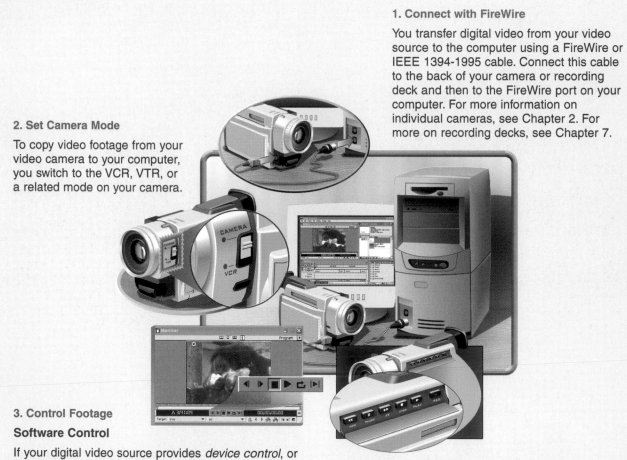

1. Connect with FireWire

You transfer digital video from your video source to the computer using a FireWire or IEEE 1394-1995 cable. Connect this cable to the back of your camera or recording deck and then to the FireWire port on your computer. For more information on individual cameras, see Chapter 2. For more on recording decks, see Chapter 7.

2. Set Camera Mode

To copy video footage from your video camera to your computer, you switch to the VCR, VTR, or a related mode on your camera.

3. Control Footage

Software Control

If your digital video source provides *device control*, or the ability to control camera playback functions, you can control the camera from your computer. Your video capture software provides buttons for controlling the play, fast forward, rewind, and stop functions of the camera.

If you have the feature, you can control your camera playback functions from your computer.

Manual Control

To control your video camera manually, you press the Play, Rewind, Fast Forward, and Stop buttons on the camera.

ANALOG SOURCE

Connect to Capture Card

Some video *capture cards*, the computer cards designed specifically for capturing video from external video sources, provide both analog and FireWire connections. With an analog connection, you plug your source directly into your computer using the appropriate composite video cables — the same cables you use to view video footage on a television from your analog video source.

Connect Through Digital Video Camera

Some digital video cameras, such as the Sony DCR VX2000, allow you to pass an analog source to a computer. You do this by connecting your analog camera to the back of the digital video camera and then connecting the digital video camera to the FireWire port on the computer. When you play the video on your analog source, it passes through the digital video camera to the computer. You must select the A/V ⇨ DV Out option, or a similar option, on the digital video camera. Check your digital video camera documentation for availability.

Record to Digital Video Source

If you cannot connect your analog video source directly to your computer, consider connecting it to your digital video camera and recording the analog video as digital. After you record your footage, you can use your digital FireWire connection to transfer it to your computer.

CAPTURE WITH APPLE IMOVIE

You can use Apple iMovie to capture digital video footage with the express purpose of editing it. Because the DV format is specific to iMovie, you should only capture footage with iMovie if you intend to edit with this program as well. As you capture video, iMovie recognizes scene changes and creates a new clip.

CAPTURE WITH APPLE IMOVIE

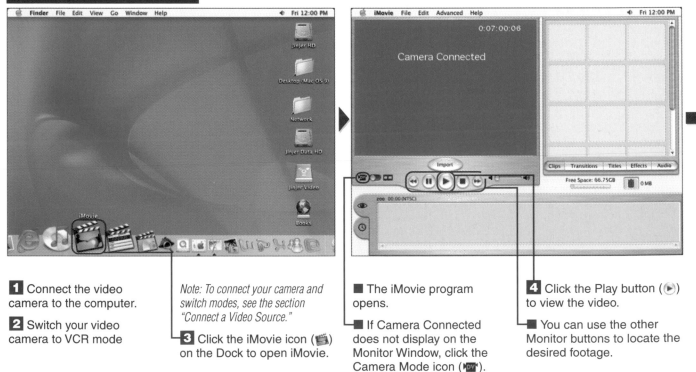

1 Connect the video camera to the computer.

2 Switch your video camera to VCR mode

Note: To connect your camera and switch modes, see the section "Connect a Video Source."

3 Click the iMovie icon (🎬) on the Dock to open iMovie.

■ The iMovie program opens.

■ If Camera Connected does not display on the Monitor Window, click the Camera Mode icon (DV).

4 Click the Play button (▶) to view the video.

■ You can use the other Monitor buttons to locate the desired footage.

Can I import clips directly into iMovie?

Yes. You select this option in the Preference dialog box, which you open by clicking **iMovie** and then **Preferences**. In the Preferences dialog box:

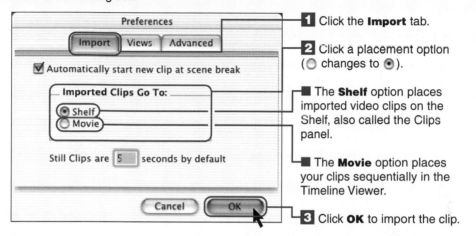

1 Click the **Import** tab.

2 Click a placement option (◯ changes to ◉).

■ The **Shelf** option places imported video clips on the Shelf, also called the Clips panel.

■ The **Movie** option places your clips sequentially in the Timeline Viewer.

3 Click **OK** to import the clip.

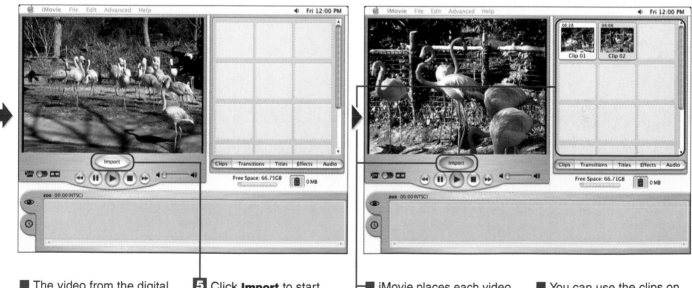

■ The video from the digital camera displays on the monitor window.

5 Click **Import** to start recording.

■ iMovie places each video clip on the Clips panel.

6 Click **Import** to stop recording.

■ The video continues playing in the Monitor window.

■ You can use the clips on the shelf to create your video project.

Note: See Chapter 7 for information on the various parts of the iMovie window. See Chapter 9 for more on creating your video project.

CAPTURE WITH WINDOWS MOVIE MAKER

Windows Movie Maker comes as a feature of Windows XP. With it, you can capture digital video and create movies that users can view with Windows Media Player.

CAPTURE WITH WINDOWS MOVIE MAKER

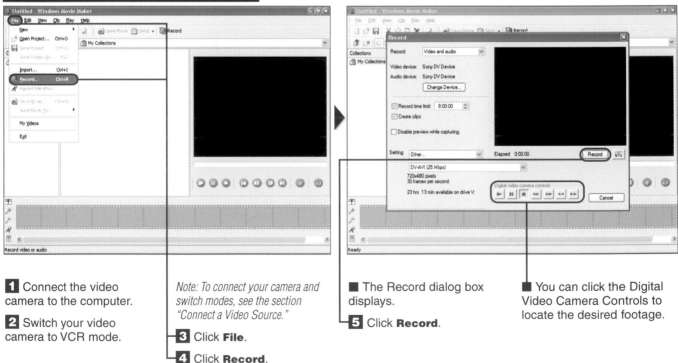

1 Connect the video camera to the computer.

2 Switch your video camera to VCR mode.

Note: To connect your camera and switch modes, see the section "Connect a Video Source."

3 Click **File**.

4 Click **Record**.

■ The Record dialog box displays.

5 Click **Record**.

■ You can click the Digital Video Camera Controls to locate the desired footage.

**How do I save my video
clips in a different format?**

By default, Movie Maker
saves your video clips in
the AVI format. To change
the file format of your video
clips, follow steps **1**
through **4** in this section to
open the Record dialog
box. Click the Settings box
☑ and click **Other**. Click
☑ in the box under the
Settings box and select
the desired format.

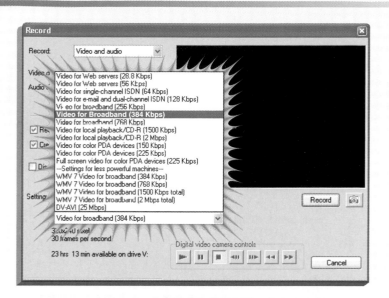

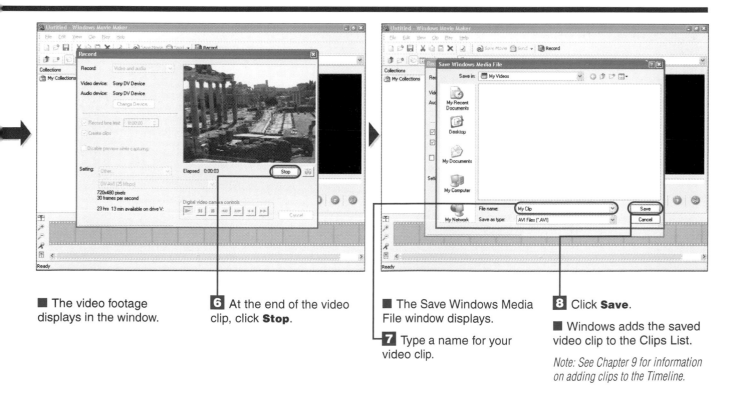

■ The video footage
displays in the window.

6 At the end of the video
clip, click **Stop**.

■ The Save Windows Media
File window displays.

7 Type a name for your
video clip.

8 Click **Save**.

■ Windows adds the saved
video clip to the Clips List.

*Note: See Chapter 9 for information
on adding clips to the Timeline.*

CAPTURE WITH ADOBE PREMIERE

You can use Adobe Premiere on either a Microsoft Windows or Mac OS operating system to capture digital video from your camera. If you use Premiere, you can save your video clips in a variety of different formats.

CAPTURE WITH ADOBE PREMIERE

1 Connect the video camera to the computer.

2 Switch your video camera to VCR mode.

Note: To connect your camera and switch modes, see the section "Connect a Video Source."

3 Click **File**.

4 Click **Capture**.

5 Click **Movie Capture**.

■ The Movie Capture dialog box displays.

6 Click the Play button (▶).

7 Click the Record button (●).

■ You can click the other Capture window controls to locate the desired footage.

How do I play my video footage in slow motion to locate my start point?

You can use the Shuttle bar to slowly move forward and backward through your footage on your video camera. To move the video, click the Shuttle bar and drag it right to move forward or left to rewind.

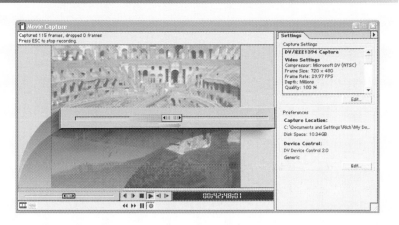

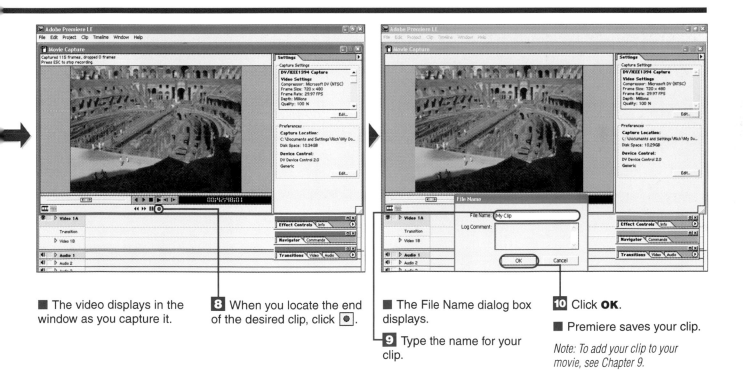

■ The video displays in the window as you capture it.

8 When you locate the end of the desired clip, click [⬤].

■ The File Name dialog box displays.

9 Type the name for your clip.

10 Click **OK**.

■ Premiere saves your clip.

Note: To add your clip to your movie, see Chapter 9.

CAPTURE WITH APPLE FINAL CUT PRO

You can use Apple Final Cut Pro to capture digital video on your Mac OS 10 computer. Although you have several methods for capturing, the easiest method involves using the Now button in the Log and Capture dialog box when you find the desired clip.

CAPTURE WITH APPLE FINAL CUT PRO

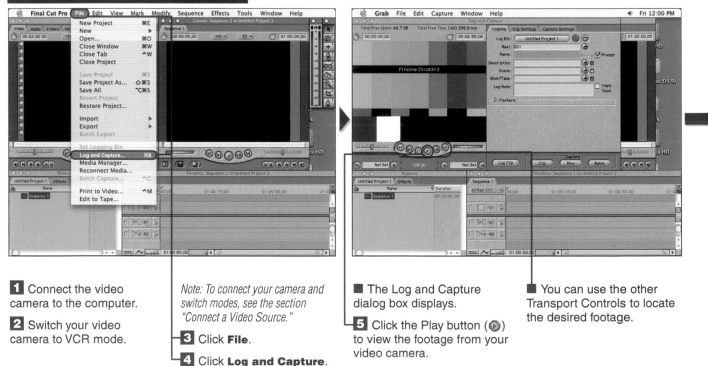

1 Connect the video camera to the computer.

2 Switch your video camera to VCR mode.

Note: To connect your camera and switch modes, see the section "Connect a Video Source."

3 Click **File**.

4 Click **Log and Capture**.

■ The Log and Capture dialog box displays.

5 Click the Play button (▶) to view the footage from your video camera.

■ You can use the other Transport Controls to locate the desired footage.

How do I find my video clip?

When you press Esc, Final Cut Pro places each video clip on your desktop in a separate window and sequentially numbers their names. The first clip becomes Untitled 0001, the second Untitled 0002, and so on. You can save the video clip by clicking **File**, **Save As,** and then typing the desired clip name. To add the clip to the current project, click and drag it into the Project window.

■ The video footage displays in the Viewer window.

Note: For more on the various parts of the Final Cut Pro window, see Chapter 7.

6 When you locate the desired clip, click **Now**.

■ The video footage plays in a full screen window.

7 At the end of the footage, press Esc.

■ Final Cut Pro completes the capture.

BATCH CAPTURE

If you have a lot of footage to capture, consider using the Batch capture mode available with most advanced editing packages, including Final Cut Pro and Premiere. When you batch capture, you log your clips — a process of marking the beginning and ending of the clip — and then your video editing package copies all the clips at once.

Although this task illustrates batch capturing with Final Cut Pro, the process is very similar with Premiere. iMovie and Movie Maker do not offer this feature.

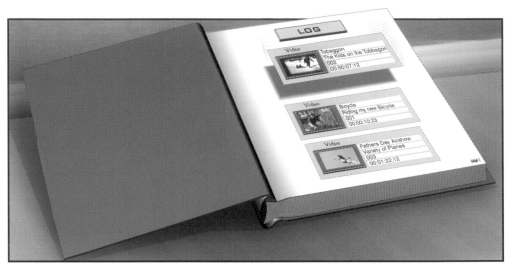

BATCH CAPTURE

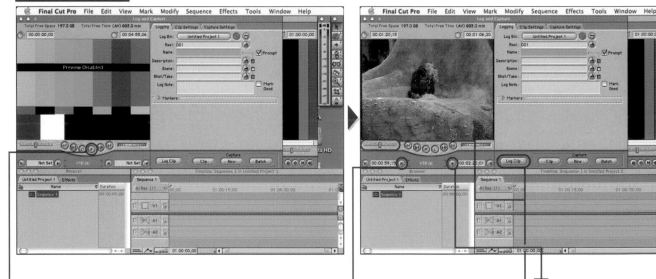

LOG CLIPS

1 In the Log and Capture dialog box, click ▶.

Note: See the section "Capture with Apple Final Cut Pro" to access the Log and Capture dialog box.

Note: Batch capturing is not available with all video cameras. Refer to your video camera documentation for more information.

■ The video footage displays in the Monitor window.

2 When you locate the desired footage, click ⬛ to mark the start of the footage.

3 When you find the end of the footage, click ⬛ to mark the end of the footage.

■ You can also move the Shuttle bar to locate the desired start and stop.

4 Click **Log Clip**.

Can I log clips for batch capturing with Premiere?

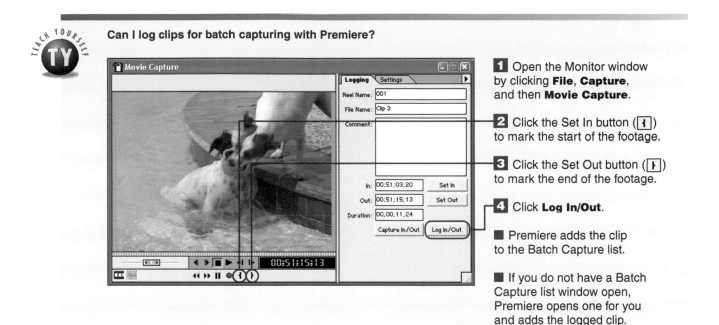

1 Open the Monitor window by clicking **File**, **Capture**, and then **Movie Capture**.

2 Click the Set In button ([↑]) to mark the start of the footage.

3 Click the Set Out button ([↑]) to mark the end of the footage.

4 Click **Log In/Out**.

■ Premiere adds the clip to the Batch Capture list.

■ If you do not have a Batch Capture list window open, Premiere opens one for you and adds the logged clip.

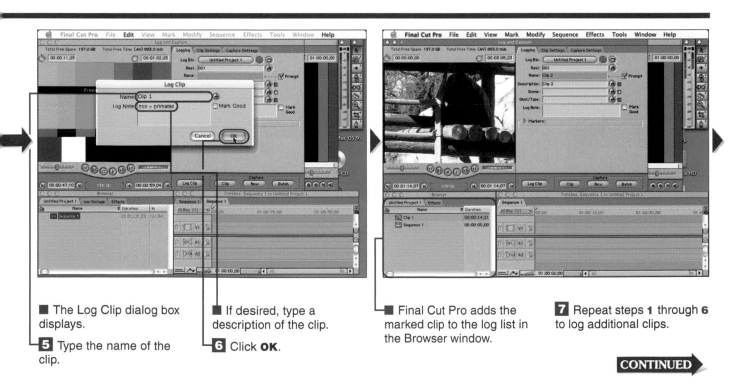

■ The Log Clip dialog box displays.

5 Type the name of the clip.

■ If desired, type a description of the clip.

6 Click **OK**.

■ Final Cut Pro adds the marked clip to the log list in the Browser window.

7 Repeat steps **1** through **6** to log additional clips.

CONTINUED ▶

BATCH CAPTURE

When you select the Batch capture option, the editing software takes the clips listed in the log, locates them on the digital camera, and copies them to your computer. Using the Batch mode, you can leave the computer to capture the clips while you take care of other issues.

BATCH CAPTURE (CONTINUED)

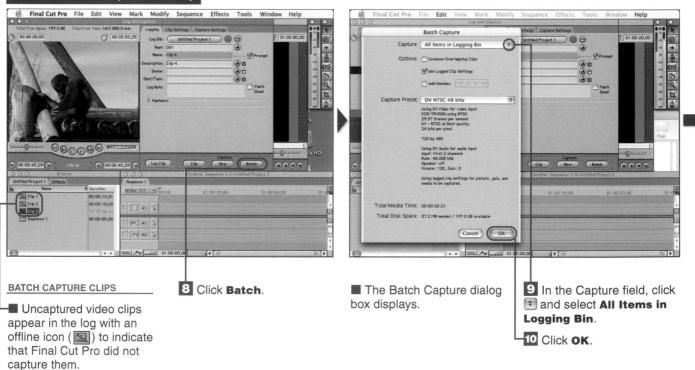

BATCH CAPTURE CLIPS

■ Uncaptured video clips appear in the log with an offline icon (▥) to indicate that Final Cut Pro did not capture them.

8 Click **Batch**.

■ The Batch Capture dialog box displays.

9 In the Capture field, click ⬍ and select **All Items in Logging Bin**.

10 Click **OK**.

How do I start a Batch capture with Premiere?

In Premiere, you start a batch capture by clicking , which you find located at the bottom center of the Batch Capture list window. When you click this button, Premiere captures all of the logged clips in the list. Each captured clip appears in the Project window.

Can I batch capture with my video camera?

Your video camera may inhibit your ability to batch capture clips. Batch capturing uses the timecode, a sequential unit of time, on the video tape to identify the start and stop of each clip. If your video camera did not record a sequential timecode from the beginning of the video tape, you need to manually capture your footage. Refer to your video camera documentation for specific timecode features of your camera.

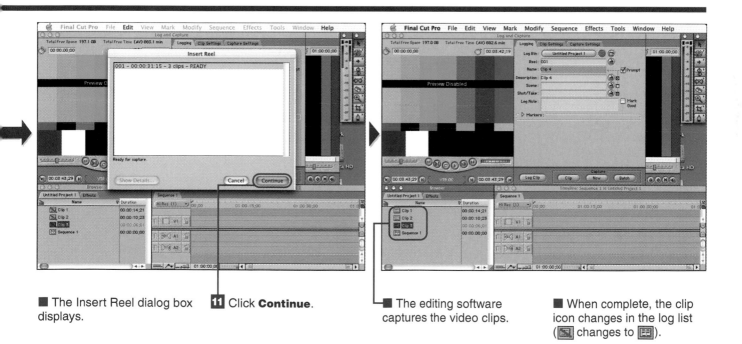

■ The Insert Reel dialog box displays.

11 Click **Continue**.

■ The editing software captures the video clips.

■ When complete, the clip icon changes in the log list.

ORGANIZE CLIPS

You can organize your video clips into different bins to make them easier to organize. You can create different bins or folders and then drag different clips into the bins.

Although this task illustrates organizing clips with Final Cut Pro, the process is very similar with Premiere and Movie Maker. You cannot create bins in iMovie.

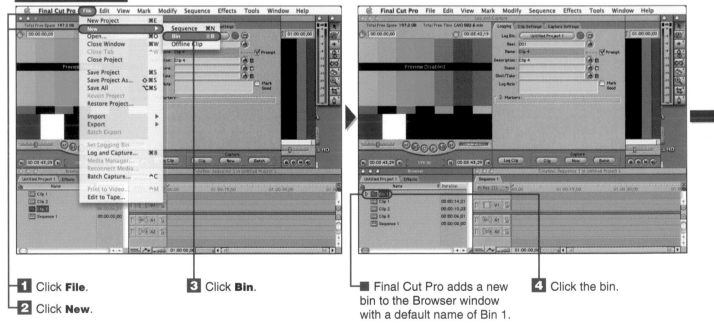

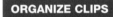
1 Click **File**.

2 Click **New**.

3 Click **Bin**.

■ Final Cut Pro adds a new bin to the Browser window with a default name of Bin 1.

4 Click the bin.

Can I organize my clips in Premiere and Movie Maker?

Premiere

Yes. Click **File**, **New**, and then **Bin** to display the Create Bin dialog box. Type the name of the new bin and click **OK**. Premiere adds the new bin to the project window. To move clips to the bin, click to select the desired clip and drag it onto the desired bin.

Movie Maker

Yes, although Movie Maker refers to bins as *collections*. Movie Maker keeps all your clips in collections that you can access from any project. To create a new collection in Movie Maker, click the collection you want as the parent to the new collection. Click **File**, **New**, and then **Collection**. Movie Maker creates a new collection inside of the selected collection. To add clips to the collection, click to select the desired clip and drag it onto the desired collection.

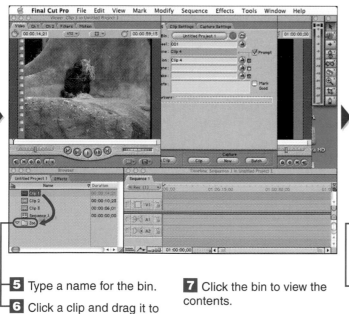

5 Type a name for the bin.

6 Click a clip and drag it to the bin.

7 Click the bin to view the contents.

■ The contents of the bin display under the bin.

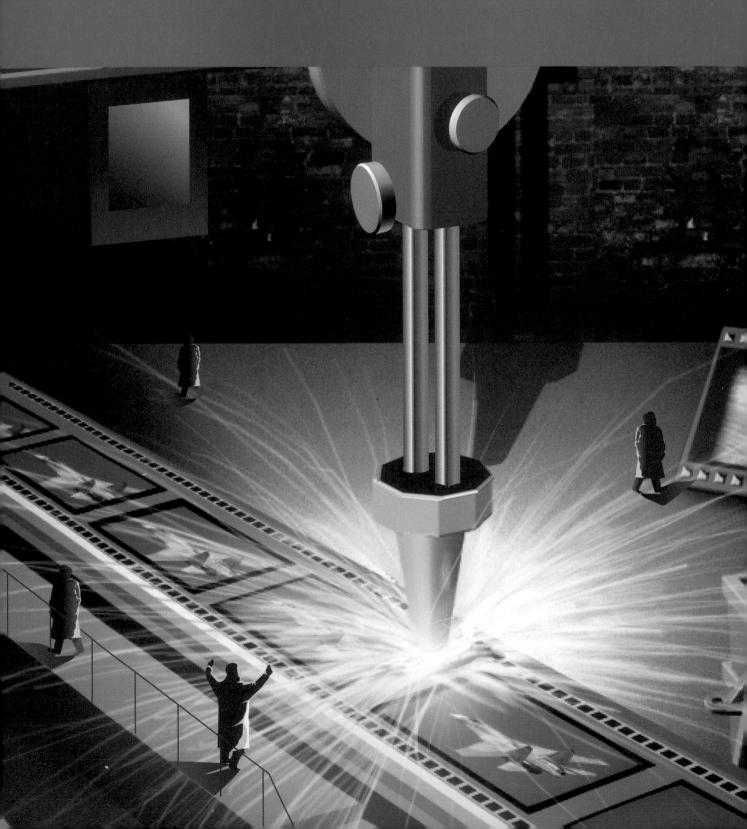

CHAPTER 9

Timeline Tasks

You use the timeline in your video-editing software to control the video clips. You can add, remove, reorder, and change the length of the clips in the timeline. This chapter looks at the different tasks you perform to create the video project and insert the desired clips.

CREATE A VIDEO PROJECT

You need to create
a *video project*, a
container for all video
clips, music clips,
special effects, and the
actual video project, in
your video-editing
software to store all
items related to your
video. Although this
section illustrates
iMovie, you can also
create a video project in
Premiere, Movie Maker,
and Final Cut Pro.

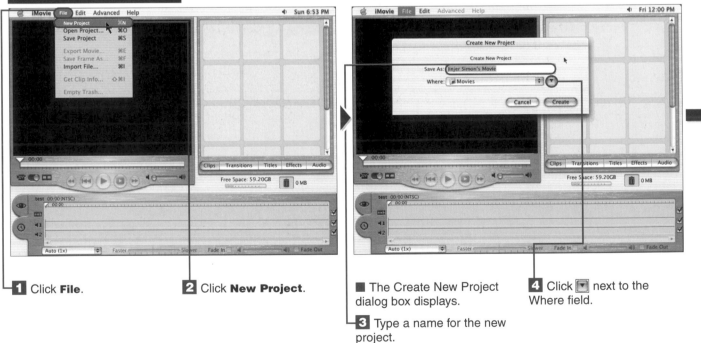

1 Click **File**.

2 Click **New Project**.

■ The Create New Project dialog box displays.

3 Type a name for the new project.

4 Click ▼ next to the Where field.

How do I create a video project in Premiere, Movie Maker, and Final Cut Pro?

Adobe Premiere

Click **File**, and then **New Project** to open the options in the Load Project Settings dialog box. Click an option (○ changes to ◉). Click **DV-NTSC** for video equipment sold in the United States and most other countries, or **DV-PAL** for equipment from European countries. Click **Standard 32kHz**, **Standard 48 kHz**, **Widescreen 32 kHz**, or **Widescreen 48 kHz**. The Widescreen option is only for video filmed in 16 by 9 ratio; otherwise, select the Standard option. The 48 kHz option is for audio filmed at 16-bit, and the 32 kHz option is for both 12- and 16-bit audio. Click **OK** to create an untitled project.

Movie Maker

Click **File**, **New**, and then **Project**. Movie Maker creates a new project, *Untitled*, which you need to name. To specify a name and location for the project, click **File**, and then **Save Project** to display the Save Project dialog box where you type the project information.

Final Cut Pro

Click **File**, and then **New Project**. Final Cut Pro creates a new untitled project. You specify a name for the project by clicking **File**, and then **Save Project As** to display the Save dialog box. Type a name for the project and click the storage location. Click **Save** to create the project.

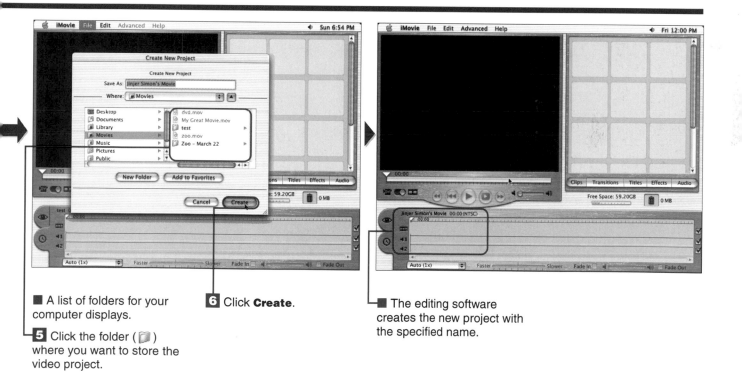

■ A list of folders for your computer displays.

5 Click the folder (🗀) where you want to store the video project.

6 Click **Create**.

■ The editing software creates the new project with the specified name.

IMPORT VIDEO CLIPS

You add video clips to a video project to create your video. You can add clips either by capturing them from a video source, as discussed in Chapter 8, or by importing the video files. When you import video clips into your video project, the original video files remain intact. The editing software creates a link back to the original video clip file. Remember that because you linked the video clip to a project, if you move a video clip file, your project can no longer access the file.

Although this section illustrates Adobe Premiere, you can also import in iMovie, Movie Maker, and Final Cut Pro. You can select a specific file type to import, although you should select the format that corresponds to the type of file you want to import into your video project.

IMPORT VIDEO CLIPS

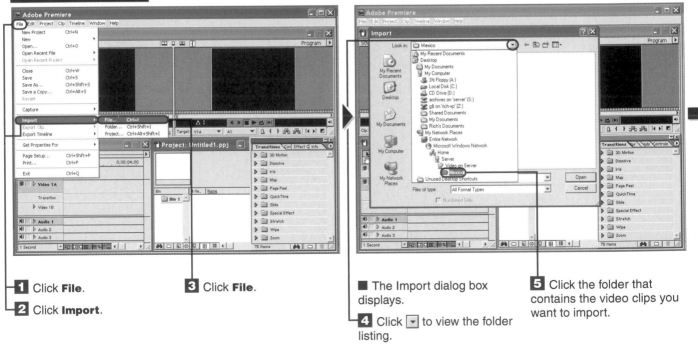

1 Click **File**.

2 Click **Import**.

3 Click **File**.

■ The Import dialog box displays.

4 Click ▼ to view the folder listing.

5 Click the folder that contains the video clips you want to import.

How do I import video clips into Final Cut Pro, Movie Maker, and iMovie?

Final Cut Pro

Click **File**, **Import**, and then **Files** to display the Choose a File dialog box. Click the desired video clip file and click **Choose**. Final Cut Pro adds the video clip to the Browser window.

Movie Maker

Click **File**, **Import** to display the Select the File to Import dialog box. Click the desired video clip and click **Open**. The video clip displays in the Collections Area.

iMovie

Click **File**, and then **Import File** to display the Import File dialog box. Click the desired video clip file and click **Import**. The selected video clip displays on the Clips panel.

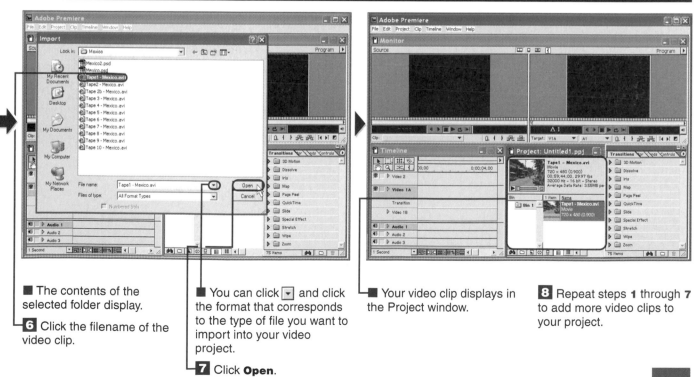

■ The contents of the selected folder display.

6 Click the filename of the video clip.

■ You can click ▾ and click the format that corresponds to the type of file you want to import into your video project.

7 Click **Open**.

■ Your video clip displays in the Project window.

8 Repeat steps **1** through **7** to add more video clips to your project.

ANATOMY OF A TIMELINE

You use the Timeline window in your video-editing software to lay out your video by arranging video and audio clips in the order you want them to play. You can add transitions, titles, and special effects, on *tracks*, or separate layers. Adobe Premiere and Final Cut Pro have ample tracks for layout. For more on audio clips, see Chapter 10. See Chapters 11, 12, and 13 for more on transitions, effects, and titles, respectively.

THE ADOBE PREMIERE TIMELINE

Edit Line

Indicates the current time position within the video.

Work Area Bar

Defines the work area portion of your video for previewing and exporting.

Time Ruler

Displays a ruler that helps you determine the start and stop points for each clip as well as the entire length of the clips. You use the Time Ruler to position your clips.

Keyframe

Marks the start or end of a clip by indicating changes in the clip's characteristics, such as the opacity of the video clip.

Transition

Shows the location of a video transition.

Video 2 Track

Contains video overlays, such as titles.

Video 1 Track

Contains the clips for the primary video track. If you use A/B editing, Video 1 track displays as Video 1A and Video 1B for showing transitions between clips. With single-track editing, Video 1 track displays as a single track with all clips and transitions on that single track.

Transition Track

Shows transitions between clips.

Audio Tracks

Contain audio clips for the video.

Title Clip

Adds a label as an overlay to the video clip in Video 1 track.

Video Clip

Represents an actual video clip sized to represent the actual clip length. The start and stop frames display for the clip.

Audio Clip

Represents an actual audio clip on the timeline. The clip size represents its actual length.

THE WINDOWS MOVIE MAKER TIMELINE

Zoom In Button

Increases the
size of the
timeline on
your display.

Play Indicator

Indicates the
current time
position within
the video.

Transition

Shows the location
of a video transition.

Video Track

Contains all video
clips and transitions
in the video.

Video Clip

Represents an actual
video clip on the
timeline. The clip size
represents its actual
length. The start and
stop frames display
for the clip.

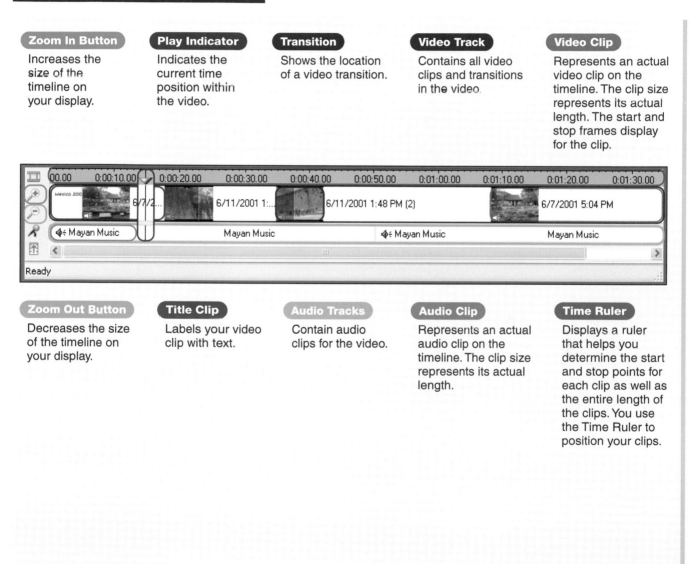

Zoom Out Button

Decreases the size
of the timeline on
your display.

Title Clip

Labels your video
clip with text.

Audio Tracks

Contain audio
clips for the video.

Audio Clip

Represents an actual
audio clip on the
timeline. The clip size
represents its actual
length.

Time Ruler

Displays a ruler
that helps you
determine the start
and stop points for
each clip as well as
the entire length of
the clips. You use
the Time Ruler to
position your clips.

ANATOMY OF A TIMELINE

Render Quality Button

Indicates the quality at which the video builds transitions and special effects. To change the Render Quality, click the button to display a menu of render quality options.

V2 Track

Contains video overlays, such as titles.

V1 Track

Contains the clips and transitions for the main video track.

Timeline Ruler

Displays a ruler that helps you determine the start and stop points for each clip as well as the entire length of the clips. You use the Timeline Ruler to position your clips.

Transition

Shows the location of a video transition.

Title Clip

Labels your video clip in the V1 track.

Playhead

Indicates the current time position within the video.

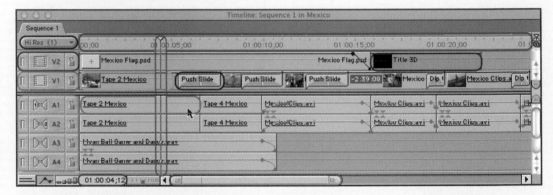

Audio Tracks

Contain audio clips for the video.

Current Timecode Field

Identifies the current position of the playhead. You can type a new timecode number to change the position of the playhead.

Video Clip

Represents an actual video clip on the timeline. The clip size represents its actual length. The start frame displays for the clip unless you play the clip.

Audio Clip

Represents an actual audio clip on the timeline. The clip size represents its actual length.

Zoom Slider

Increases or decreases the size of the timeline on the display. You drag the thumb tabs ( ) on the sides of the slider to change the timeline size.

THE APPLE IMOVIE TIMELINE

Video Track

Contains all of
the clips and
transitions for
the video.

Playhead

Indicates the
current time
position within
the video.

Title Clip

Contains a text
label added to the
video either as a
separate clip or
an overlay of a
video clip.

Timeline Ruler

Displays a ruler that
helps you determine
the start and stop
points for each clip
as well as the entire
length of the clips.
You use the Timeline
Ruler to position
your clips.

Video Clip

Represents an actual
video clip on the
timeline. The clip size
represents the actual
clip length within the
video. The start
frame displays for
the clip unless you
play the clip.

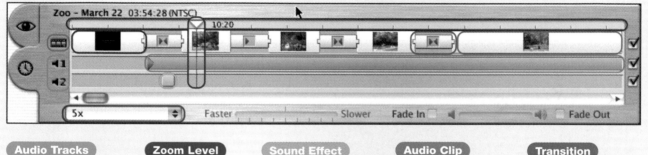

Audio Tracks

Contain audio clips
for the video. iMovie
provides two separate
audio tracks for adding
sound to your video.

Zoom Level

Indicates the
current zoom level
for the timeline. To
change the zoom
level, click and
select the desired
zoom level.

Sound Effect

Adds a built-in sound
to the video. iMovie
provides several
different sound effects
that you can add to
your video.

Audio Clip

Represents an actual
audio clip on the
timeline. The clip size
represents the actual
clip length in relation
to the entire video.

Transition

Shows the location
of a video transition.

ADD CLIPS TO THE TIMELINE

You add clips to your timeline to create the actual video. You can create a video that contains only one clip or a multitude of different video, audio, and still shots. Keep in mind that video clips play in the order you list them on the timeline.

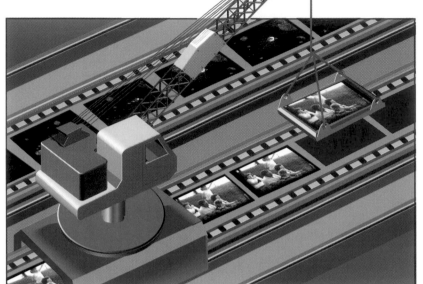

Although, this example uses Final Cut Pro and iMovie to illustrate how to add clips to a timeline, you use the same click-and-drag technique to add clips in Adobe Premiere and Movie Maker.

For more information concerning the various parts of a specific program's window, see Chapter 7. For more information about the parts of a timeline, see the section "Anatomy of a Timeline."

ADD CLIPS TO THE TIMELINE

USING FINAL CUT PRO

1 Click the clip you want to add to the video.

■ If the Browser window does not display click **Window**, and then **Browser**.

2 Drag the clip to the desired location on the timeline.

■ As you drag the clip, it appears grayed out under the cursor.

3 Release the mouse button.

■ The video clip inserts in the timeline at the location of the mouse.

How do I add clips to the timeline with Premiere and Movie Maker?

Premiere

Click the desired clip in the Project Bin window and drag it to the appropriate location on the timeline. As you drag, a black line shows the clip's location. Release the mouse button to place the clip. Keep in mind that when you add a video clip to the timeline, Adobe places the audio portion of the clip on the corresponding Audio track.

Movie Maker

Click the desired clip in the Collections area and drag it to the appropriate location on the timeline. As you drag, a black line shows the clip's location. Release the mouse button to place the clip.

USING IMOVIE

1 Click **Clips**.

■ The Clips panel displays.

2 Click the clip you want to add and drag it to the desired location on the timeline.

■ The clip appears grayed out under the cursor and a blue bar shows the clip's insertion point on the timeline.

3 Release the mouse button.

■ The video clip inserts in the timeline at the location of the insertion point.

137

TRIM A CLIP

You can trim frames from the beginning and end of any video clip to shorten it. When you trim a video clip, you need to mark the new start and end points within the clip.

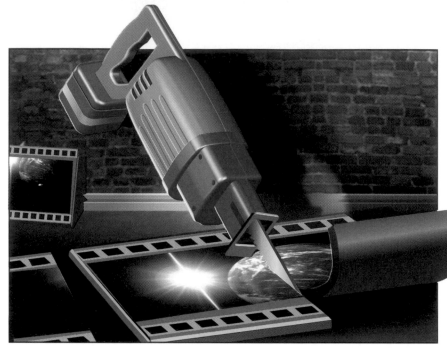

Although this section uses Adobe Premiere to illustrate how to trim clips, you can also trim clips in iMovie, Final Cut Pro, and Movie Maker.

For specific information concerning the various parts of a program's window, see Chapter 7. For more on the specific parts of a timeline, see the section "Anatomy of a Timeline."

TRIM A CLIP

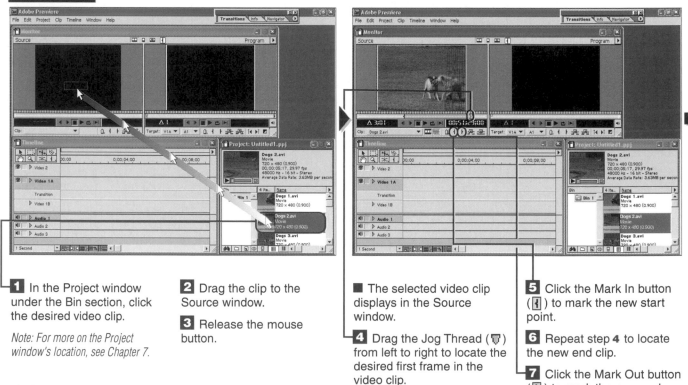

1 In the Project window under the Bin section, click the desired video clip.

Note: For more on the Project window's location, see Chapter 7.

2 Drag the clip to the Source window.

3 Release the mouse button.

■ The selected video clip displays in the Source window.

4 Drag the Jog Thread (▽) from left to right to locate the desired first frame in the video clip.

5 Click the Mark In button ([|) to mark the new start point.

6 Repeat step **4** to locate the new end clip.

7 Click the Mark Out button (|]) to mark the new end point.

How do I trim clips in Final Cut Pro, iMovie, and Movie Maker?

Final Cut Pro

In the Browser window, click the video clip and drag it to the Viewer window. Release the mouse button. Drag the Playhead (▽) under the viewer window from left to right to locate the starting frame in the video clip. Click ⬤. Drag the Playhead to the final frame. Click ⬤. Drag the video clip from the Viewer window to the desired location on the timeline.

iMovie

Here, you specify the frames to remove from the video clip using the crop marks (◁). Click the desired video clip in the Clips panel. The clip displays in the Monitor window. Drag (↖) below the Scrubber bar (▬▬) to display ◁. Drag the beginning ◁ to the first clip you want

to trim and the ending ◁ to the last clip. The yellow area between the crop marks indicates the frames that iMovie retains; iMovie removes the blue area outside the crop marks. Click **Edit**, and then **Clear**. Drag the clip to the timeline.

Movie Maker

Here, you split clips from the timeline. Play the video on the timeline. When you locate the frame you want to trim, click **Clip**, and then **Set Start Trim Point**. Locate the last frame to remove and click **Clip**, and then **Set End Trim Point**. Movie Maker removes the selected frames from the video. To undo the process, click **Clip**, and then **Clear Trim Points**.

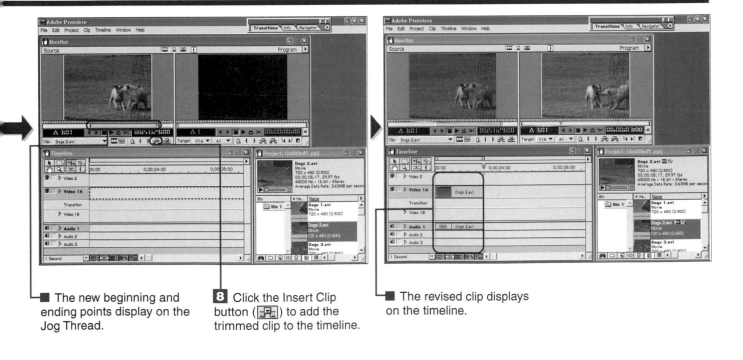

■ The new beginning and ending points display on the Jog Thread.

8 Click the Insert Clip button (⊞) to add the trimmed clip to the timeline.

■ The revised clip displays on the timeline.

CHANGE THE ORDER OF CLIPS

You can change the order of clips in your video on the timeline. You change the order by moving a video clip either in front of or behind another clip. Although this section illustrates changing the order of clips with Movie Maker, you use the same click-and-drag technique in Adobe Premiere and Final Cut Pro.

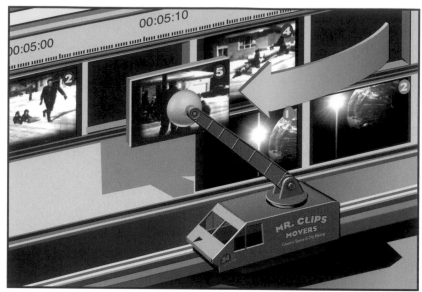

If you want to reorder clips in iMovie, you need to remove the clip from the timeline and add it again at the desired location. See the section "Cut and Paste Clips on the Timeline" for more information.

CHANGE THE ORDER OF CLIPS

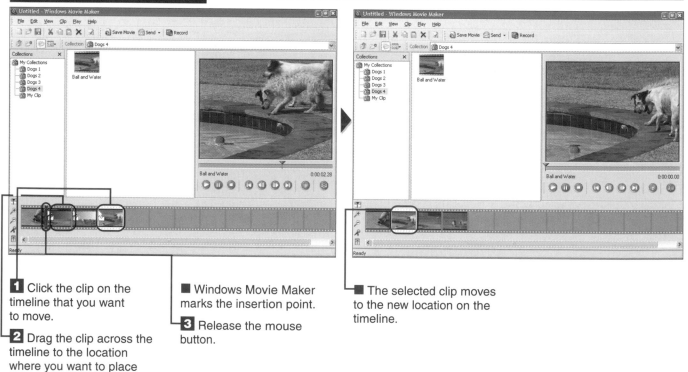

1 Click the clip on the timeline that you want to move.

2 Drag the clip across the timeline to the location where you want to place the clip.

■ Windows Movie Maker marks the insertion point.

3 Release the mouse button.

■ The selected clip moves to the new location on the timeline.

ADD TRACKS TO THE TIMELINE

To insert overlays and special effects in your video, you must add additional video tracks to your timeline. You can only add tracks to a timeline in Adobe Premiere and Final Cut Pro.

Although this section illustrates adding tracks in Final Cut Pro, you can use the same steps to add them in Adobe Premiere. For more on adding overlays, see the section "Create a Video Overlay." For more on special effects, see Chapter 12.

ADD TRACKS TO THE TIMELINE

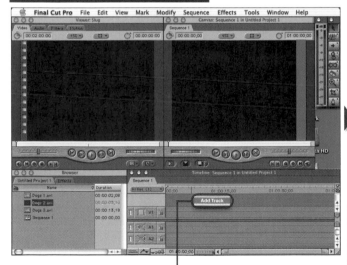

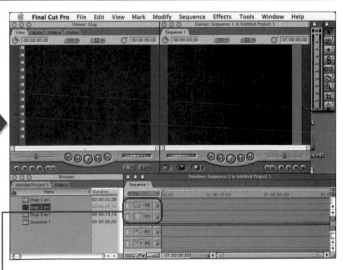

1 Press [Control] and click the mouse in the video track area of the Timeline window.

■ In Premiere, right-click the video tracks to display a menu.

■ A menu displays.

2 Click **Add Track**.

■ In Premiere, click **Add Video Track**.

■ A new track inserts into the timeline.

CREATE A VIDEO OVERLAY

You can create a video *overlay*, which allows two video clips to play simultaneously. To do this, you place the clip you want to overlay in a track above the current video track. To have both clips show at once, you must change the current clip's opacity by adjusting the Opacity Rubberband in the clip's keyframe.

You can only create a video overlay in Adobe Premiere and Final Cut Pro. Although this section illustrates adding video overlays in Adobe Premiere, you can use the same steps to add them in Final Cut Pro. You must place overlay clips in a separate video track. See the section "Add Tracks to the Timeline" for information on adding additional video tracks.

CREATE A VIDEO OVERLAY

1 Click the video clip in the Bin section of the Project window.

■ In Final Cut Pro, click the video clip in the Browser window.

2 Drag the clip to the Video 2 track on the timeline.

■ In Final Cut Pro, drag the clip to the V2 track.

Note: For more on the various parts of Adobe Premiere and Final Cut Pro, see Chapter 7.

3 Release the mouse button.

■ The clip appears on the timeline.

4 Click the Display Opacity Rubberbands icon (▣).

■ If necessary, click ▷ to expand the track (▷ changes to ▽).

■ In Final Cut Pro, click the overlay clip and click the Clip Overlays button (▱).

Can I make the video overlay last as long as another video clip?

Yes. If you want your video overlay to last as long as the track below, you need to adjust the speed that the track overlay plays. To do so, click the Rate Stretch tool (). Click the edge of your overlay and drag it to the desired length. Adobe Premiere adjusts the speed that the clip plays to make it last the amount of time you select on the timeline.

5 Click and drag the Rubberband to adjust the opacity.

■ In Final Cut Pro, click the white opacity line, which appears at the top of the clip, and drag it down to adjust the opacity.

■ In Adobe Premiere, the lower the rubberband, the more transparent the video clip appears.

■ When you play your video, the overlayed video clip plays on top of the track below it.

Note: If your overlay does not play in your monitor window, you must render the video. See Chapter 11 for more information.

SPLIT CLIPS INTO MULTIPLE SCENES

You can split any video clip into two or more clips. You can split clips to remove video from the center of a clip, or to rearrange events by moving the new clips on the timeline. In Adobe Premiere and Final Cut Pro, when you split the clip, you separate it with the Razor tool.

Although both iMovie and Movie Maker also allow you to split clips, they both provide slightly different methods for doing so.

SPLIT CLIPS INTO MULTIPLE SCENES

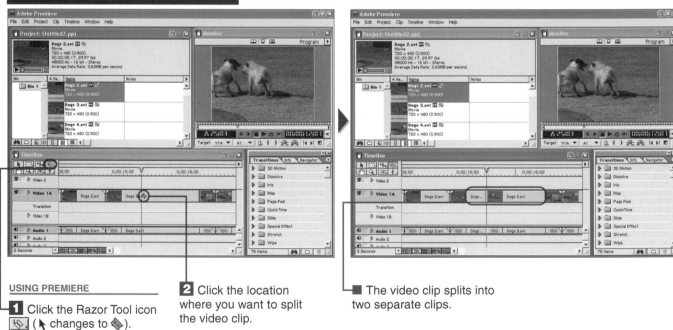

<u>USING PREMIERE</u>

1 Click the Razor Tool icon (✎) (▸ changes to ◈).

2 Click the location where you want to split the video clip.

■ The video clip splits into two separate clips.

How do I split clips in Final Cut Pro and Movie Maker?

Final Cut Pro

In the Canvas window, click ▽ to play the video until you find the desired split location. In the Tools palette, click the Razor Blade icon ( ). For more on the Tools palette, see Chapter 7. Click the location where you want to split the video clip. The video clip splits into two separate clips on the timeline.

Movie Maker

In the Collections area, click the clip you want to split. The selected clip displays in the Monitor window. Drag the Playhead ( ) to the location where you want to split the clip. Click the Split Clip button ( ). The video clip splits into two separate clips in the Collections area. For more on the various parts of the Movie Maker window, see Chapter 7.

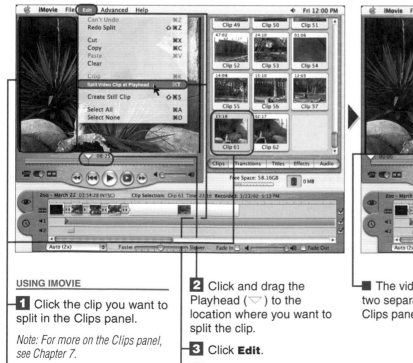

USING IMOVIE

1 Click the clip you want to split in the Clips panel.

Note: For more on the Clips panel, see Chapter 7.

■ The selected video clip displays in the Monitor window.

2 Click and drag the Playhead (▽) to the location where you want to split the clip.

3 Click **Edit**.

4 Click **Split Video Clip at Playhead**.

■ The video clip splits into two separate clips in the Clips panel.

CHANGE THE TIMELINE VIEW

You can zoom in and out on your timeline to change the perspective. For example, if you have a 30 minute movie, you can have the timeline adjusted to 6 minute intervals so that you can view the entire movie timeline. If you want to move or split individual clips on the timeline, you may find it easier to zoom in so the clip appears larger on the timeline.

You can select a zoom range from 1 frame to 6 minutes in Adobe Premiere. You can zoom in and out on the timeline in Adobe Premiere, Final Cut Pro, iMovie, and Movie Maker. For more on the various parts of an individual program, see Chapter 7. For more on timelines, see the section "Anatomy of a Timeline."

CHANGE THE TIMELINE VIEW

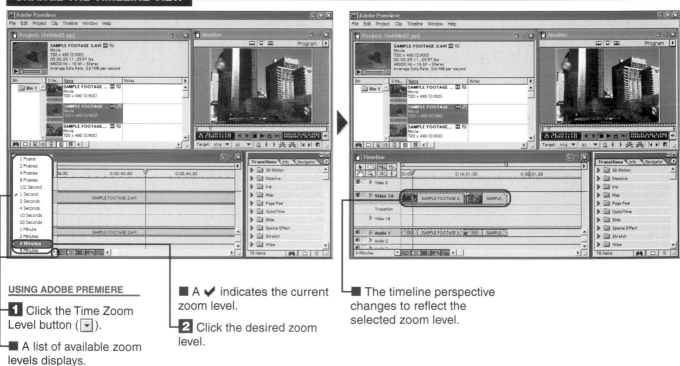

USING ADOBE PREMIERE

1 Click the Time Zoom Level button (▾).

■ A list of available zoom levels displays.

■ A ✔ indicates the current zoom level.

2 Click the desired zoom level.

■ The timeline perspective changes to reflect the selected zoom level.

How do I zoom the timeline in iMovie and Movie Maker?

iMovie

To display the Zoom menu, click 🔽 in the Zoom Level box. See the section "Anatomy of a Timeline" for the box's exact location. iMovie displays a check mark (☑) next to the current zoom level. Click the appropriate zoom level for the timeline. The timeline perspective changes to reflect the selected zoom level. You can select a zoom level from 1 to 50 times, with 50 being the largest or closest zoom level.

Movie Maker

To zoom in the timeline, click the Zoom In button (🔍). To zoom out the timeline, click the Zoom Out button (🔍). See the section "Anatomy of a Timeline" for the exact location of these buttons. Each click of the button zooms the timeline to the next perspective. Movie Maker provides zoom levels between 1/3 of a second and 1 hour and 20 minutes.

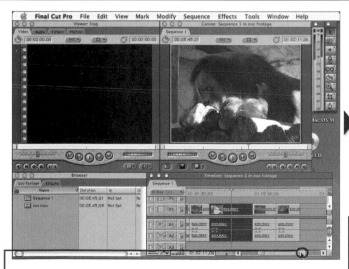

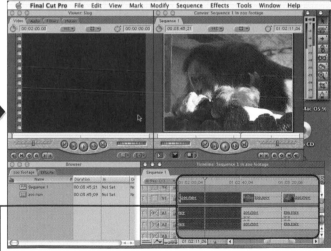

USING FINAL CUT PRO

1 Click a thumb tab (▥) on the Zoom Slider.

2 Drag ▥.

■ You can drag ▥ toward the center of the Zoom Slider to zoom in, and in the opposite direction to zoom out.

■ The timeline perspective changes to reflect the adjustments.

DELETE CLIPS FROM THE TIMELINE

You can delete clips from your timeline that you no longer want in your video. Deleting clips from the timeline does not remove them from your video project. The clips remain in the video project allowing you to add them to another location.

Although this section illustrates deleting video clips in Final Cut Pro, you can use the same steps to delete them in Premiere, iMovie, and Movie Maker.

DELETE CLIPS FROM THE TIMELINE

1 Click the clip you want to remove.

2 Press Delete.

Note: On some keyboards the Delete key is labeled Del.

■ The program removes the clip from the timeline.

You can use the cut and paste process to move clips on the timeline. When you cut a clip, you remove it from that location on the timeline. You can move the Playhead to another location on the timeline and paste the cut clip in that location.

This section illustrates cutting and pasting using iMovie, which is the best method for moving clips in this program. Although you can also use this method in Final Cut Pro, Premiere, and Movie Maker, the best method for moving clips in those packages involves clicking and dragging the clip. See the section "Change the Order of Clips" for more information.

CUT AND PASTE CLIPS ON THE TIMELINE

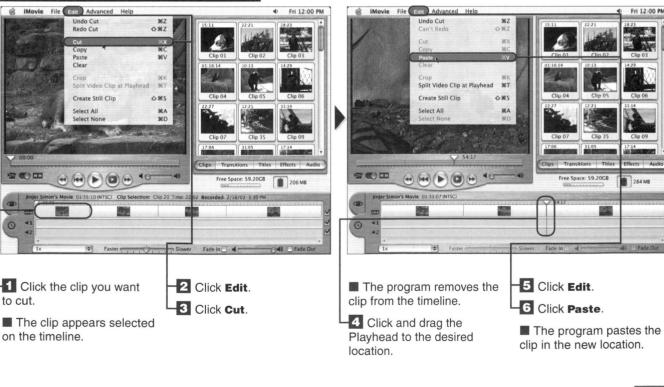

1 Click the clip you want to cut.

■ The clip appears selected on the timeline.

2 Click **Edit**.

3 Click **Cut**.

■ The program removes the clip from the timeline.

4 Click and drag the Playhead to the desired location.

5 Click **Edit**.

6 Click **Paste**.

■ The program pastes the clip in the new location.

CHAPTER 10

Adding and Synchronizing Sound

You modify the sound for your video by editing the existing sounds and adding new sounds, such as music files. You can synchronize sounds to play when an event occurs in the video. This chapter looks at the different tasks you perform to refine your video's sound quality.

MUSIC FILE TYPES

You can add music to your video from different sources. Music helps to set the mood of your video. You can open music from several different file types.

Be careful when using copyrighted music. You can use copyrighted music that you have purchased for personal videos, but you cannot sell your videos without acquiring appropriate permissions.

MP3

MP3, or Moving Picture Experts Group Audio Layer III, is the sound format standard for creating CD-quality music in a compressed format. You can capture music

files from CDs and save them as MP3 files using MP3 player software available on the Internet for download. You can also find MP3 files available for download from many different sites on the Internet. Typically you pay a fee to download an MP3 file to your computer.

WAV

WAV, or Windows Audio, files store an uncompressed CD-quality audio file. If possible, use WAV files instead of MP3s because the compression used to create an MP3 reduces the quality of the audio file. When saving CD-audio, consider creating WAV files instead of MP3s to ensure the highest quality of sound for your video. See the section "Convert CD Audio to WAV Format Using Roxio SoundStream" for more information on creating WAV files.

DV

You can capture the audio tracks from a *DV*, or digital video, file. When you import a digital video file into your video editing software, you can specify that you only want to capture the audio portion of the video by selecting the Audio Only option. See Chapter 2 for more information about the DV format.

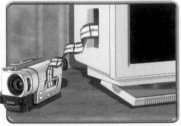

MOV

MOV, or QuickTime Movie, files typically contain both audio and video tracks. You can import the audio portion of a MOV file.

AIFF

AIFF, or Audio Interchange File Format, files are audio files you create on a Macintosh computer. AIFF files can provide CD-quality audio in an uncompressed format, similar to a WAV file.

AUDIO QUALITY

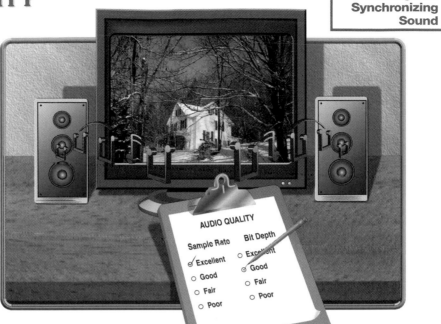

As you work with digital audio within your video editing software, you need to consider the different audio attributes. You must select attributes, such as the sample rate and the bit depth, that best match your audio files.

Sample Rate

The *sample rate* indicates the number of times per second that a computer reads and records a sound. The higher the sample rate, the better the sound quality. But a higher sample rate also means a larger file size. You select the sample rate based upon the source of your audio files. Sample rates are measured in Kilo-Hertz, or kHz.

Sample Rate	Description
8 kHz–22.225 kHz	Range for multimedia files you create on a computer.
32 kHz and 48 kHz	Digital video from a digital video camera. Select the setting that matches the audio settings on your digital video camera. 48 kHz provides higher quality audio.
44.1 kHz	Music CDs or microphone input.

Bit Depth

The bit depth defines the number of data bits, from 8 to 16, that describe each sample of the audio stream. You cannot select a higher bit depth, which translates into more dynamic sound, than the original source. Lower bit depth does not necessarily translate into a smaller file size because it may actually create a larger file during conversion. Most CODECs are designed for 16-bit audio. See Chapter 7 for more information about CODECs.

Bit Depth	Description
8-bit	Lowest quality sound. Best for sound files that you transmit over the Internet.
12-bit	Optional bit rate for working with digital video.
16-bit	Highest quality bit rate. Select this rate, if possible, to achieve the best results.

ADD AUDIO CLIPS IN ADOBE PREMIERE

You can add different sounds to your video by placing audio clips in appropriate locations on the timeline. You add audio clips to the timeline in Premiere in basically the same fashion as video clips, but you place the audio clips in one of the audio tracks. For more information on video clips and the video timeline, see Chapter 9.

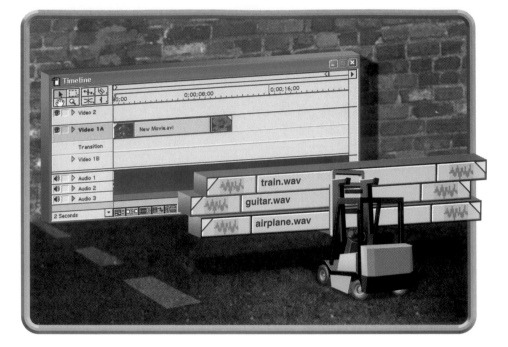

ADD AUDIO CLIPS IN ADOBE PREMIERE

1 Click **File**.

2 Click **Import**.

3 Click **File**.

■ The Import dialog box displays.

4 Click the filename of the audio file you want to import.

5 Click **Open**.

**Why should I place the audio
clip in a separate audio track?**

When you add your video clips
to the timeline, the audio
associated with the video clip
moves to the corresponding
audio track. In other words, the
video in Video 1A has
corresponding audio in Audio 1.
To maintain that audio, you add
the new audio clip to a separate
audio track and both tracks play
with the audio.

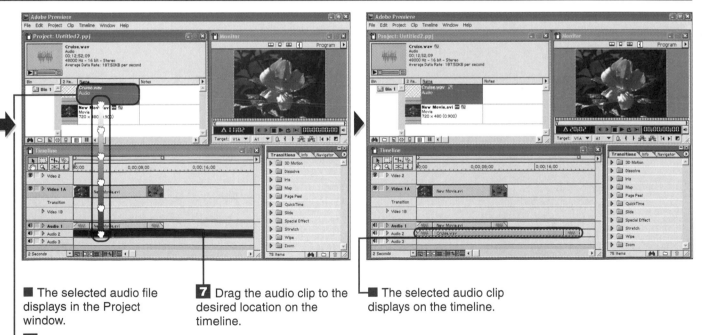

■ The selected audio file
displays in the Project
window.

6 Click the audio clip.

7 Drag the audio clip to the
desired location on the
timeline.

■ The selected audio clip
displays on the timeline.

ADD AUDIO CLIPS IN FINAL CUT PRO

You can add different sounds to your video in Final Cut Pro by placing audio clips in appropriate locations on the timeline. You add audio clips to the timeline in basically the same fashion as video clips, but you place the audio clips in one of the audio tracks. For more information on video clips and the video timeline, see Chapter 9.

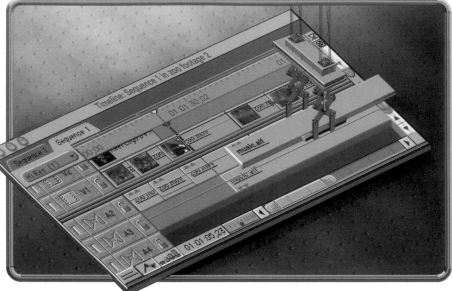

ADD AUDIO CLIPS IN FINAL CUT PRO

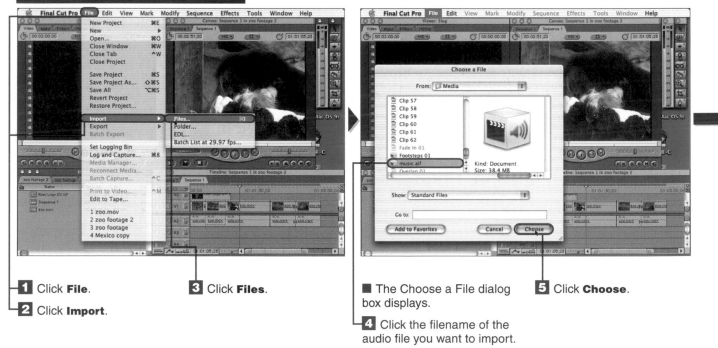

1 Click **File**.

2 Click **Import**.

3 Click **Files**.

■ The Choose a File dialog box displays.

4 Click the filename of the audio file you want to import.

5 Click **Choose**.

Why does Final Cut Pro place the audio clip on two audio tracks?

Final Cut Pro uses two audio tracks for your audio clip so you can customize the right and left channels to produce stereo sound. You can adjust the volume for each channel using the Volume Level Indicator.

Left Channel Icon

You specify the left channel and speaker for each track by clicking and dragging the left channel icon (▥).

Right Channel Icon

You specify the right channel and speaker for each track by clicking and dragging the right channel icon (▥).

Volume Level Indicator

Click the Volume Level Indicator (▴▴) and drag it up or down to adjust the volume to a desired level. The volume level appears as you drag the Indicator.

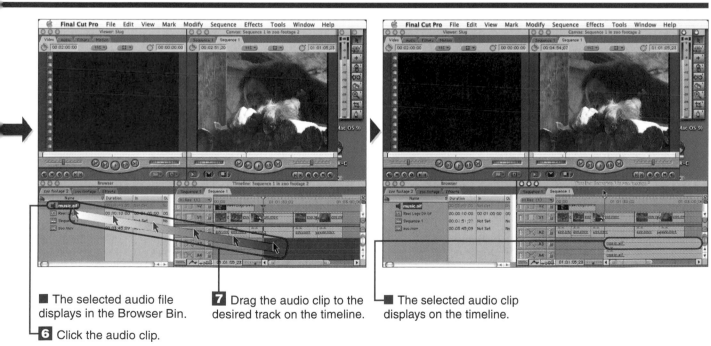

■ The selected audio file displays in the Browser Bin.

6 Click the audio clip.

7 Drag the audio clip to the desired track on the timeline.

■ The selected audio clip displays on the timeline.

ADD AUDIO CLIPS IN MOVIE MAKER

You can add different sounds to your video in Movie Maker by placing audio clips in the appropriate location on the audio track of the timeline. To add audio clips, you first import the clips into the Clips List. From the Clips List, you drag the desired audio clip to the audio track. For more information on video clips and the timeline, see Chapter 9.

ADD AUDIO CLIPS IN MOVIE MAKER

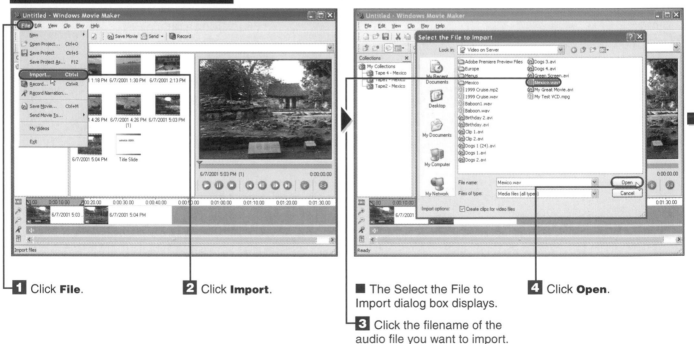

1 Click **File**.

2 Click **Import**.

■ The Select the File to Import dialog box displays.

3 Click the filename of the audio file you want to import.

4 Click **Open**.

**Can I overlap audio clips in
Windows Movie Maker?**

Yes. When you overlay portions of
two audio clips, Windows Movie
Maker creates a transition between
the two overlapped audio clips by
playing the two clips together.
To overlap two clips, click the
second clip and drag it over the
portion of the first clip that you
want to play together.

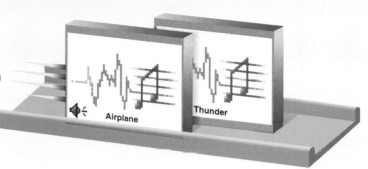

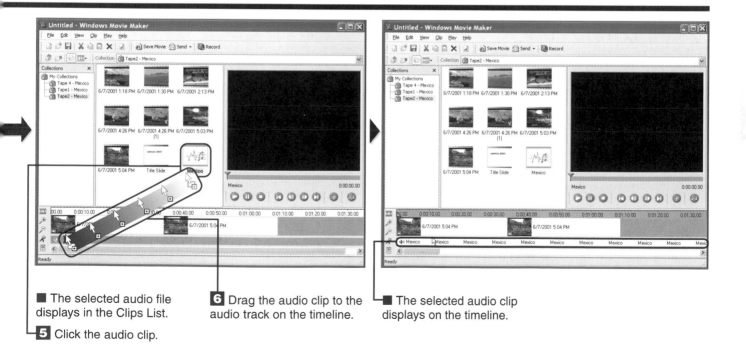

■ The selected audio file
displays in the Clips List.

5 Click the audio clip.

6 Drag the audio clip to the
audio track on the timeline.

■ The selected audio clip
displays on the timeline.

ADD AUDIO CLIPS IN IMOVIE

You can add different sounds to your video in iMovie by placing audio clips in the appropriate locations on one of the two audio tracks of the timeline. To add audio clips, you import the clips into iMovie. iMovie accepts only audio clips in the AIFF format. See the section "Using QuickTime to Convert Audio to AIFF Format" for more information.

ADD AUDIO CLIPS IN IMOVIE

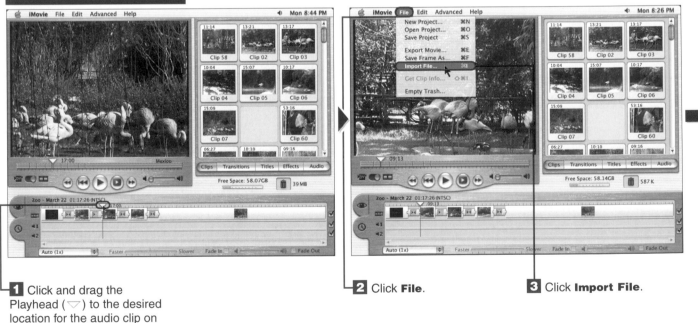

1 Click and drag the Playhead (▽) to the desired location for the audio clip on the timeline.

2 Click **File**.

3 Click **Import File**.

Can I attach an audio clip to a specific video clip?

Yes. Not only can you attach the audio clip to the video clip, but you can also specify the location in the video clip where you want the audio clip to start. You do this by locking the audio clip to the video clip:

1 Click and drag ▽ to the location where the audio should start.

2 Click and drag the audio clip so that its start lines up with ▽.

3 Click **Advanced**.

4 Click **Lock Audio Clip at Playhead**.

■ Little pins (▶) display on the timeline indicating the two clips are locked.

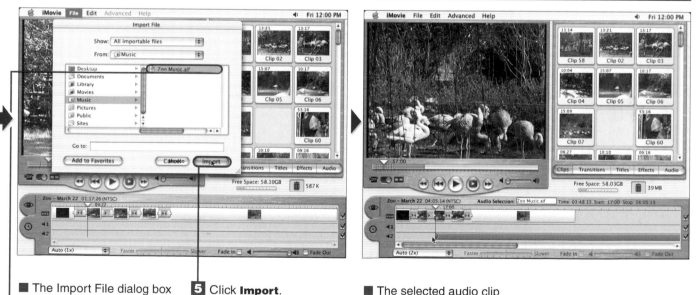

■ The Import File dialog box displays.

4 Click the filename of the audio file you want to import.

5 Click **Import**.

■ The selected audio clip displays on the timeline.

CONVERT CD AUDIO TO WAV FORMAT USING ROXIO SOUNDSTREAM

You can use Roxio SoundStream to convert audio on CDs to WAV files that you can import into Adobe Premiere or Microsoft Movie Maker as your audio clips. These Microsoft Window video editing packages do not recognize the CDDA format you use to store music on CDs. For this reason, you must use another application, such as Roxio SoundStream, to convert the files.

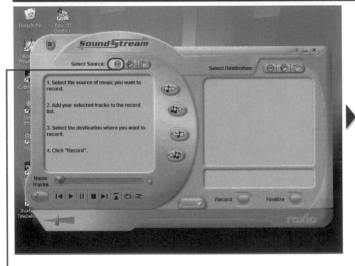

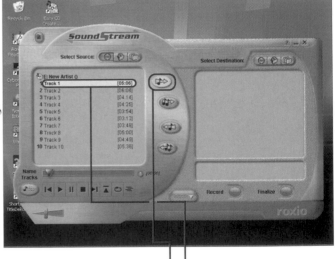

1 After opening Roxio SoundStream, click the Select Music CD As Source button (⊙).

Note: See your product instructions for more on installing and opening Roxio SoundStream.

■ A list of the music tracks on the audio CD displays with each track representing a separate piece of music.

2 Click the desired music track.

3 Click the Add Selected button (⊡).

**The tracks display numerically.
How do I know which track to
select?**

You can determine which track is
which by previewing them within
SoundStream. To listen to a
particular track, click the desired
track and then click the Play
button (▶).

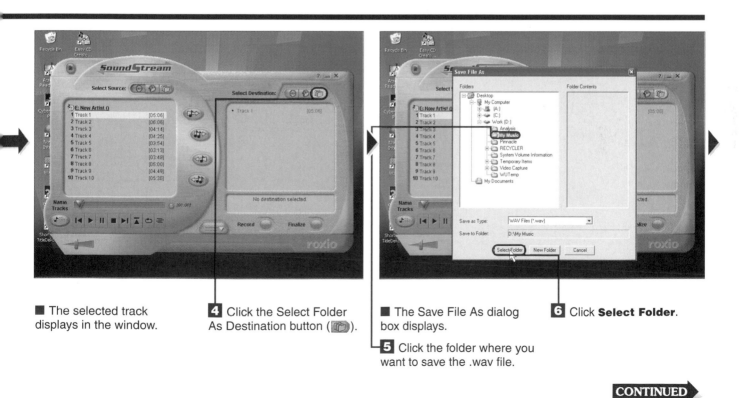

■ The selected track
displays in the window.

4 Click the Select Folder
As Destination button (📁).

■ The Save File As dialog
box displays.

5 Click the folder where you
want to save the .wav file.

6 Click **Select Folder**.

CONTINUED ▶

CONVERT CD AUDIO TO WAV FORMAT USING ROXIO SOUNDSTREAM

You need to save CD audio files as .wav files because the .wav format produces a CD-quality file that you can insert in your video. If you use SoundStream to create audio files for other purposes, such as to transfer files over the Internet, you may want to save them file as MP3, which is a compressed format.

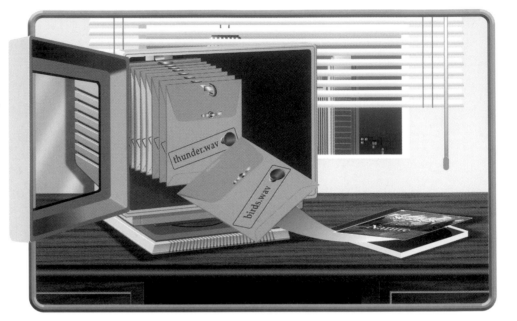

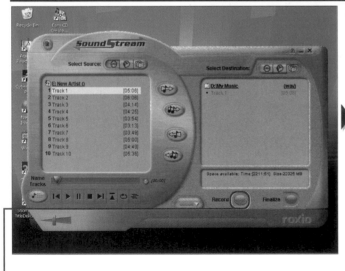

7 Click the Record button (⬤).

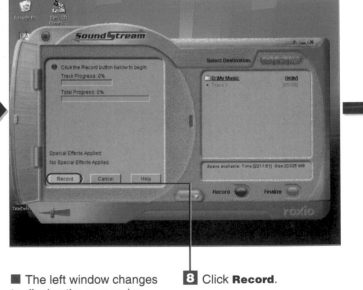

■ The left window changes to display the conversion process.

8 Click **Record**.

The Record window indicates No Special Effects applied. Can I add special effects to the audio track?

Yes, you can actually add special effects to your track by clicking the Show Option Drawer button ( ) to display options for equalizing your audio and adding special effects.

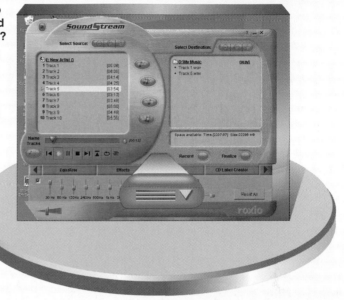

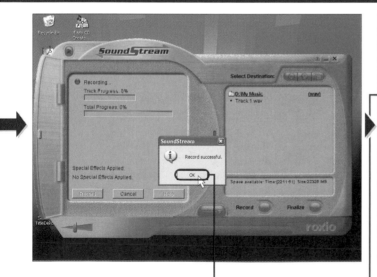

■ When the file converts to WAV format, Roxio SoundStream displays a message box.

9 Click **OK**.

■ The converted track displays.

■ You can repeat steps **2** through **9** to convert additional CD tracks.

USING QUICKTIME TO CONVERT AUDIO TO AIFF FORMAT

You can use QuickTime on your Macintosh computer to convert any type of audio, including music CDs, to AIFF format. You want to use this file format because it creates a CD-quality audio file that you can import into Final Cut Pro, Adobe Premiere, and iMovie. Keep in mind, the only audio file type that you can import into iMovie is AIFF; therefore you need to follow these steps to convert audio files that you want to use.

USING QUICKTIME TO CONVERT AUDIO TO AIFF FORMAT

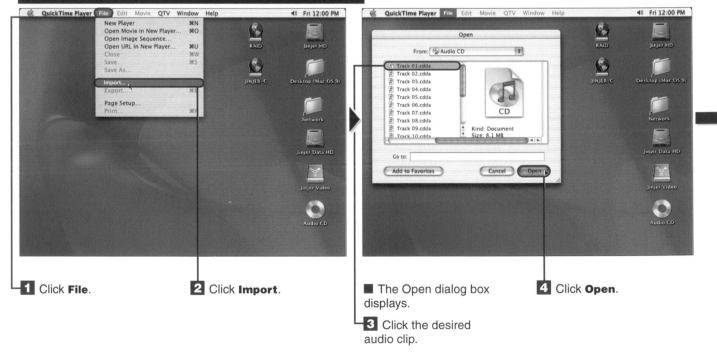

1 Click **File**.

2 Click **Import**.

■ The Open dialog box displays.

3 Click the desired audio clip.

4 Click **Open**.

Adding and
Synchronizing **10**
Sound

Can I use QuickTime on my Microsoft Windows operating system to save audio from a CD?

No, QuickTime cannot save CD audio files under the Microsoft Windows operating system. But you can purchase several programs, such as Roxio SoundStream, for that specific purpose. See the section "Convert CD Audio to WAV Formats Using Roxio SoundStream" for more information.

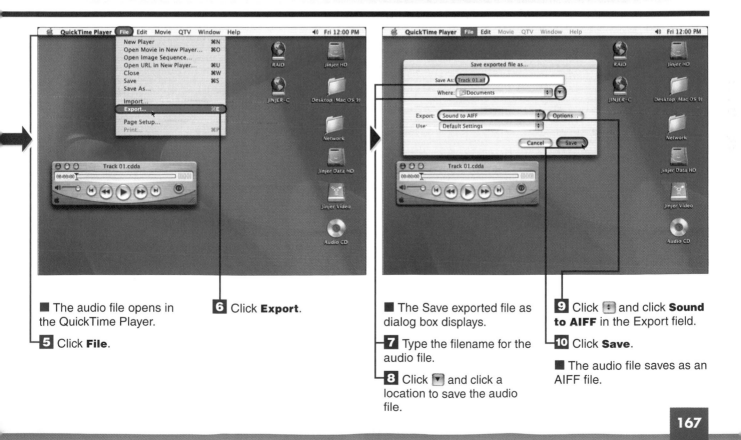

■ The audio file opens in the QuickTime Player.

5 Click **File**.

6 Click **Export**.

■ The Save exported file as dialog box displays.

7 Type the filename for the audio file.

8 Click ▼ and click a location to save the audio file.

9 Click 🔼 and click **Sound to AIFF** in the Export field.

10 Click **Save**.

■ The audio file saves as an AIFF file.

IMPORT CD AUDIO INTO FINAL CUT PRO

You can import CD audio files directly into your video using Final Cut Pro. This eliminates the need to convert the files before using them. Although only Final Cut Pro allows you to import audio directly from a CD, you can record audio from a CD in iMovie. See the section "Record CD Audio in iMovie" for more information.

IMPORT CD AUDIO INTO FINAL CUT PRO

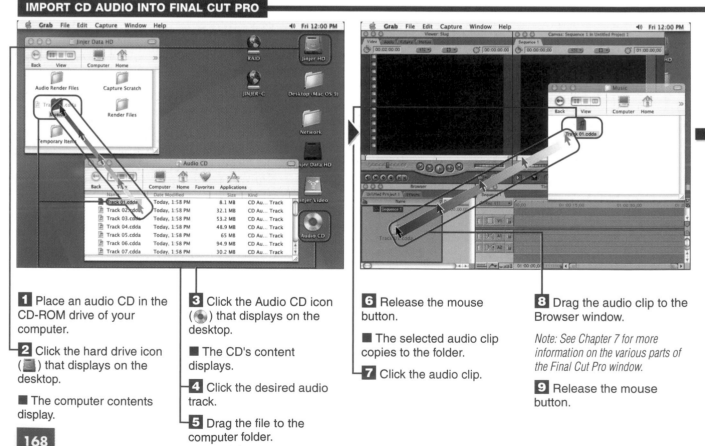

1 Place an audio CD in the CD-ROM drive of your computer.

2 Click the hard drive icon (🖥) that displays on the desktop.

■ The computer contents display.

3 Click the Audio CD icon (🔘) that displays on the desktop.

■ The CD's content displays.

4 Click the desired audio track.

5 Drag the file to the computer folder.

6 Release the mouse button.

■ The selected audio clip copies to the folder.

7 Click the audio clip.

8 Drag the audio clip to the Browser window.

Note: See Chapter 7 for more information on the various parts of the Final Cut Pro window.

9 Release the mouse button.

Why do I need to follow the steps in this section, when clicking File and then Import imports CD audio directly into Final Cut Pro?

You can import files directly into Final Cut Pro from a CD by clicking **File**, **Import**, and then locating the CD audio in the Import dialog box. However, this method does not copy the CD audio from the CD; this means that whenever you edit your video, you must insert the CD in your computer's CD-ROM drive.

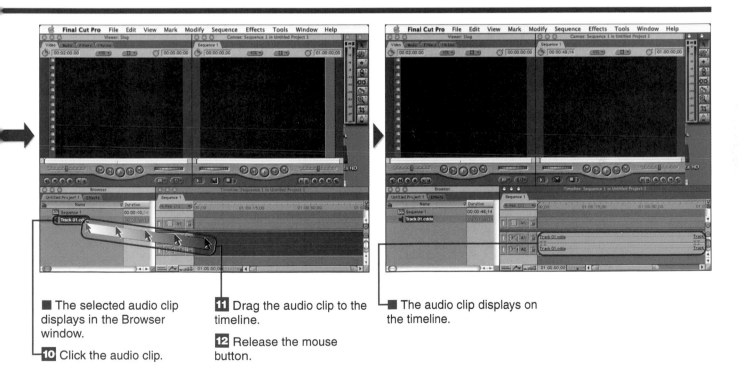

■ The selected audio clip displays in the Browser window.

10 Click the audio clip.

11 Drag the audio clip to the timeline.

12 Release the mouse button.

■ The audio clip displays on the timeline.

USING DEFAULT SOUNDS IN IMOVIE

You can use the default sounds provided with iMovie in your video. You can use these sounds when you want to create a quick sound effect, such as a dog barking or lightning striking. Because iMovie makes these sounds short, you may want to use them in combination with other sounds. Unfortunately, the other programs do not provide built-in sounds like iMovie.

USING DEFAULT SOUNDS IN IMOVIE

1 Click **Audio**.

■ The Audio Panel displays.

2 Click and drag the slider (●) to locate the desired sound effect.

3 Click the desired sound effect.

Can I have more than one sound effect playing at a time?

Yes, you can combine sound effects by overlaying them on the timeline to create a more dynamic sound. For example, if you want to make the sound of barking dogs last longer, you can add another sound effect after the first one.

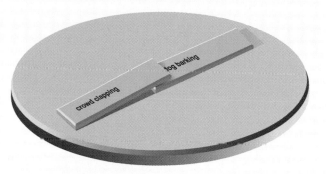

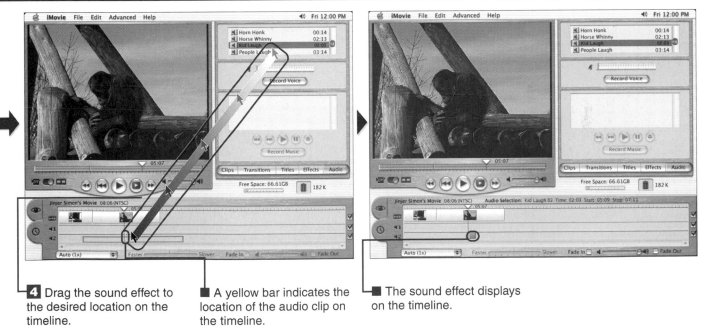

4 Drag the sound effect to the desired location on the timeline.

■ A yellow bar indicates the location of the audio clip on the timeline.

5 Release the mouse button.

■ The sound effect displays on the timeline.

RECORD CD AUDIO IN iMOVIE

You can record audio directly from a CD for use within your movie from the Audio Panel in iMovie. When you use this feature in iMovie, you can capture an entire track from the CD or just a portion. You can also insert various sounds that iMovie has available. See the section "Using Default Sounds in iMovie" for more information.

Although iMovie is the only editing package that allows you to record audio from a CD, you can import audio files from a CD using Final Cut Pro. See "Import CD Audio into Final Cut Pro" for more information.

RECORD CD AUDIO IN iMOVIE

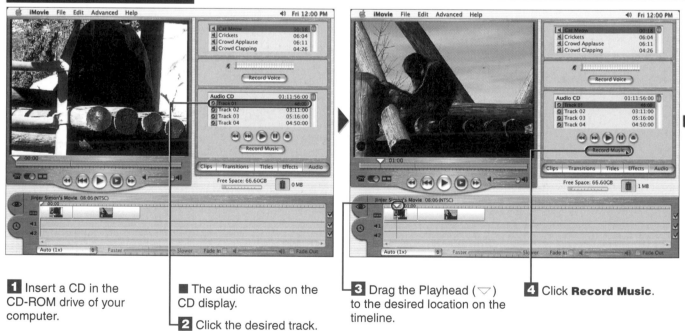

1 Insert a CD in the CD-ROM drive of your computer.

■ The audio tracks on the CD display.

2 Click the desired track.

3 Drag the Playhead (▽) to the desired location on the timeline.

4 Click **Record Music**.

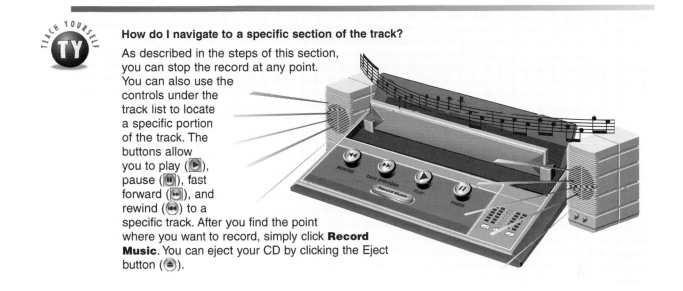

How do I navigate to a specific section of the track?

As described in the steps of this section, you can stop the record at any point. You can also use the controls under the track list to locate a specific portion of the track. The buttons allow you to play (▶), pause (❚❚), fast forward (▶▶), and rewind (◀◀) to a specific track. After you find the point where you want to record, simply click **Record Music**. You can eject your CD by clicking the Eject button (⏏).

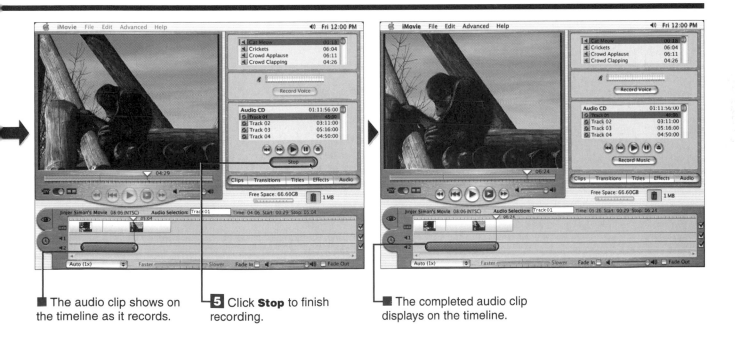

■ The audio clip shows on the timeline as it records.

5 Click **Stop** to finish recording.

■ The completed audio clip displays on the timeline.

RECORD NARRATION IN IMOVIE

You can use an external microphone to record narration for your video in iMovie. When you do so, your program records and adds the narration to the timeline at the location of the Playhead in iMovie. When iMovie records audio, it adds it to the timeline as an orange audio clip.

RECORD NARRATION IN IMOVIE

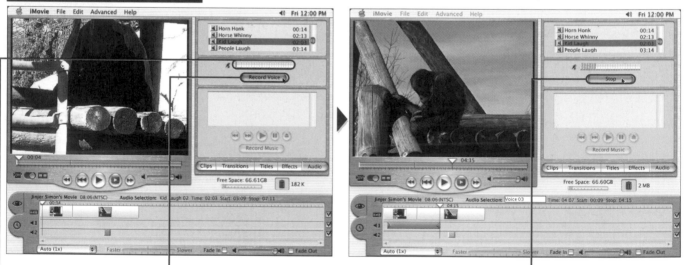

1 Connect an external microphone.

■ If you properly connect the microphone, the audio level displays.

Note: For more information on connecting your microphone, see your Macintosh documentation.

2 Click **Record Voice**.

3 Record the desired narration in the microphone.

■ The narration displays on the timeline as an orange bar.

4 When you complete your narration, click **Stop**.

You can use an external microphone to record narration for your video in Movie Maker. When you do so, Movie Maker places the audio clip in the current Clips List. You can add the narration clip to your timeline in the same fashion you add other audio clips.

RECORD NARRATION IN MOVIE MAKER

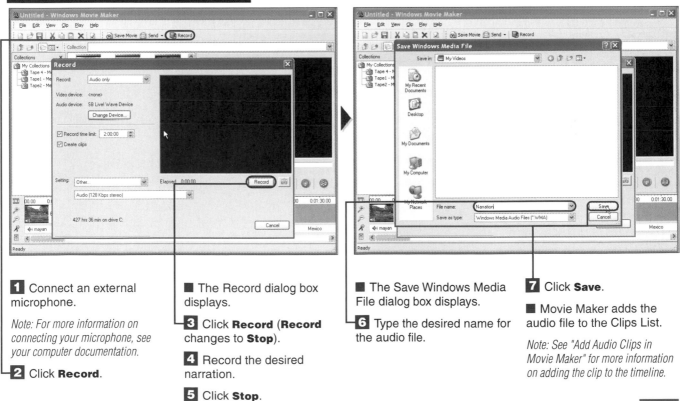

1 Connect an external microphone.

Note: For more information on connecting your microphone, see your computer documentation.

2 Click **Record**.

■ The Record dialog box displays.

3 Click **Record** (**Record** changes to **Stop**).

4 Record the desired narration.

5 Click **Stop**.

■ The Save Windows Media File dialog box displays.

6 Type the desired name for the audio file.

7 Click **Save**.

■ Movie Maker adds the audio file to the Clips List.

Note: See "Add Audio Clips in Movie Maker" for more information on adding the clip to the timeline.

RECORD NARRATION IN PREMIERE

You can use an external microphone to record narration for your video in Premiere. Unlike most video editing packages, Premiere does not directly provide the ability to record audio from a microphone. In order to do so, you must use either a Premiere plug-in program or the Windows Sound Recorder that comes with the Microsoft Windows operating system. After you record the audio file, you can import it into Premiere like any other audio clip.

These steps illustrate creation of a narration clip using the Windows Sound Recorder. If you have a plug-in loaded, refer to the corresponding documentation.

RECORD NARRATION IN PREMIERE

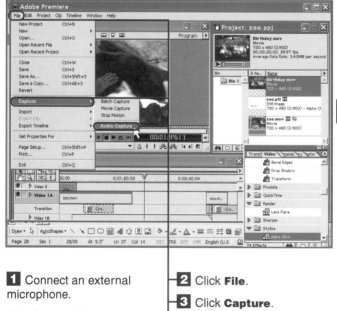

1 Connect an external microphone.

Note: For more information on connecting your microphone, see your computer documentation.

2 Click **File**.

3 Click **Capture**.

4 Click **Audio Capture**.

■ The Audio Capture dialog box displays.

5 Click the audio capture plug-in.

Note: You can find the Windows Sound Recorder, sndrec32.exe, in the System32 folder of your Windows system folder.

6 Click **Open**.

■ Premiere remembers this selection and automatically opens the same audio capture program in the future.

**Can I listen to the audio clip before
adding it to the timeline?**

Yes, Premiere allows you to listen to
your audio clips directly from the
Project window. To do so, click the
desired clip to display the Preview
option. Click the Play button (▶)
and the clip begins to play.

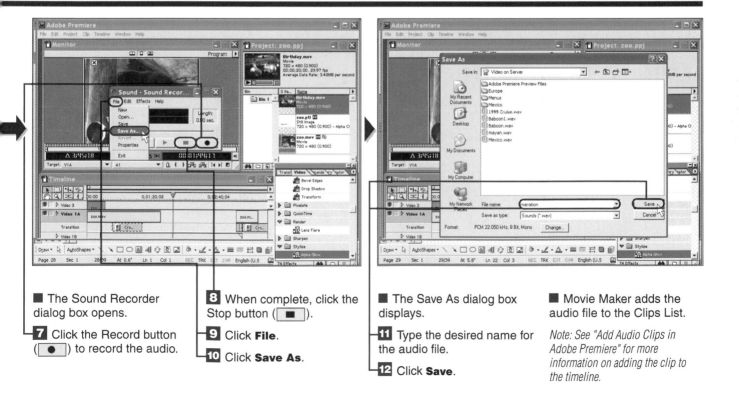

■ The Sound Recorder
dialog box opens.

7 Click the Record button
(●) to record the audio.

8 When complete, click the
Stop button (■).

9 Click **File**.

10 Click **Save As**.

■ The Save As dialog box
displays.

11 Type the desired name for
the audio file.

12 Click **Save**.

■ Movie Maker adds the
audio file to the Clips List.

*Note: See "Add Audio Clips in
Adobe Premiere" for more
information on adding the clip to
the timeline.*

RECORD NARRATION IN FINAL CUT PRO

You can use an external microphone to record narration for your video in Final Cut Pro. To capture audio only, you must first create an audio preset that you can use for all captures. The audio preset instructs Final Cut Pro to capture audio only from the specified microphone. Therefore, you need to make sure you connect your microphone before creating the preset. After you create the audio preset, you select it each time you want to capture audio only.

RECORD NARRATION IN FINAL CUT PRO

CREATE AUDIO PRESET

1 Connect an external microphone.

Note: For more information on connecting your microphone, see your computer documentation.

2 Click **Final Cut Pro**.

3 Click **Audio/Video Settings**.

■ The Audio/Video Settings dialog box displays.

4 Click the **Capture Presets** tab.

Can I change the settings for a capture preset after I create it?

Yes, you can modify any of the capture presets at anytime:

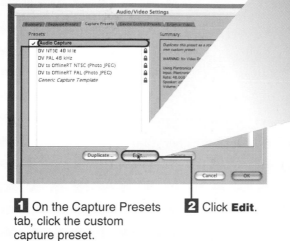

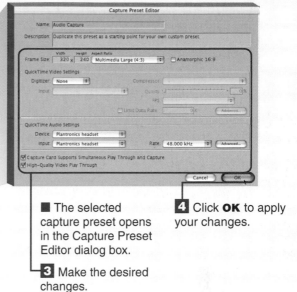

■ The selected capture preset opens in the Capture Preset Editor dialog box.

4 Click **OK** to apply your changes.

1 On the Capture Presets tab, click the custom capture preset.

2 Click **Edit**.

3 Make the desired changes.

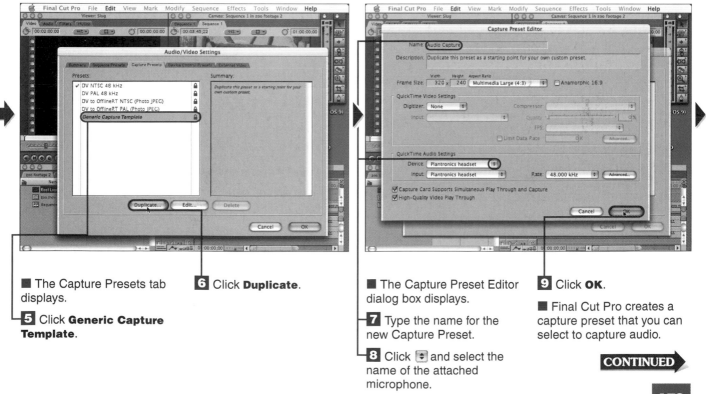

■ The Capture Presets tab displays.

5 Click **Generic Capture Template**.

6 Click **Duplicate**.

■ The Capture Preset Editor dialog box displays.

7 Type the name for the new Capture Preset.

8 Click ⬦ and select the name of the attached microphone.

9 Click **OK**.

■ Final Cut Pro creates a capture preset that you can select to capture audio.

CONTINUED

RECORD NARRATION IN FINAL CUT PRO

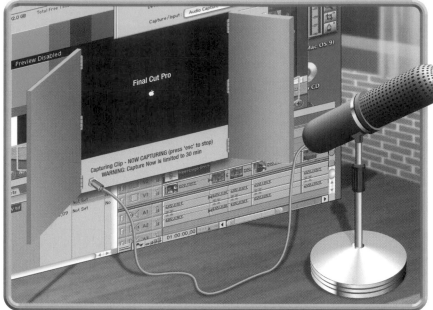

In Final Cut Pro, you record narration, or any other audio from the microphone, in the same fashion that you capture video from a video camcorder. To record from the microphone, you must select the capture preset that you created for the microphone. This instructs Final Cut Pro as to the location of the capture.

After you create your audio clip from the microphone, you must import it into Final Cut Pro using the same process as any other audio clip. See "Add Audio Clips in Final Cut Pro" for more information.

RECORD NARRATION IN FINAL CUT PRO (CONTINUED)

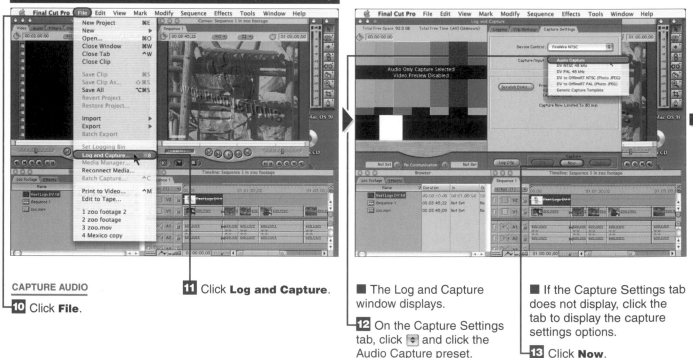

CAPTURE AUDIO

10 Click **File**.

11 Click **Log and Capture**.

■ The Log and Capture window displays.

12 On the Capture Settings tab, click ⬍ and click the Audio Capture preset.

■ If the Capture Settings tab does not display, click the tab to display the capture settings options.

13 Click **Now**.

**Can I add the audio clip to the timeline
directly from the audio window?**

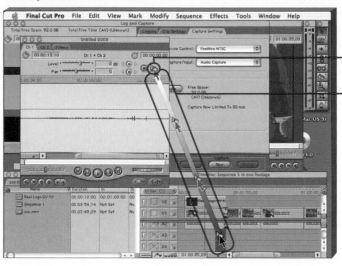

1 Click the Drag Hand
button ( ).

2 Drag to the desired
location on the timeline.

■ The audio clip moves to
timeline.

*Note: If you have not already saved
the audio clip, the Save window
displays so you can save the clip
before adding it to the timeline.*

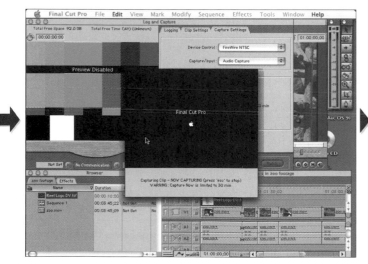

■ The Capturing window
displays.

14 Record the desired
narration.

15 When complete,
press Esc.

■ The recorded audio clip
displays in the audio window.

*Note: See "Add Audio Clips in Final
Cut Pro" for more information on
adding the clip to the timeline.*

ADJUST AUDIO LEVEL

You can adjust the audio level for a specific audio clip to make it play either louder or softer. This adjustment only affects the selected audio clip. The remaining clips still play at the original audio level.

Although this section illustrates adjusting the Audio Level in iMovie and Final Cut Pro, you can also adjust the audio levels using Movie Maker and Premiere. Because iMovie uses the DV format, you can make your audio either a part of the video track, or place it in a separate audio track.

ADJUST AUDIO LEVEL

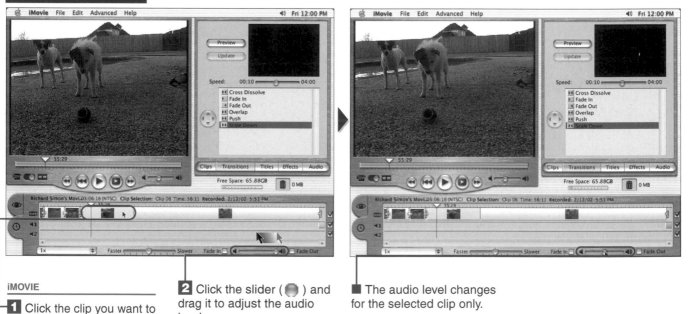

iMOVIE

1 Click the clip you want to adjust.

2 Click the slider ( ) and drag it to adjust the audio level.

■ The audio level changes for the selected clip only.

How can I adjust the Audio Levels in Movie Maker or Premiere?

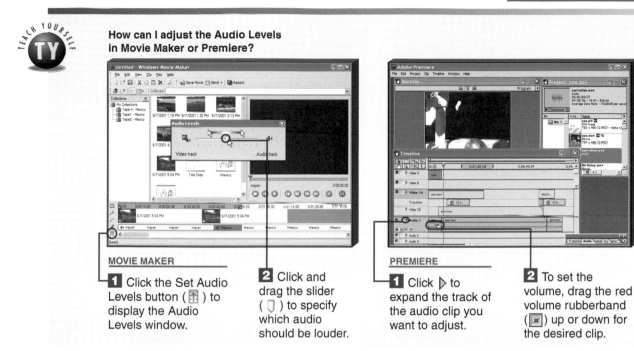

MOVIE MAKER

1 Click the Set Audio Levels button (🎚) to display the Audio Levels window.

2 Click and drag the slider (🎚) to specify which audio should be louder.

PREMIERE

1 Click ▷ to expand the track of the audio clip you want to adjust.

2 To set the volume, drag the red volume rubberband (▨) up or down for the desired clip.

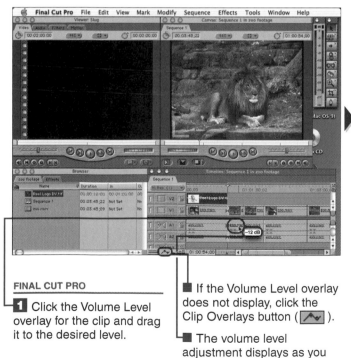

FINAL CUT PRO

1 Click the Volume Level overlay for the clip and drag it to the desired level.

■ If the Volume Level overlay does not display, click the Clip Overlays button (〰).

■ The volume level adjustment displays as you drag the Volume Level overlay.

■ The volume adjusts for the selected audio clip.

FADE AUDIO IN AND OUT

You can fade audio in and out within your video so that it does not abruptly start or stop. By fading your audio, you create a smoother transition between each audio track.

Although this section illustrates the fading technique in iMovie and Premiere, you can also fade audio using Final Cut Pro. Movie Maker does not provide the ability to fade your audio clips.

FADE AUDIO IN AND OUT

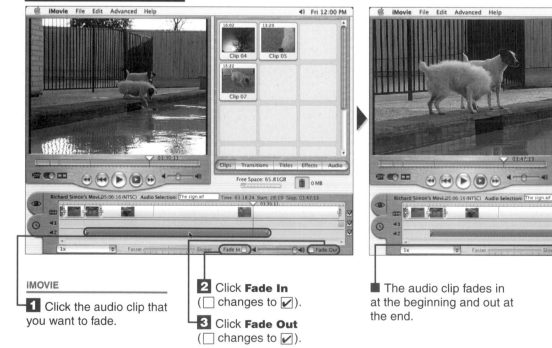

IMOVIE

1 Click the audio clip that you want to fade.

2 Click **Fade In** (☐ changes to ☑).

3 Click **Fade Out** (☐ changes to ☑).

■ The audio clip fades in at the beginning and out at the end.

How can I fade an audio clip in Final Cut Pro?

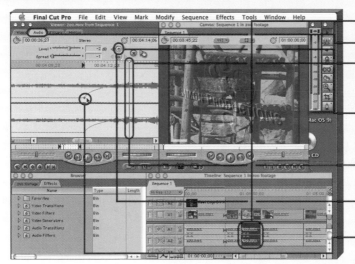

1 Click the audio clip.

2 Click the **Audio** tab.

3 Click and drag the Playhead (▽) to where you want to start the fade.

4 Click the Ins/Del Keyframe button (⊚) to display a pink handle (─◆─).

5 Click and drag ▽ to the end of the fade area.

6 Click ⊚ to add a second handle.

7 Click a handle and drag it up or down to create the fade.

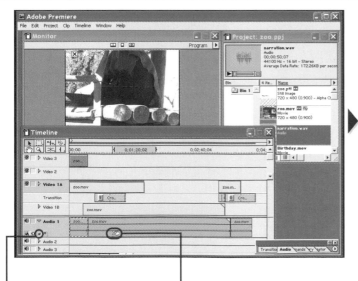

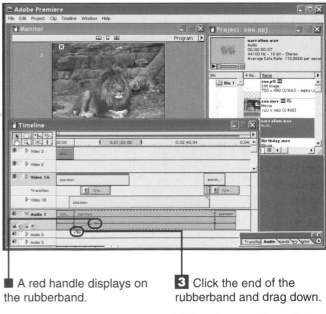

PREMIERE

1 Click the red Volume Rubberband icon (▣) to displays the rubberband on the audio track.

■ If the track is not expanded, click the ▷ next to the track to expand (▷ changes to ▽).

2 Click the rubberband at the location where you want to end/start the fade to add a new handle.

■ A red handle displays on the rubberband.

3 Click the end of the rubberband and drag down.

■ Premiere creates a fade.

TRIM AN AUDIO CLIP

You can reduce the
length of an audio track
by trimming it in the
timeline. When you trim
it, you remove audio
from either the
beginning or ending,
depending upon where
you decide to trim.

Although this section
illustrates trimming an audio
clip in iMovie and Premiere,
you can also trim an audio
clip using Movie Maker and
Final Cut Pro.

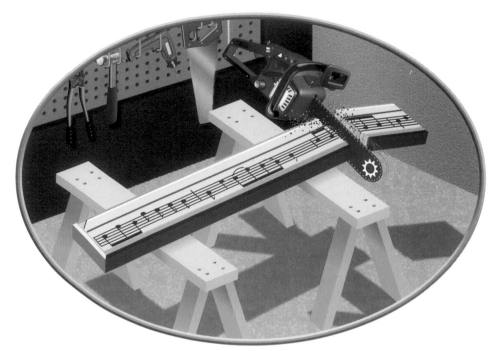

TRIM AN AUDIO CLIP

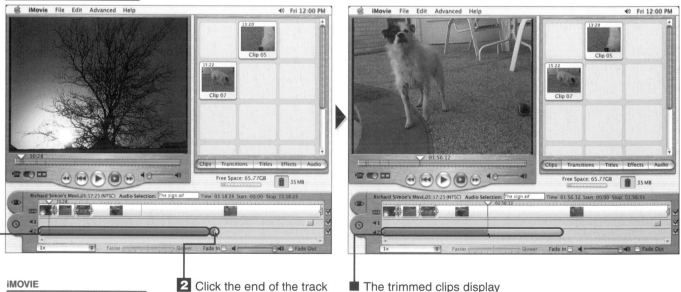

iMOVIE

1 Click the audio clip that
you want to trim.

2 Click the end of the track
and drag it to the location
where you want to trim.

■ You can also click and
drag the beginning of the
audio clip.

■ The trimmed clips display
in dark purple on the
timeline, and the portion you
trimmed off displays in a
lighter shade.

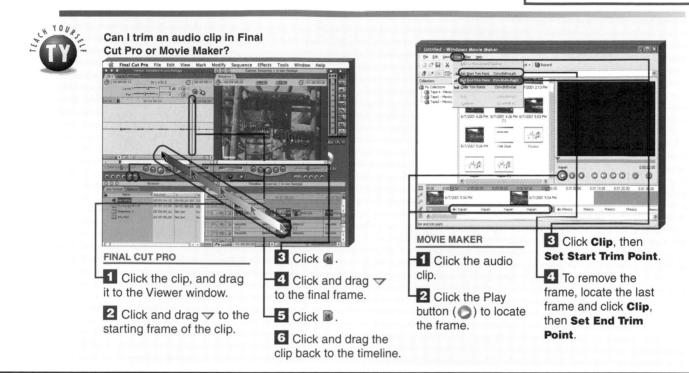

FINAL CUT PRO

1 Click the clip, and drag it to the Viewer window.

2 Click and drag ▽ to the starting frame of the clip.

3 Click ▣.

4 Click and drag ▽ to the final frame.

5 Click ▣.

6 Click and drag the clip back to the timeline.

MOVIE MAKER

1 Click the audio clip.

2 Click the Play button (▶) to locate the frame.

3 Click **Clip**, then **Set Start Trim Point**.

4 To remove the frame, locate the last frame and click **Clip**, then **Set End Trim Point**.

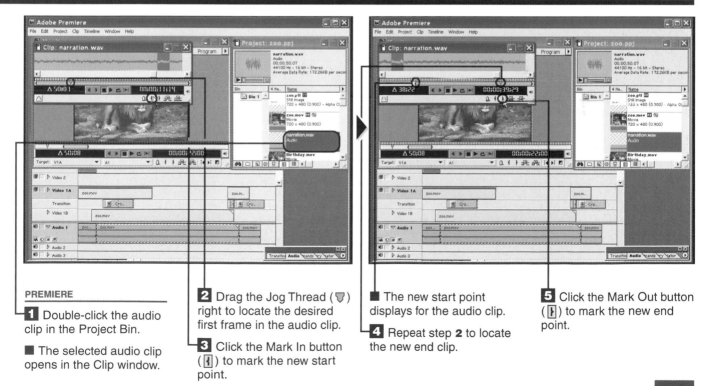

PREMIERE

1 Double-click the audio clip in the Project Bin.

■ The selected audio clip opens in the Clip window.

2 Drag the Jog Thread (▽) right to locate the desired first frame in the audio clip.

3 Click the Mark In button (▣) to mark the new start point.

■ The new start point displays for the audio clip.

4 Repeat step **2** to locate the new end clip.

5 Click the Mark Out button (▣) to mark the new end point.

MIX AUDIO TRACKS

You can mix different audio clips to change between different sounds in your video. To mix the sounds, you use at least two different audio clips and place them on separate audio tracks. After you have your audio clips, you decide where you want each clip to start playing. If you want to alternate between two audio clips, you can separate one clip and insert the second clip in between.

Although this section illustrates mixing audio tracks using Adobe Premiere, you can also mix audio clips using Final Cut Pro.

MIX AUDIO TRACKS

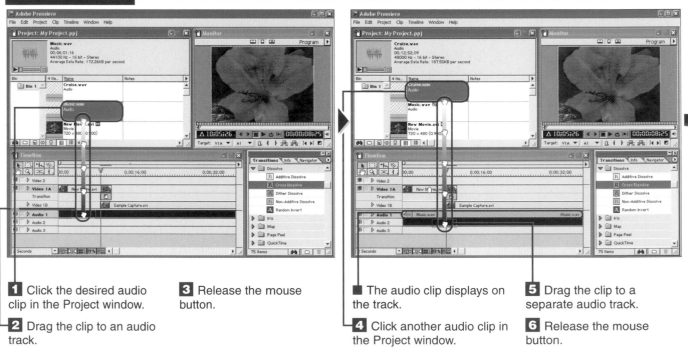

1 Click the desired audio clip in the Project window.

2 Drag the clip to an audio track.

3 Release the mouse button.

■ The audio clip displays on the track.

4 Click another audio clip in the Project window.

5 Drag the clip to a separate audio track.

6 Release the mouse button.

Can I disable the sound of an audio track without removing the audio clips?

Yes, you can disable any audio track to allow you to isolate the sound from a specific audio track. To disable the sound for a particular audio track, click the Toggle Track Output icon ( ) for the selected audio track. Clicking silences the corresponding audio track.

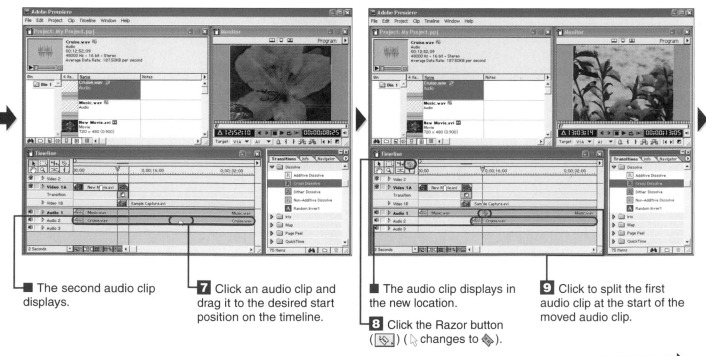

■ The second audio clip displays.

7 Click an audio clip and drag it to the desired start position on the timeline.

■ The audio clip displays in the new location.

8 Click the Razor button ( ) (changes to).

9 Click to split the first audio clip at the start of the moved audio clip.

MIX AUDIO TRACKS

You split audio tracks using the Razor in Adobe Premiere. When you use this option, the audio clip separates at the specified location. After you split the audio clip, you can move the separated clips anywhere on the timeline. You can also remove sections of an audio clip using the Clear option.

MIX AUDIO TRACKS (CONTINUED)

■ The first audio clip splits at the specified location.

10 Click the Selection Tool button (▶).

11 Click the split section of the audio clip (▷ changes to a ⌢ as you drag the clip).

12 Drag the audio clip to the desired location on the timeline.

■ The split audio clip moves to the new location.

13 Click ✎ (▷ changes to ◆).

14 Click to split the second audio clip at the start of the moved audio clip.

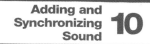

How do I mix audio clips in Final Cut Pro?

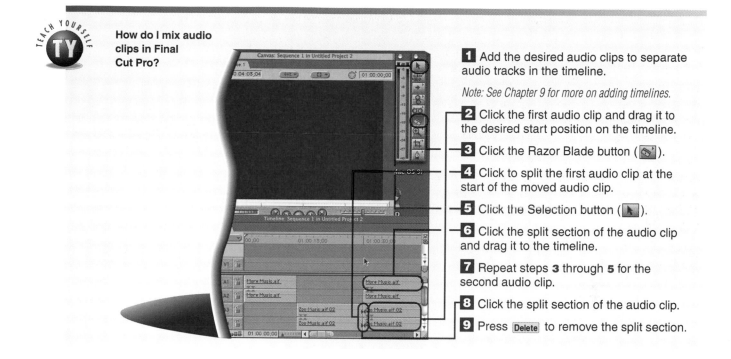

1 Add the desired audio clips to separate audio tracks in the timeline.

Note: See Chapter 9 for more on adding timelines.

2 Click the first audio clip and drag it to the desired start position on the timeline.

3 Click the Razor Blade button (⬛).

4 Click to split the first audio clip at the start of the moved audio clip.

5 Click the Selection button (⬛).

6 Click the split section of the audio clip and drag it to the timeline.

7 Repeat steps **3** through **5** for the second audio clip.

8 Click the split section of the audio clip.

9 Press Delete to remove the split section.

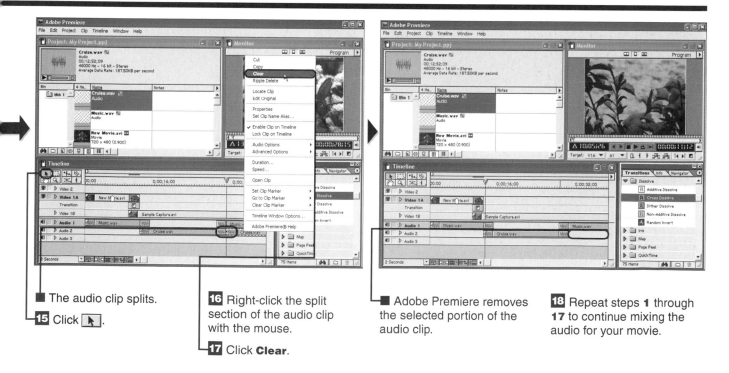

■ The audio clip splits.

15 Click ⬛.

16 Right-click the split section of the audio clip with the mouse.

17 Click **Clear**.

■ Adobe Premiere removes the selected portion of the audio clip.

18 Repeat steps **1** through **17** to continue mixing the audio for your movie.

WORK WITH SOUND FILTERS

You can use filters to improve the quality of your sound. You want to apply filters to make your audio more clear and noise-free.

Although the steps in this section illustrate working with filters in Final Cut Pro, you can also use Adobe Premiere to equalize, compress, and reduce noise in your audio clips.

WORK WITH SOUND FILTERS

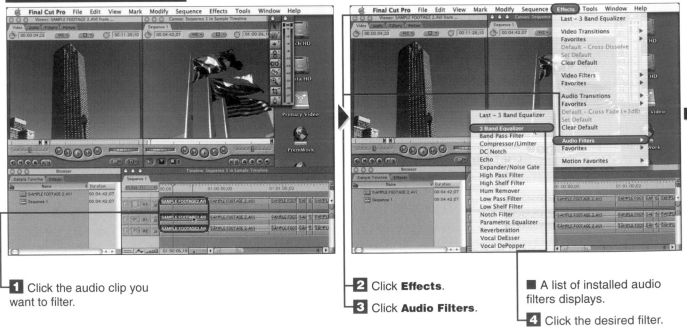

1 Click the audio clip you want to filter.

2 Click **Effects**.

3 Click **Audio Filters**.

■ A list of installed audio filters displays.

4 Click the desired filter.

How do I use sound filters in Premiere?

You can apply any of the built-in audio filters
to an audio clip. To view audio filters:

1 Click **Window**.

2 Click **Show
Audio Effects**.

■ The Audio tab
displays a list of
available filters.

3 Click the desired
filter and drag it
onto the audio clip
in the timeline.

■ Premiere applies
the selected audio
filter to the audio clip.

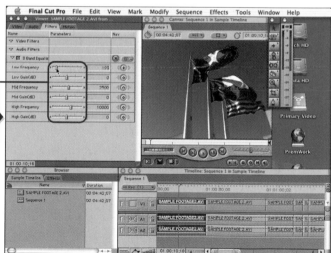

■ A red line displays above
the timeline indicating that
Final Cut Pro made changes
to the clip.

5 Double-click the audio
clip on the timeline.

■ The filter settings display
on the Filter tab of the Viewer
window.

■ You can adjust the settings
for the filter by clicking and
dragging the appropriate
slider (🖑).

■ You can apply additional
filters to the same audio clip
so that the assigned filters
display on the Filters tab.

CHAPTER 11

Adding Transitions

You can use different transitions, or visual effects, in your video to make the movement between different video clips more appealing. You add a transition so that your video moves smoothly from one scene to the next. This chapter looks at the different tasks you perform to create and work with transitions in your video project.

UNDERSTANDING TRANSITIONS

You can add any type of transition to create a desired visual effect for your video. No matter which transition you select, they all provide the same end result of producing a connection between two video clips. Transitions fall into nine different categories, with several variations of each category available on advanced editing packages such as Adobe Premiere and Apple Final Cut Pro.

Dissolve

Dissolves create the effect of one video clip blending into the next clip.

Iris

An Iris transition creates the effect of the iris opening in a pattern to reveal the second clip.

Map

A Map transition uses a specified color to transition between video clips.

Page Peel

A Page Peel transition creates the effect of the first clip peeling away to reveal the second clip.

Slide

A Slide transition shows the first clip sliding off the screen as the second clip displays.

Stretch

A Stretch transition squeezes the first clip off as the second clip stretches across the screen.

Wipe

A Wipe transition spreads across the screen to reveal the second video clip.

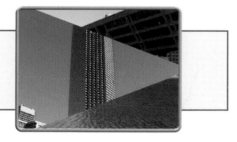

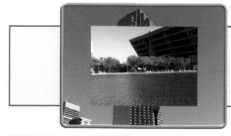

Zoom

A Zoom transition zooms one video clip in or out of the other video clip.

3-D Effect

A 3-D transition gives a 3-D look to the transition between video clips. A common 3-D transition creates a 3-D cube effect of changing video clips.

ADD A TRANSITION IN ADOBE PREMIERE

You can add a transition to your video to control the look as one video clip ends and the next one starts. Using a transition, you eliminate the abrupt start and stop of each video clip and create the sense of one video clip flowing into the next.

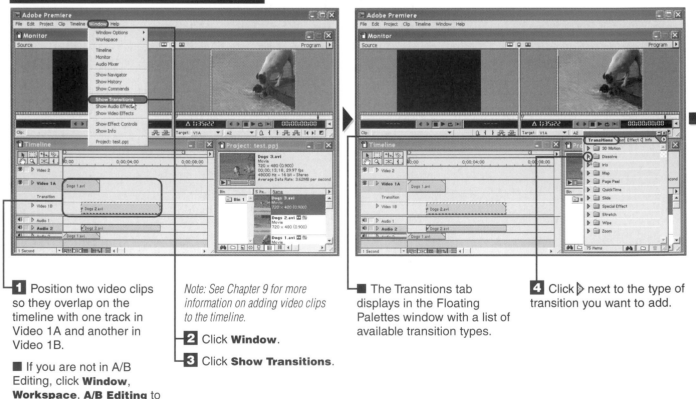

You add a transition to the timeline by inserting it between two video clips. In Adobe Premiere, you place the transition on the Transition track between Video 1A and Video 1B.

ADD A TRANSITION IN ADOBE PREMIERE

1 Position two video clips so they overlap on the timeline with one track in Video 1A and another in Video 1B.

■ If you are not in A/B Editing, click **Window**, **Workspace**, **A/B Editing** to switch modes.

Note: See Chapter 9 for more information on adding video clips to the timeline.

2 Click **Window**.

3 Click **Show Transitions**.

■ The Transitions tab displays in the Floating Palettes window with a list of available transition types.

4 Click ▷ next to the type of transition you want to add.

Why do I have black frames in my transition?

When you add transitions, you need to match the length of the overlapped video in the two video tracks. When you add a transition, Adobe Premiere automatically sizes the transition to match this length. If you move a video after inserting a transition, the transition picks up blank frames for the portion where you have no video clip. To correct this problem, move video clips so that they both overlap.

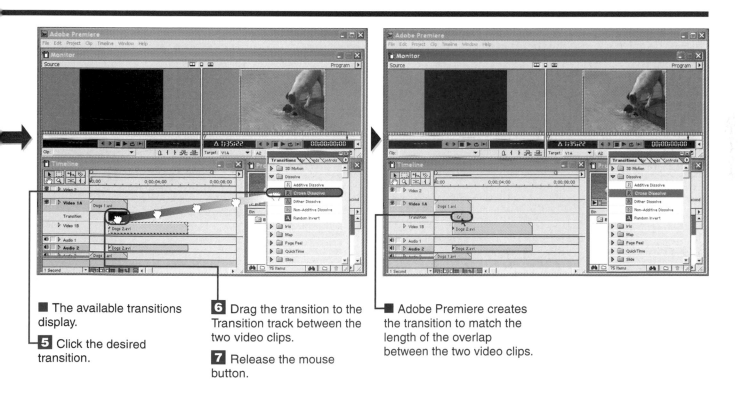

■ The available transitions display.

5 Click the desired transition.

6 Drag the transition to the Transition track between the two video clips.

7 Release the mouse button.

■ Adobe Premiere creates the transition to match the length of the overlap between the two video clips.

ADD A TRANSITION IN IMOVIE

You can add a transition to your video in iMovie. By doing so, you create a smooth changeover between two different video clips. You can select from any one of the six transitions that iMovie provides on the Transition panel.

This example illustrates the addition of a Push transition. A Push transition gives the appearance of one video clip pushing the other clip off of the screen from the top, bottom, or one of the sides. You can add all iMovie transitions using the steps in this section.

ADD A TRANSITION IN IMOVIE

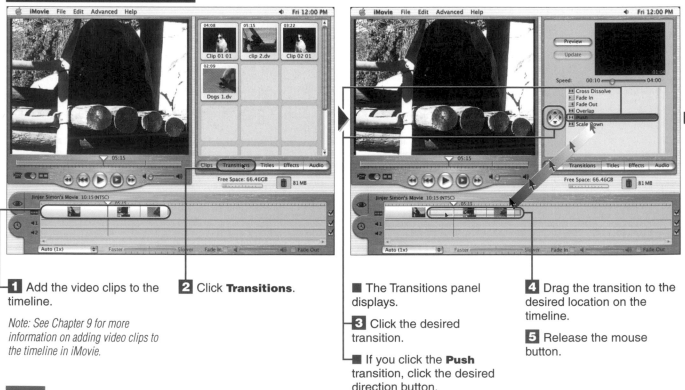

1 Add the video clips to the timeline.

Note: See Chapter 9 for more information on adding video clips to the timeline in iMovie.

2 Click **Transitions**.

■ The Transitions panel displays.

3 Click the desired transition.

■ If you click the **Push** transition, click the desired direction button.

4 Drag the transition to the desired location on the timeline.

5 Release the mouse button.

Can I make the transition last longer?

Yes, iMovie allows you to control the amount of time that it takes to play the transition. You can make the transition faster or slower. Keep in mind that iMovie removes the amount of time that the transition takes to play from the actual video clips. For example, if you set your transition to take two seconds to play, iMovie overlaps the first and second clips by two seconds. You can adjust the speed of the transition by clicking and dragging the Speed slider (). Dragging to the left decreases the time, while dragging it to the right increases the time.

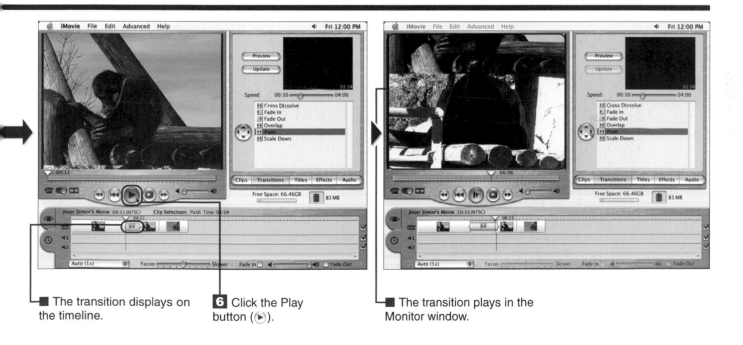

■ The transition displays on the timeline.

6 Click the Play button ().

■ The transition plays in the Monitor window.

ADD A TRANSITION IN FINAL CUT PRO

You can use transitions in Final Cut Pro to create a smooth flow from one video clip to another. For example, you can use a Cross Dissolve transition to create the appearance of one video clip fading into another video clip. When you work with transitions in Final Cut Pro, you need to overlay your two video clips for the amount of time you want your video transition to last.

ADD A TRANSITION IN FINAL CUT PRO

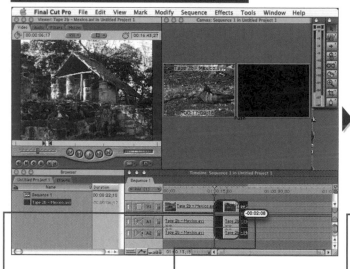

1 Click and drag one video clip so it overlays the end of another video clip.

Note: See Chapter 9 for more information on adding video clips to the timeline in Final Cut Pro.

■ Final Cut Pro indicates the amount of overlapping time.

2 Release the mouse button to place the clip.

■ The overlapped video clips display on the timeline.

3 Click and drag the Playhead (∨) to the start of the overlaid video clips.

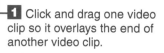

How do I make the transition start at the edit point?

By default, when you add a transition to the timeline, Final Cut Pro centers the transition around the edit point. You can have the transition start at the edit point or finish at the edit point. To change the alignment of the transition, press `Ctrl` and click the transition with the mouse to display a menu. Click the desired alignment for the transition in the menu. As the menu options indicate, **Start On Edit** starts the transition at the edit point, **Center On Edit** centers it around the edit point, and **End On Edit** has the transition end at the edit point.

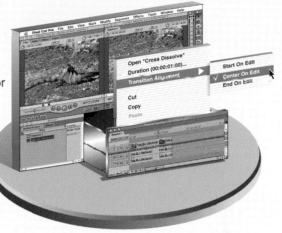

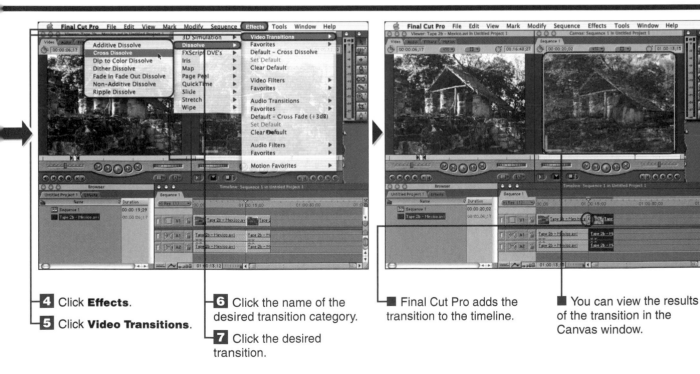

◄■ **4** Click **Effects**.

◄■ **5** Click **Video Transitions**.

■ **6** Click the name of the desired transition category.

■ **7** Click the desired transition.

■ Final Cut Pro adds the transition to the timeline.

■ You can view the results of the transition in the Canvas window.

CREATE A TRANSITION IN WINDOWS MOVIE MAKER

Although it does not have built-in transitions like other video editing packages, you can create a transition between video clips in Windows Movie Maker. To do so, you simply overlap two different video clips, and Windows Movie Maker automatically creates a cross dissolve between the two clips. The transition lasts for the amount of time you overlap the clips on the timeline.

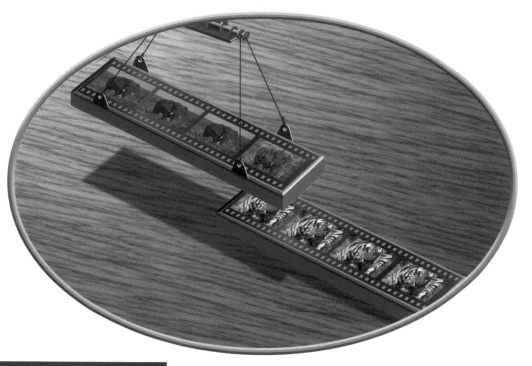

CREATE A TRANSITION IN WINDOWS MOVIE MAKER

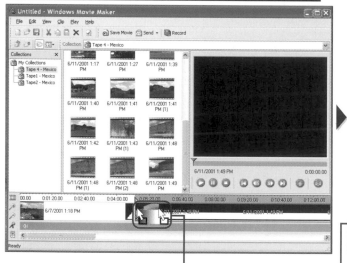

1 Add video clips to the timeline.

Note: See Chapter 9 for more information on working with the timeline in Windows Movie Maker.

2 Click the second clip and drag it until it overlaps the first clip.

■ The two clips overlap on the timeline, and the amount of overlap determines the transition time.

MOVE A TRANSITION

You can move a transition to any location on your timeline, for example, when you want to position the transition between a different set of clips. Because the transition remains the same length, you may need to resize it after you reposition it. To resize the transition, see the section "Change the Length of a Transition."

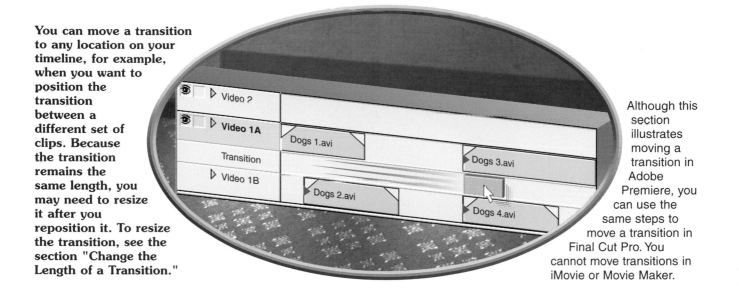

Although this section illustrates moving a transition in Adobe Premiere, you can use the same steps to move a transition in Final Cut Pro. You cannot move transitions in iMovie or Movie Maker.

MOVE A TRANSITION

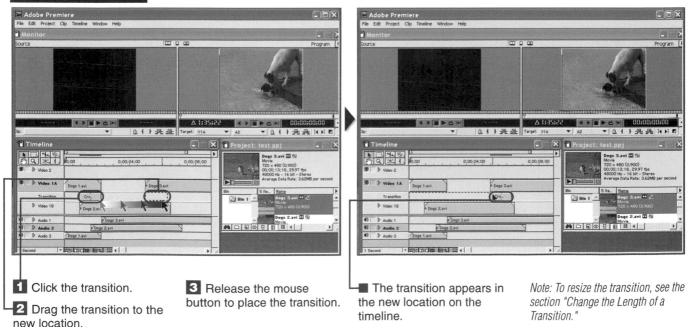

1 Click the transition.

2 Drag the transition to the new location.

3 Release the mouse button to place the transition.

■ The transition appears in the new location on the timeline.

Note: To resize the transition, see the section "Change the Length of a Transition."

CHANGE THE LENGTH OF A TRANSITION

You can resize any transition after adding it to your video. You resize the transition by making it either longer or shorter. You resize when you want the transition to take up more or less time in your video.

Although this section illustrates resizing a transition in Premiere, you can use the same steps to resize a transition in Final Cut Pro. In iMovie, you resize a transition using the Speed slider. See the section "Add a Transition in iMovie" for more information. The length of a transition in Movie Maker is determined by the size of the overlap. See "Create a Transition in Windows Movie Maker" for more information.

CHANGE THE LENGTH OF A TRANSITION

1 Click the transition on the side you want to resize.

■ In Premiere, the cursor changes to ◄⊡►.

2 Drag the transition until you size it to match the overlaid video clips.

■ The transition resizes.

■ When working in A/B Editing in Premiere, the transition should match the overlap size between the two clips.

You can remove any transitions you add to your video. Although the following steps illustrate how to remove a transition in Adobe Premiere, you use the exact same steps to remove a transition from Final Cut Pro and iMovie.

Keep in mind that you create a transition in Movie Maker by overlapping clips. To remove a transition from Movie Maker, you simply move the second clip off of the first clip so that the two no longer overlap.

REMOVE A TRANSITION

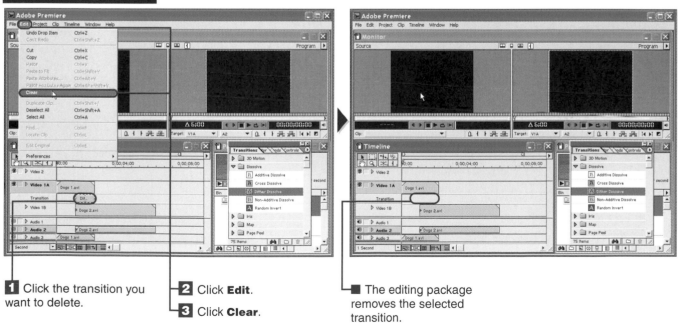

1 Click the transition you want to delete.

2 Click **Edit**.

3 Click **Clear**.

■ The editing package removes the selected transition.

You can customize the settings for each transition that you add in Adobe Premiere. When you customize the settings, you change items such as the size and color of the border that displays around the video clips during the transition.

You customize the settings for each transition by selecting the transition and then opening the corresponding dialog box for the transition. Premiere applies all changes you make in the dialog box to the selected transition.

Although this section uses the Iris Points Settings dialog box to illustrate how to change settings, you can use these steps to change the settings of other transitions.

CUSTOMIZE TRANSITION SETTINGS IN ADOBE PREMIERE

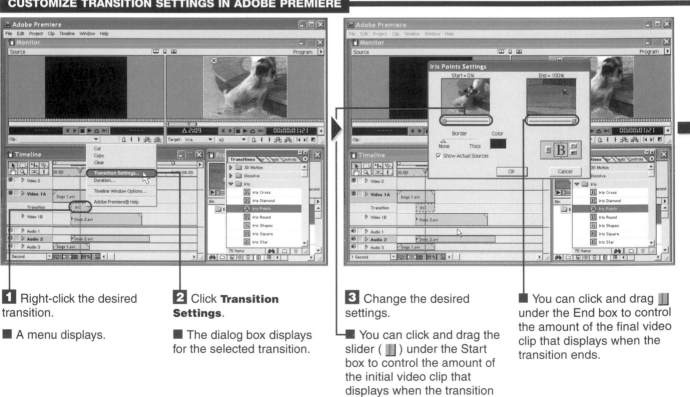

1 Right-click the desired transition.

■ A menu displays.

2 Click **Transition Settings**.

■ The dialog box displays for the selected transition.

3 Change the desired settings.

■ You can click and drag the slider (▓) under the Start box to control the amount of the initial video clip that displays when the transition starts.

■ You can click and drag ▓ under the End box to control the amount of the final video clip that displays when the transition ends.

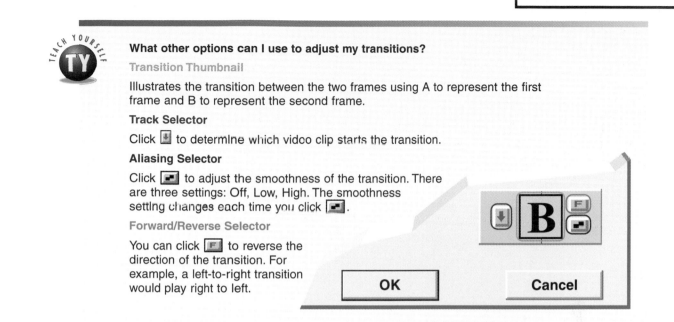

What other options can I use to adjust my transitions?

Transition Thumbnail

Illustrates the transition between the two frames using A to represent the first frame and B to represent the second frame.

Track Selector

Click ⬇ to determine which video clip starts the transition.

Aliasing Selector

Click ◼ to adjust the smoothness of the transition. There are three settings: Off, Low, High. The smoothness setting changes each time you click ◼.

Forward/Reverse Selector

You can click F to reverse the direction of the transition. For example, a left-to-right transition would play right to left.

■ You can click and drag the slider (△) to control the amount of border that displays around the transition.

■ You can click **Show Actual Sources** (☐changes to ☑) to quickly see the actual beginning and ending frames in the windows above the Start and End sliders.

4 Click the color swatch.

■ The Color Picker dialog box appears.

5 Click to select the desired color.

6 Click **OK** to close the Color Picker dialog box.

7 Click **OK** in the settings dialog box.

■ When you insert a transition, Adobe Premiere applies your settings.

Note: To insert a transition, see the section "Add a Transition in Adobe Premiere."

CHANGE TRANSITION SETTINGS IN FINAL CUT PRO

You can customize specific settings for each transition in Final Cut Pro using the Transition Editor. With this editor, you can change settings such as duration and direction of the transition. Each transition also provides custom settings you can adjust, such as direction and border color.

CHANGE TRANSITION SETTINGS IN FINAL CUT PRO

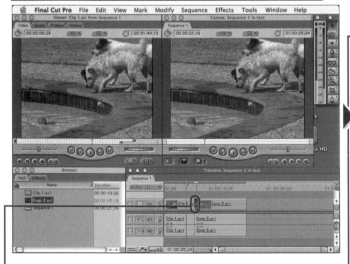

■1 Double-click the desired transition.

■ The Transition Editor appears with the name of the selected transition on a tab.

■2 Make the desired modifications to the settings.

■ You can view the current length of the transition here.

■ Click and drag the sliders (📐) to control the amount of the initial or final video clip that displays at the start or end of the transition. A percentage displays next to the slider.

What other options can I use to adjust my transitions?

Alignment Buttons

You can click these buttons to lay out the transition to the left
(◄), center (▲), or right (►) in relation to the edit point.

Recent Clips

You can click this button
(▦) to display a list
of the recently used clips.

Drag Head

You can click this button (▣)
to place the displayed transition
in another location on the timeline.
To do so, click the button and drag it
to the desired location on the timeline.

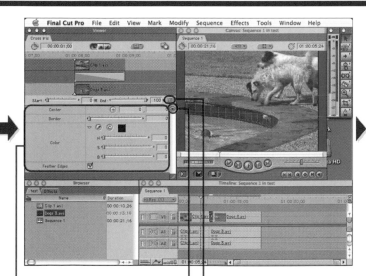

■ You change settings
specific to your transition in
this area.

■ To reverse the direction
of the transition, click the
Reverse Transition
button (▤).

■ To reset the transition,
click the Reset button (▣).

■ Final Cut Pro updates
your transition settings as
you make the changes on
the tab.

DUPLICATE A TRANSITION

You can use the same transition in multiple locations in your video by copying it and pasting it in the desired location. You may find this especially useful if you want to reuse an already customized transition.

Although these steps illustrate duplicating a video transition in Premiere, you can perform the same steps in Final Cut Pro. Movie Maker and iMovie do not provide the ability to duplicate a transition.

DUPLICATE A TRANSITION

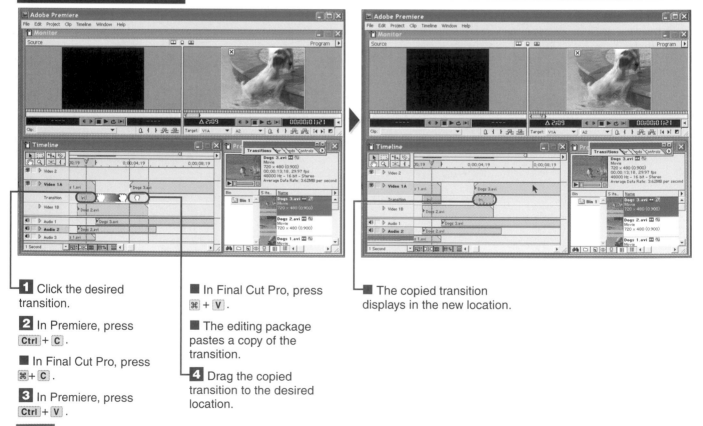

1 Click the desired transition.

2 In Premiere, press Ctrl + C.

■ In Final Cut Pro, press ⌘ + C.

3 In Premiere, press Ctrl + V.

■ In Final Cut Pro, press ⌘ + V.

■ The editing package pastes a copy of the transition.

4 Drag the copied transition to the desired location.

■ The copied transition displays in the new location.

You can *render*, or build,
your video to combine video
clips with transitions and
special effects. Video editing
packages require you to
render your video before you
can view some transitions
and other special effects.

Premiere and Final Cut Pro
require you to render most
transitions, whereas iMovie
renders transitions
automatically when you add
them. In Premiere and Final Cut
Pro, if the Render bar is red
above a transition, you need to
render it before viewing.

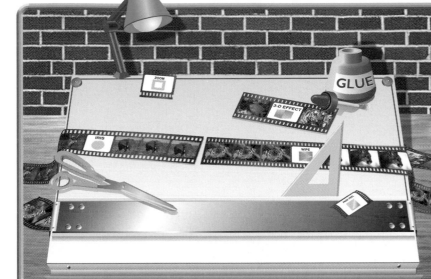

RENDER A TRANSITION

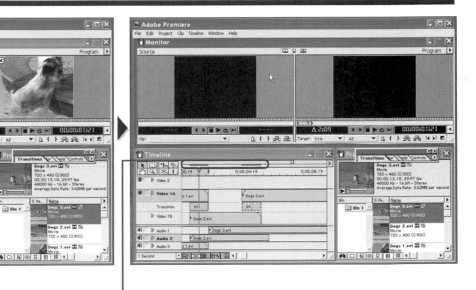

1 In Premiere, click
Timeline.

■ In Final Cut Pro click
Sequence.

2 In Premiere, click
Render Work Area.

■ In Final Cut Pro, click
Render Selection.

■ The editing software
renders the video and the
Render bar changes color
when the process completes.

■ In Premiere, the Render
bar turns green upon
completion.

■ In Final Cut Pro, the
Render bar turns blue
upon completion.

CHAPTER 12

Adding Special Effects

You can add different special effects to your video clip to change the clip's appearance. You can do anything from changing the coloring of the video clip, to actually inserting other graphic images. This chapter looks at the different tasks you can perform to add special effects to your video clips.

UNDERSTANDING SPECIAL EFFECTS

You can use standard video filters, provided with video editing software, to create different visual effects and change the quality of a series of frames in a video clip. Adobe Premiere, Final Cut Pro, and iMovie all provide different video filters you can apply to your video clips. Movie Maker does not provide any special effects. Although you may find the list of available filters extensive, they fall into eleven basic categories.

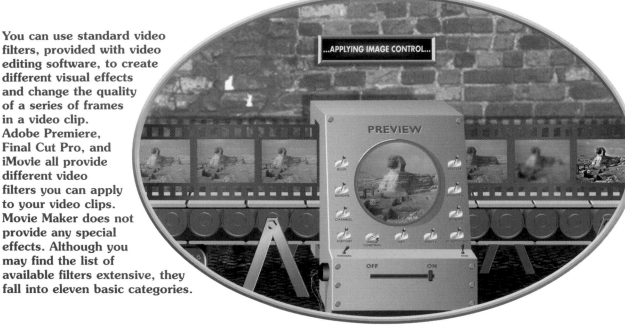

Blur

Blur filters allow you to create an out-of-focus look to your video clips. You can use blurred images as background images.

Border

You can use Border filters to add a frame around the edges of your video clip. Use these effects anytime you want to make your video clip stand out from its background.

Channel

Channel filters change different color channels (RGB) within your clips to create specific effects. For example, you may apply a blur to specific colors of your video clip.

Distort

You can use Distort filters to alter the shape of your video clips. These filters allow you to create different texture effects within your video clips.

Image Control

You can use Image Control filters to alter the level of black, white, and other colors in your video clips. These filters range from color correcting filters that compensate for too much or too little light, to filters that make your video clip look old fashioned by applying a sepia tint.

UNDERSTANDING SPECIAL EFFECTS

Key

With Key filters, you can isolate foreground images by removing the background. Typically, you use a key filter with an image shot in front of a solid color background, such as a blue screen. You can then place a different background behind the image. To learn more about using a blue screen to replace a background with one of your choosing, see Chapter 7.

Matte

You can use Matte filters to mask or blank out specific areas of your clip. You can also use a matte filter to make additional adjustments to your clips before applying keys. You should use this filter anytime you need to remove or replace portions of your video clip.

Perspective

You can use Perspective filters to change the clip spatially by rotating, mirroring, or even creating an apparent 3-D perspective. Use these types of effects when you want to give a video clip a different viewpoint.

Render

You can use Render filters to add effects such as a lens flare. A lens flare effect creates the effect of the sun or a bright light shining directly on the camera lens. You can use this effect to create the appearance of shooting your video on a bright sunny day.

Sharpen

Sharpen filters improve the contrast in your video clips to make the images appear more in focus. By sharpening the video clip, you make the areas of the video where color changes occur more apparent. You can create unique effects by over sharpening your video clip.

Stylize

You can create extreme changes in the appearance of your video clips using Stylize filters. For example, if you apply an embossed effect, the video clip has the appearance of being stamped on the screen.

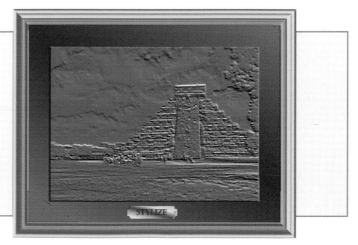

APPLY AN EFFECT IN IMOVIE

You can apply an effect to change the appearance of a selected video clip in iMovie. For example, you can apply a Sepia Tone effect to make your video clip look like an old movie. When you apply effects to your video clip, you can select what portion of the video clip receives the effect.

APPLY AN EFFECT IN IMOVIE

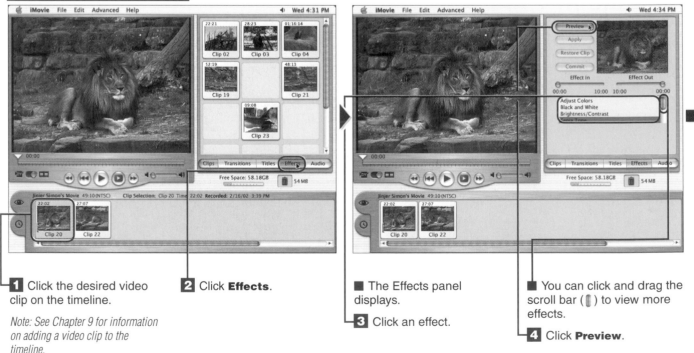

1 Click the desired video clip on the timeline.

Note: See Chapter 9 for information on adding a video clip to the timeline.

2 Click **Effects**.

■ The Effects panel displays.

3 Click an effect.

■ You can click and drag the scroll bar ( ) to view more effects.

4 Click **Preview**.

Can I apply multiple effects to the same video clip?

Yes, to do so, after applying the first video effect to the selected video clip, click **Commit**. Now you can apply another effect to the same video clip. If you do not click **Commit**, the new effect you select replaces the original effect.

As long as you have not saved the video, you can still undo the effects by clicking **File**, **Undo**. When you use the Undo command, iMovie removes the effects in reverse order and therefore removes the last committed effect first.

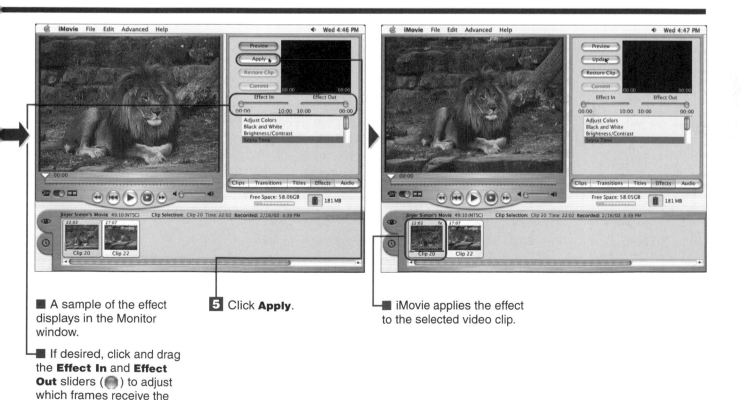

■ A sample of the effect displays in the Monitor window.

■ If desired, click and drag the **Effect In** and **Effect Out** sliders (◉) to adjust which frames receive the video effect.

5 Click **Apply**.

■ iMovie applies the effect to the selected video clip.

APPLY AN EFFECT IN ADOBE PREMIERE

You can apply an effect in
Adobe Premiere to create
a unique and interesting
video clip. Effects allow
you to enhance or alter
the selected video image.

You apply the effect by
selecting one of the built-in
video filters. For example, a
lens flare creates the
appearance of light reflecting
off the lens of a camera
creating a bright flare.

APPLY AN EFFECT IN ADOBE PREMIERE

1 Click the desired video
clip on the timeline.

*Note: See Chapter 9 for more
information on working with video
clips on the timeline.*

2 Click **Window**.

3 Click **Show Video
Effects**.

■ The **Video** tab displays in
the floating palettes window.

4 Click ▷ next to the effect
category you want to apply
(▷ changes to ▽) to view a
list of filters.

■ This example illustrates
the selection of the Render
category.

5 Click the filter that you
want to apply.

6 Drag the filter to the
selected video clip.

Can I adjust the video effect to only apply to a portion of my video clip?

Yes, you can apply the video effect to the entire video clip or only a portion of the clip. By default, it applies to the entire video clip. To change that setting, click ▷ to display the keyframe for the Video Frame. Click the edge of the video effect line and drag it to locate the start and stop of the effect.

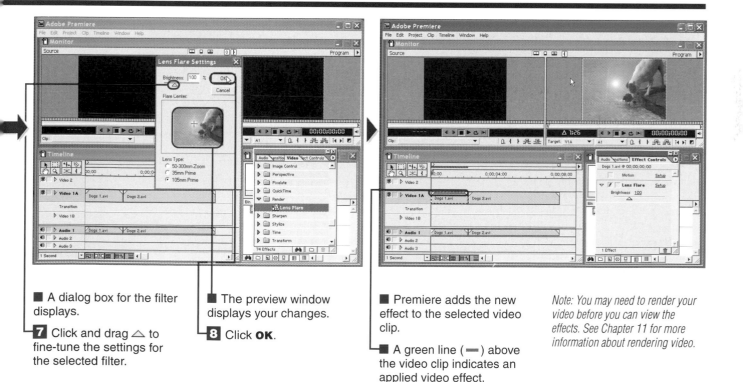

■ A dialog box for the filter displays.

7 Click and drag △ to fine-tune the settings for the selected filter.

■ The preview window displays your changes.

8 Click **OK**.

■ Premiere adds the new effect to the selected video clip.

■ A green line (▬) above the video clip indicates an applied video effect.

Note: You may need to render your video before you can view the effects. See Chapter 11 for more information about rendering video.

APPLY AN EFFECT IN FINAL CUT PRO

You can apply an effect to change the appearance of your video clips in Final Cut Pro using a variety of filters. When you do so, you alter your video clip enhancing its appearance. For example, you can use the Ripple effect to give your video clips a wavy, distorted appearance.

Ripple Effect

APPLY AN EFFECT IN FINAL CUT PRO

1 Click the video clip you want to change.

■ The selected video clip displays in the Viewer window.

2 Click the **Effects** tab in the Browser window.

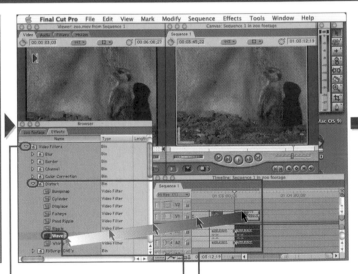

■ The available video effects display.

3 Click the arrow next to the **Video Filter** (▷ changes to ▽).

■ The list of available video filter categories displays.

4 Click the arrow next to a category (▷ changes to ▽).

■ The filters display.

5 Click the filter and drag it onto the selected clip on the Timeline window.

Can I tweak the effects of the filter I want to apply to the video clip?

Yes, you can customize all filters that you apply in Final Cut Pro. See the following steps to modify the setting for a filter. Keep in mind, once you make modifications, you must render the video clip again to see the results.

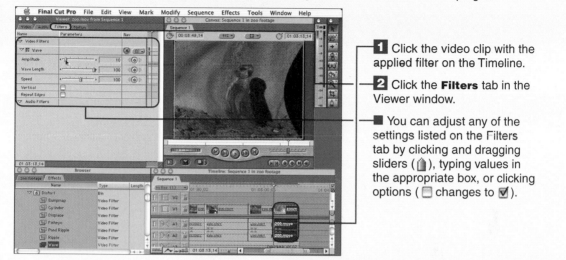

1 Click the video clip with the applied filter on the Timeline.

2 Click the **Filters** tab in the Viewer window.

■ You can adjust any of the settings listed on the Filters tab by clicking and dragging sliders ( ), typing values in the appropriate box, or clicking options (changes to ☑).

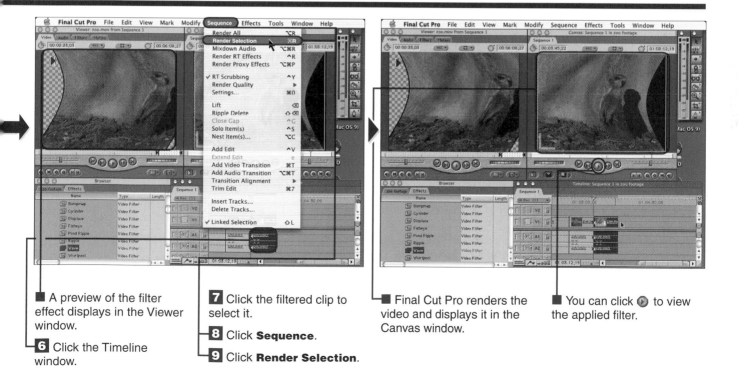

■ A preview of the filter effect displays in the Viewer window.

6 Click the Timeline window.

7 Click the filtered clip to select it.

8 Click **Sequence**.

9 Click **Render Selection**.

■ Final Cut Pro renders the video and displays it in the Canvas window.

■ You can click to view the applied filter.

COLOR CORRECT A VIDEO CLIP

You can correct the colors in any video clip by applying a color-correcting filter and making the desired adjustments. With a color-correcting filter, you can adjust the attributes such as the hue, saturation, and brightness of the image. This helps you correct for instances where you have too much light, over-exposure, or not enough light.

Although this example uses Adobe Premiere to illustrate correcting a color, you can do something similar in Final Cut Pro and iMovie.

COLOR CORRECT A VIDEO CLIP

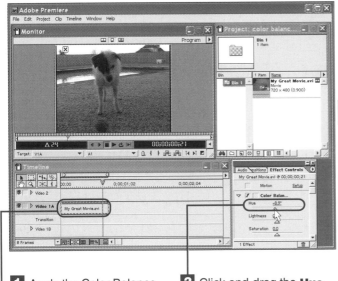

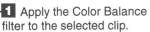 Apply the Color Balance filter to the selected clip.

Note: See the section "Apply an Effect in Adobe Premiere" for more information about adding video filters.

2 Click and drag the **Hue** slider (△) to shift the colors in the image.

■ The effects of the Hue adjustment display in the Monitor window.

3 Click and drag the **Lightness** slider (△) to shift the brightness of the video clip.

■ The clip becomes brighter when you shift it to the right and darker when you shift it to the left.

What exactly changes when I adjust the color attributes in Premiere?

Hue	Shifts the position of the colors on the color wheel.
Lightness	Changes the brightness, with higher levels creating brighter video clips.
Saturation	Changes the color intensity to make the image either duller or more vibrant. Remember that an oversaturation of colors, especially red, can create a smeared effect on your video footage.

 How do I color correct a video clip in iMovie and Final Cut Pro?

iMovie

First, apply the Adjust Color effect per the steps in the section "Apply an Effect in iMovie." As you drag the sliders for **Hue Shift**, **Color**, and **Lightness**, your adjustments display in the preview window at the top of the panel.

Final Cut Pro

First, apply the Color Corrector video filter in the Color Correction category per the steps in the section "Apply an Effect in Final Cut Pro." Next, click the **Color Corrector** tab in the Viewer window and drag the **Whites**, **Mids**, **Blacks**, and **Sat** sliders to correct the color of the clip.

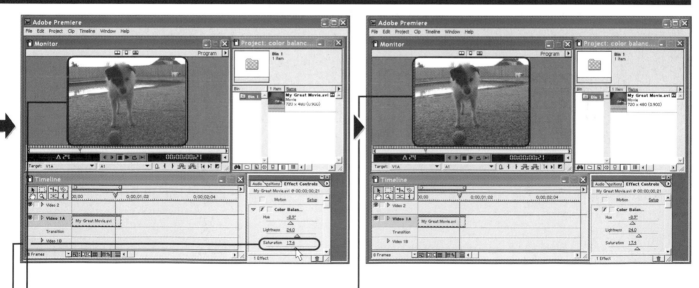

■ The effects of the Lightness adjustment display in the Monitor window.

4 Click and drag the **Saturation** slider (△) to adjust the color intensity of the image.

■ The colors become more intense when the slider moves right and duller when the slider moves left.

■ The effects of the Saturation adjustment display in the Monitor window.

Note: You need to render your video before you can view the effects. See Chapter 11 for more information about rendering video.

CREATE A VIDEO WATERMARK

You can add *watermark* images to your video clips in Adobe Premiere and Final Cut Pro. Watermarking is what you see on the television when the station adds their logo to a show. In Adobe Premiere, you do this by adjusting the transparency settings for an overlaid clip.

In Final Cut Pro, you can create a Video Watermark by adjusting the transparency settings for the image and then adding the Embossing effect to it. See the section "Apply an Affect in Final Cut Pro" for more information on adding embossing to the image. See Chapter 9 for information on placing the watermark image to the V2 track.

CREATE A VIDEO WATERMARK

1 Click the timeline location for the watermarked image.

2 Click the watermark clip in the Project window and drag it to an overlay track on the timeline — typically Video 2 in Premiere or V2 in Final Cut Pro.

Note: See Chapter 7 for more on the various parts of the Adobe Premiere window.

Note: See Chapter 9 for more information on adding clips to the timeline.

■ The watermark image clip displays on the timeline.

3 Click and drag the edge of the clip to resize it, matching the amount of time you want it to display in the video.

How do I create a Video Watermark in Final Cut Pro?

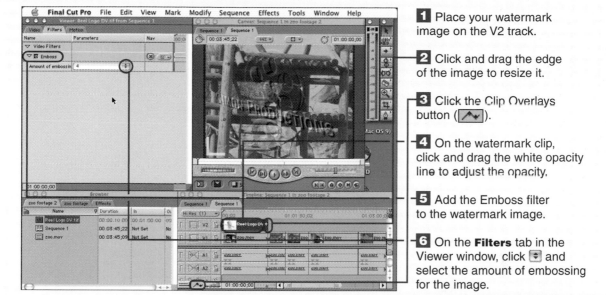

1 Place your watermark image on the V2 track.

2 Click and drag the edge of the image to resize it.

3 Click the Clip Overlays button (⬦).

4 On the watermark clip, click and drag the white opacity line to adjust the opacity.

5 Add the Emboss filter to the watermark image.

6 On the **Filters** tab in the Viewer window, click ⬦ and select the amount of embossing for the image.

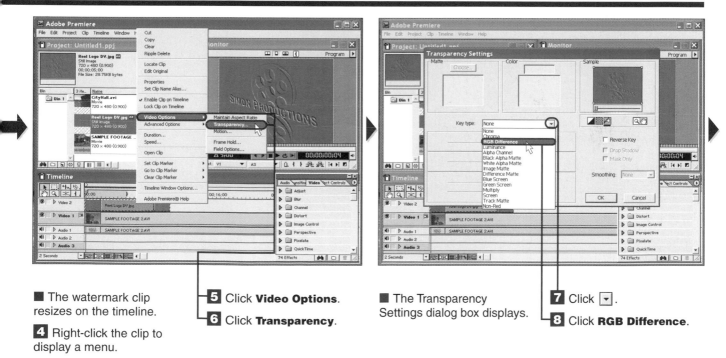

■ The watermark clip resizes on the timeline.

4 Right-click the clip to display a menu.

5 Click **Video Options**.

6 Click **Transparency**.

■ The Transparency Settings dialog box displays.

7 Click ▾.

8 Click **RGB Difference**.

CONTINUED

CREATE A VIDEO WATERMARK

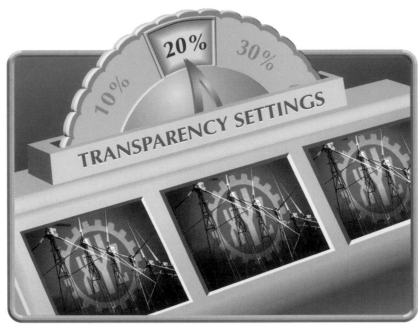

When you create a video watermark, you make the image see-through using one of the transparency keys in Adobe Premiere. You select the transparency key on the Transparency Settings dialog box. The key specifies how to create the transparency. One setting, the RGB Difference key, helps you easily apply transparency.

You need to specify the type of smoothing you want to apply to the edges of the transparent image. You can select **None** to produce sharp edges, **Low** to make edges smooth, or **High** to produce the smoothest edges of all.

CREATE A VIDEO WATERMARK (CONTINUED)

9 Click the transparent color for your watermark image.

■ The ⌖ changes to 🖉 when you drag over the image.

■ The Sample window reflects the results of selecting the transparency color.

10 Drag the △ to increase the range of transparent colors with higher values producing more colors in the transparent image.

Can I see how the watermark looks on my video clip before rendering it?

Yes, the Transparency Settings dialog box provides the option of seeing your video clip with the watermarked image displayed on top. Click ▨ to display the video clip.

Do I need to select High Smoothing?

No, you can select from three levels of smoothing depending upon how sharp you want the edges to appear between your watermarked image and the video clip. If you mainly have text for your watermark, you should click **None** to produce the sharpest edges. Click **Low** for softer edges, and **High** for the softest edges.

11 Click ▾.

12 Click a Smoothing option.

13 Click **OK**.

■ Adobe Premiere applies the settings to the clip.

Note: You need to render the video to view the effects of the clip. See Chapter 14 for information on previewing a video.

CREATE A CHROMA KEY

You can use a Chroma Key video filter to place an image from one video clip on top of another video clip. To create a Chroma key effect, you need an image that you filmed in front of a solid background, preferably blue or green. For more about the actual filming process, see Chapter 7.

Although this example illustrates this technique with Final Cut Pro, you can also use Adobe Premiere to create a Chroma Key. For more on adding clips to timelines, see Chapter 9. You can make additional adjustments by changing the other key options in the Transparency Settings dialog box.

CREATE A CHROMA KEY

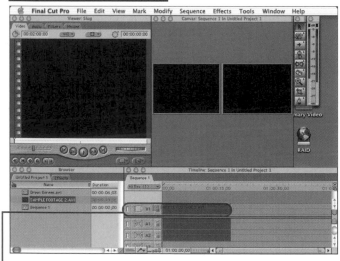

1 Click and drag the background video clip to V1.

Note: See Chapter 9 for more information on adding clips to the timeline.

2 Press Ctrl and click the mouse ( ) on the timeline.

■ A menu displays.

3 Double-click the chroma-key video clip to add it to the Viewer window.

4 Click and drag the In Point button ( ) to select the first frame for the chroma key video clip.

5 Click and drag the Out Point button ( ) to select the last frame for the chroma key video clip.

6 Click **Add Track**.

232

How do I create a Chroma Key in Adobe Premiere?

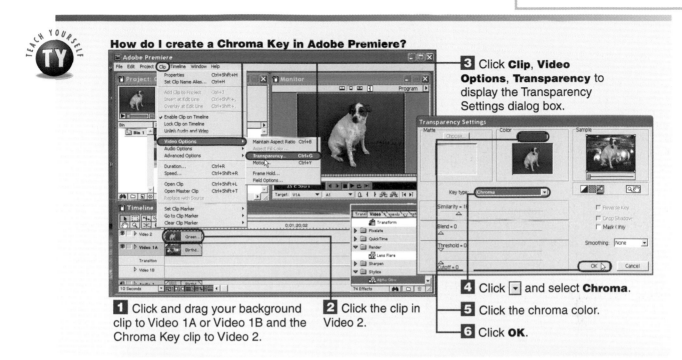

3 Click **Clip**, **Video Options**, **Transparency** to display the Transparency Settings dialog box.

4 Click ⬇ and select **Chroma**.

5 Click the chroma color.

6 Click **OK**.

1 Click and drag your background clip to Video 1A or Video 1B and the Chroma Key clip to Video 2.

2 Click the clip in Video 2.

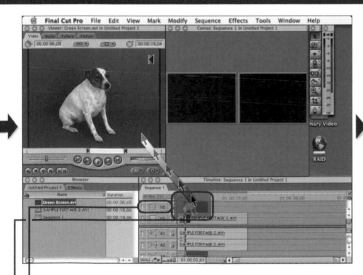

■ A V2 track appears on the timeline.

7 Click and drag the clip from Viewer to V2 track on the timeline.

Note: See Chapter 7 for more information on Final Cut Pro video tracks.

■ The clip displays on the timeline.

8 Click and drag the Playhead at the beginning of the video clip in the V2 track.

9 Click the clip in V2 track.

CONTINUED ▶

CREATE A CHROMA KEY

To finalize the effect, you must apply the Chroma Keyer filter to your video clip. With a Chroma Key effect, you make the solid background transparent, which allows you to place the image on another background.

CREATE A CHROMA KEY (CONTINUED)

⑩ Click **Effects**.

⑪ Click **Video Filters**.

⑫ Click **Key**.

⑬ Click **Chroma Keyer**.

■ Final Cut Pro adds the filter to the selected clip.

⑭ Click the **Chroma Keyer** tab.

**Can I reverse the effect so my
image becomes transparent?**

Yes, once you specify the chroma
key color for your video clip, you
can reverse the effect by clicking
the Invert Selection button ().

■ The Chroma Keyer tab
displays.

15 Click the Select Color
icon (▦).

16 Click the transparent
color in the Canvas window.

■ In this example, the
transparent color is green.

■ If the background color is
not solid and different
shades exist, you can also
adjust the color saturation in
the Sat bar and the
lumination in the Luma bar
by clicking a color.

■ The video clip's
background becomes
transparent and the
background image appears.

235

CHAPTER 13

Inserting Titles and Animation

You can add different types of titles to your video. You can use titles to provide specific information about your video, such as the production staff, location of the video footage, and so on. You can overlay titles directly on a video clip or create separate clips containing scrolling titles. This chapter looks at the different tasks you perform to add titles to your video.

ADD A TITLE SLIDE IN WINDOWS MOVIE MAKER

You can add a title slide to your video to provide specific text information, such as the name of the video, subject names, or even the video's location. You can add title slides to your video in Windows Movie Maker by creating a title slide in Microsoft Paint, or some other graphics package, and importing the slide into Windows Movie Maker. Your title slide can consist of just text or a combination of text and graphics.

ADD A TITLE SLIDE IN WINDOWS MOVIE MAKER

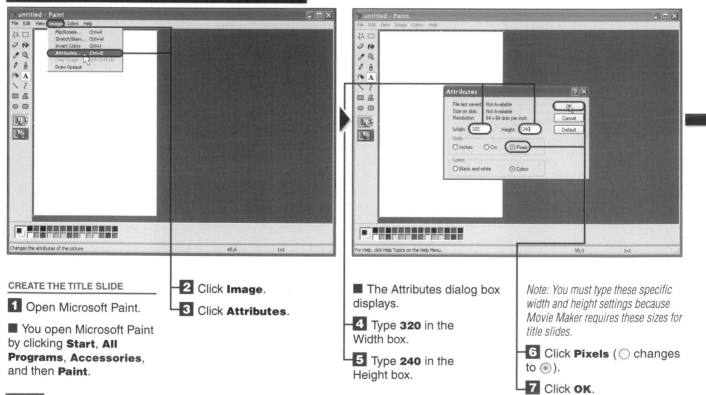

CREATE THE TITLE SLIDE

1 Open Microsoft Paint.

■ You open Microsoft Paint by clicking **Start**, **All Programs**, **Accessories**, and then **Paint**.

2 Click **Image**.

3 Click **Attributes**.

■ The Attributes dialog box displays.

4 Type **320** in the Width box.

5 Type **240** in the Height box.

Note: You must type these specific width and height settings because Movie Maker requires these sizes for title slides.

6 Click **Pixels** (○ changes to ⊙).

7 Click **OK**.

How do I change the look of the text?

You can select a font type, size, and color for your text in Microsoft Paint.

Font Type and Size

Click ⌄ of either the Font type box or the Font size box, and select the desired attribute.

Color Bar

To select a font color, click the desired color on the Colors bar.

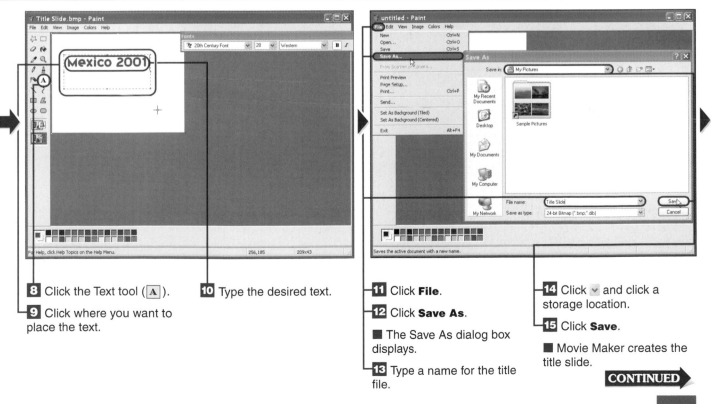

8 Click the Text tool (▲).

9 Click where you want to place the text.

10 Type the desired text.

11 Click **File**.

12 Click **Save As**.

■ The Save As dialog box displays.

13 Type a name for the title file.

14 Click ⌄ and click a storage location.

15 Click **Save**.

■ Movie Maker creates the title slide.

CONTINUED

ADD A TITLE SLIDE IN WINDOWS MOVIE MAKER

You can import graphic files into Windows Movie Maker. After you do so, you can place the title clip anywhere on the timeline simply by clicking and dragging it.

Unlike Adobe Premiere, iMovie, and Final Cut Pro, Windows Movie Maker's titling options are limited to a stationary title. For more on titling with the other three programs, see the other sections in this chapter.

ADD A TITLE SLIDE IN WINDOWS MOVIE MAKER (CONTINUED)

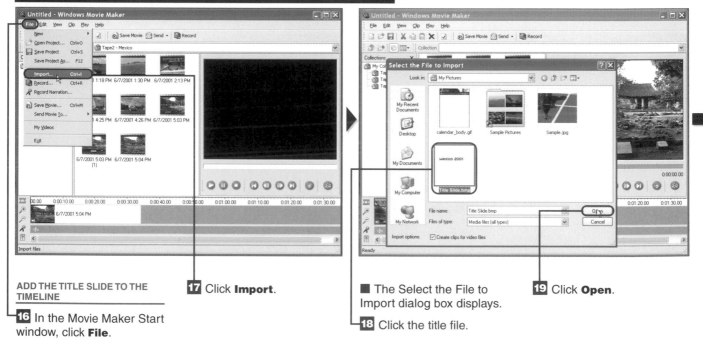

ADD THE TITLE SLIDE TO THE TIMELINE

16 In the Movie Maker Start window, click **File**.

17 Click **Import**.

■ The Select the File to Import dialog box displays.

18 Click the title file.

19 Click **Open**.

Can I make the title slide display over the top of another video clip?

Yes, if you use the two clips to create a transitional effect. Click the clip and drag it over the second clip. If desired, you can make your title slide last longer by clicking the End Trim icon (◢) and dragging it to the right. This allows you to create a title clip the same length as the video clip you want to overlay. For more on adding clips and transitions to your Movie Maker timeline, see Chapters 9 and 11, respectively.

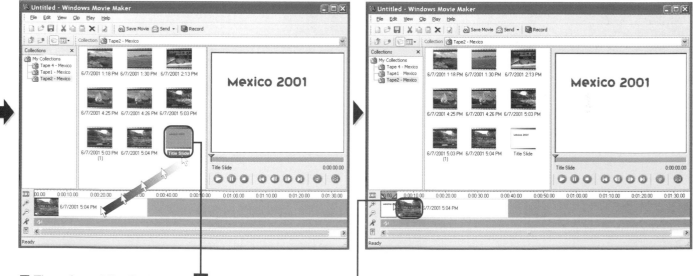

■ The selected file displays in the Clips List.

Note: For more information on the various parts of the Movie Maker window, see Chapter 7.

20 Click the title slide and drag it to the appropriate location on the timeline.

■ The title slide displays on the timeline.

OVERLAY A TITLE IN IMOVIE

You can quickly overlay a title on a clip in iMovie using one of the built-in title options to label the clips in your video. When you overlay the title, you place text on top of a video clip.

You use the built-in titling options to customize how the title text appears. For example, when you select the centering option, you specify that you want a title centered on the clip. You can customize not only the text of the title but also the font and color information.

OVERLAY A TITLE IN IMOVIE

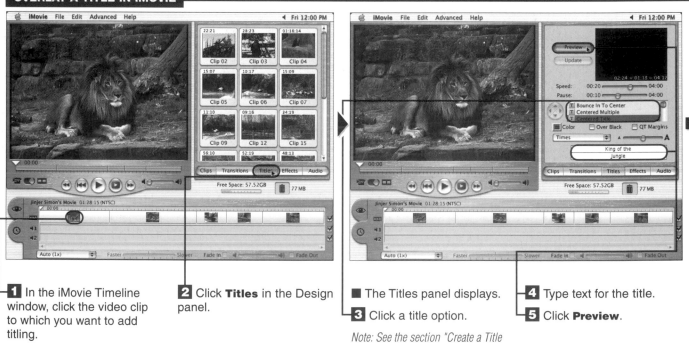

1 In the iMovie Timeline window, click the video clip to which you want to add titling.

2 Click **Titles** in the Design panel.

■ The Titles panel displays.

3 Click a title option.

Note: See the section "Create a Title Clip in iMovie" for more information on various title options.

4 Type text for the title.

5 Click **Preview**.

Can I change the color of the text?

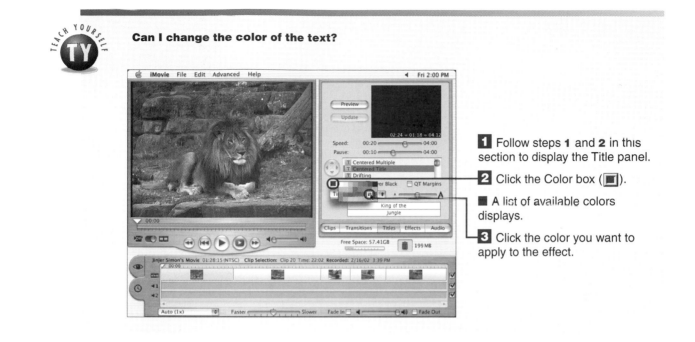

1 Follow steps **1** and **2** in this section to display the Title panel.

2 Click the Color box (■).

■ A list of available colors displays.

3 Click the color you want to apply to the effect.

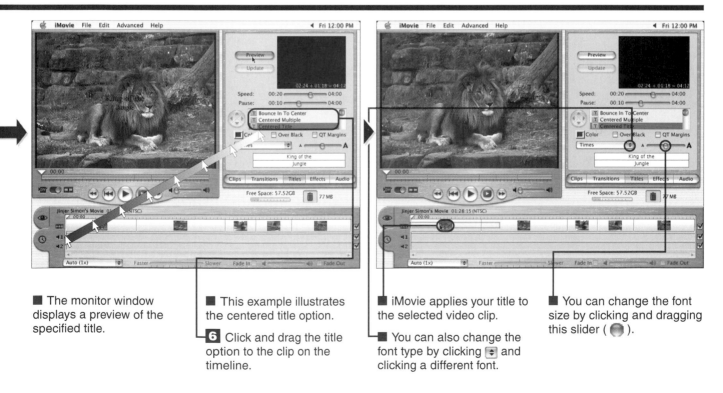

■ The monitor window displays a preview of the specified title.

■ This example illustrates the centered title option.

6 Click and drag the title option to the clip on the timeline.

■ iMovie applies your title to the selected video clip.

■ You can also change the font type by clicking ⊕ and clicking a different font.

■ You can change the font size by clicking and dragging this slider (⬤).

CREATE A TITLE CLIP IN IMOVIE

You can create a separate title slide to your video in iMovie. This type of titling displays on a black background, and works well when you want to add credits to your movie. For example, you can create rolling credits that resemble the scrolling credits you see at the end of movies in a theater. You do not have to place a title clip at the end of the video — you can place it before or after any video clip.

CREATE A TITLE CLIP IN IMOVIE

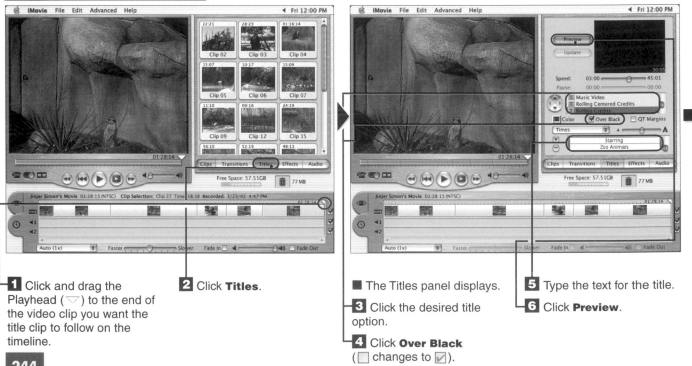

1 Click and drag the Playhead (▽) to the end of the video clip you want the title clip to follow on the timeline.

2 Click **Titles**.

■ The Titles panel displays.

3 Click the desired title option.

4 Click **Over Black** (☐ changes to ☑).

5 Type the text for the title.

6 Click **Preview**.

What title options are available in iMovie?

iMovie provides 13 different titling options. You can either create a separate title clip or overlay all of the title options. For more on overlaying titles, see the section "Overlay a Title in iMovie."

Title Option	Description
Bounce In To Center	Brings title lines together in the center either from the sides, top, or bottom.
Centered Multiple	Fades multiple title lines in the center.
Centered Title	Fades in a centered title.
Drifting	Title drifts into the center of the screen.
Flying Letters	Letters fly in one at a time.
Flying Words	Words fly into the center of the screen.
Music Video	Places a block of text in the corner of the screen.
Rolling Centered Credits	Titles roll up the center of the screen.
Rolling Credits	Titles roll on the screen.
Scroll with Pause	Titles scroll into the center, pause, and then scroll off the screen.
Scrolling Block	Scrolls a block of text across the screen.
Stripe Subtitle	Displays the title in a white stripe across the bottom of the screen.
Typewriter	Title is typed onto the screen.

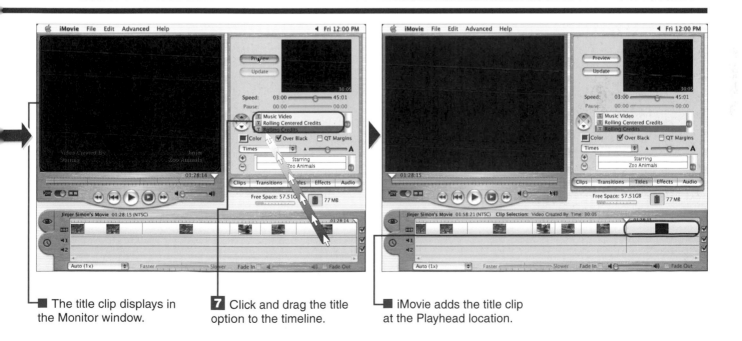

■ The title clip displays in the Monitor window.

7 Click and drag the title option to the timeline.

■ iMovie adds the title clip at the Playhead location.

OVERLAY A TITLE IN ADOBE PREMIERE

You can use the Title window in Adobe Premiere to create a title for your video. You use titles to label clips or provide additional information for your viewer. When you create a title, it becomes a separate clip in your project, and you must save it with a name.

The Title window represents a screen layout. You position your titles in the window to correspond to the location on the screen where you want your title to display.

OVERLAY A TITLE IN ADOBE PREMIERE

CREATE A TITLE

1 Click **File**.

2 Click **New**.

3 Click **Title**.

■ The Title window displays.

4 Click the Type Tool button (T).

5 Click where you want to locate the title.

6 Type your title.

■ You can change the text color by clicking here and selecting a new color.

Can I add shadowing to my text?

Not only can you add a text shadow, you can also select the placement of the shadow.

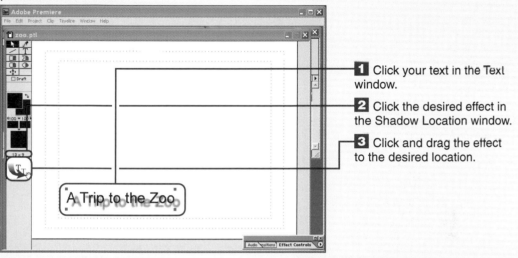

1 Click your text in the Text window.

2 Click the desired effect in the Shadow Location window.

3 Click and drag the effect to the desired location.

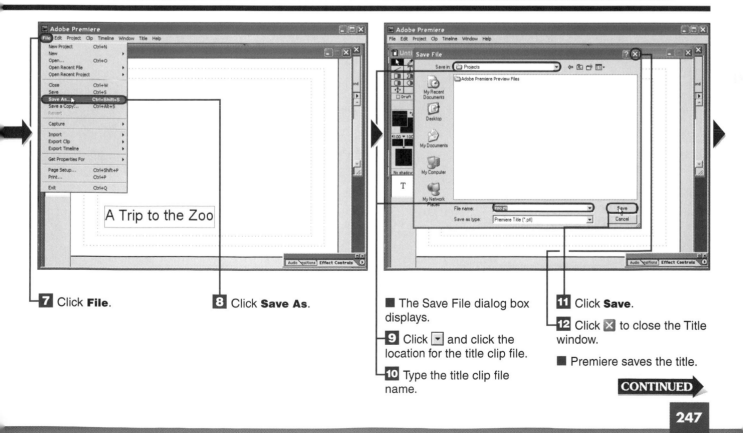

7 Click **File**.

8 Click **Save As**.

■ The Save File dialog box displays.

9 Click ▼ and click the location for the title clip file.

10 Type the title clip file name.

11 Click **Save**.

12 Click ✕ to close the Title window.

■ Premiere saves the title.

CONTINUED

OVERLAY A TITLE IN ADOBE PREMIERE

You overlay your created titles by dragging them from the Project window to the desired location on the timeline. After placing the title on the timeline, you must size it to match the clips you want to overlay.

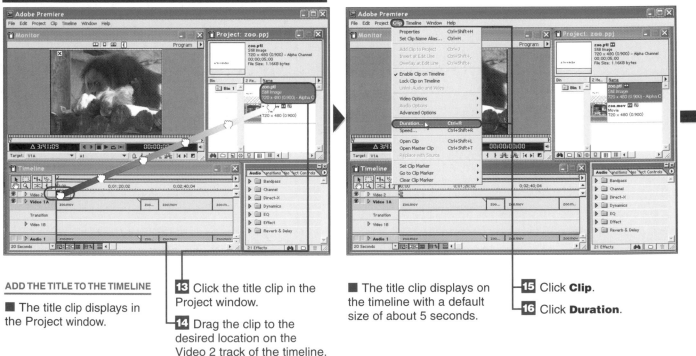

ADD THE TITLE TO THE TIMELINE

■ The title clip displays in the Project window.

13 Click the title clip in the Project window.

14 Drag the clip to the desired location on the Video 2 track of the timeline.

■ The title clip displays on the timeline with a default size of about 5 seconds.

15 Click **Clip**.

16 Click **Duration**.

Why do I need to place the title clip on the Video 2 track in Adobe Premiere?

By default, Video 2 track is a *superimposition* track, which means that when you place a title clip on this track, Premiere makes the clip's empty portions transparent. Because they are opaque, any videos in Video 1A and Video 1B become visible through the transparent portions of your title clip, thus creating the overlay effect.

■ The Clip Duration dialog box displays.

17 Type the desired duration for the clip.

18 Click **OK**.

■ Adobe Premiere resizes the title clip on the timeline.

Note: You need to render the video to view the title. See Chapter 14 for information on previewing a video.

ADD MOTION TO A TITLE IN ADOBE PREMIERE

You can make any title move within your video using the Motion Settings dialog box in Adobe Premiere. For example, you may want to have titles scroll across the screen. You specify the direction of movement for the title using *keyframes*, which represent key points in the video.

All video clips have a start and end keyframe, which you move to specify the title's path of movement. You can adjust the motion path by adding more keyframes to the motion path.

ADD MOTION TO A TITLE IN ADOBE PREMIERE

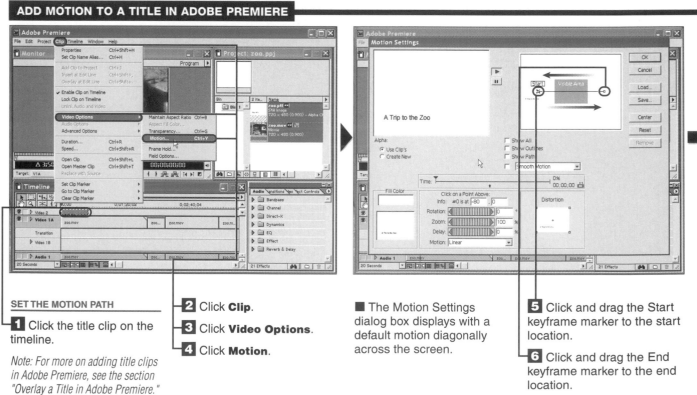

SET THE MOTION PATH

1 Click the title clip on the timeline.

Note: For more on adding title clips in Adobe Premiere, see the section "Overlay a Title in Adobe Premiere."

2 Click **Clip**.

3 Click **Video Options**.

4 Click **Motion**.

■ The Motion Settings dialog box displays with a default motion diagonally across the screen.

5 Click and drag the Start keyframe marker to the start location.

6 Click and drag the End keyframe marker to the end location.

Can I see how the moving title will look on my video without rendering?

Yes, the Motion Settings dialog box allows you to preview the title motion as you adjust the settings. To preview the motion, click **Show All** (☐ changes to ☑). Adobe Premiere displays the video clip with the moving title in the Preview window in the Motion Settings dialog box.

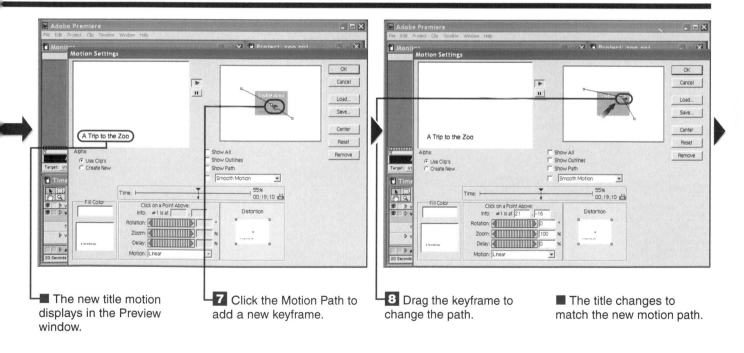

■ The new title motion displays in the Preview window.

7 Click the Motion Path to add a new keyframe.

8 Drag the keyframe to change the path.

■ The title changes to match the new motion path.

CONTINUED ▶

ADD MOTION TO A TITLE IN ADOBE PREMIERE

You can control the speed of the movement of the title between each of the keyframes on the Motion Path. By doing this, you can make the title appear to move faster to a spot on the screen and then move slower to the next location. You can also add keyframes to make the title stop in a location on the screen for a certain amount of time. You accomplish this by creating two keyframes and overlapping them.

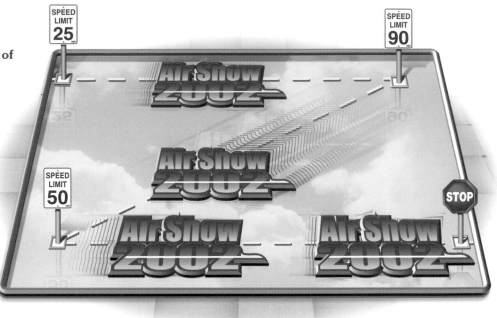

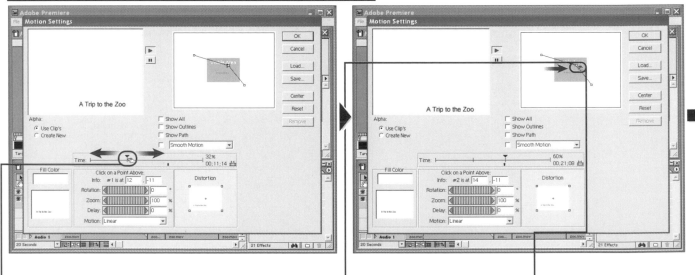

DELAY SPEED BETWEEN KEYFRAMES

9 Click and drag the keyframe marker (▼) on the Motion Timeline to adjust the delay speed.

■ Drag the marker to the left to increase speed between the start keyframe and the selected keyframe.

■ Drag the marker to the right to decrease speed between the start keyframe and the selected keyframe.

MAKE THE TITLE STOP

10 Click the Motion Path to add another keyframe.

11 Drag the keyframe on top of the existing keyframe.

Can I reuse these motion settings for another clip?

Yes, you can save your settings and apply them to another
video or title clip.

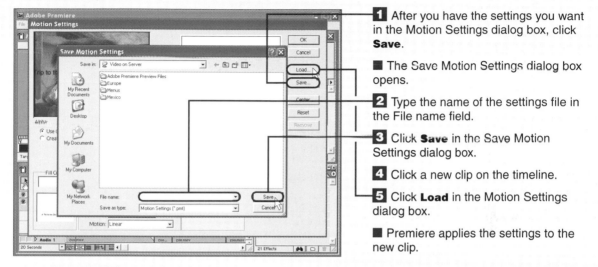

1 After you have the settings you want
in the Motion Settings dialog box, click
Save.

■ The Save Motion Settings dialog box
opens.

2 Type the name of the settings file in
the File name field.

3 Click **Save** in the Save Motion
Settings dialog box.

4 Click a new clip on the timeline.

5 Click **Load** in the Motion Settings
dialog box.

■ Premiere applies the settings to the
new clip.

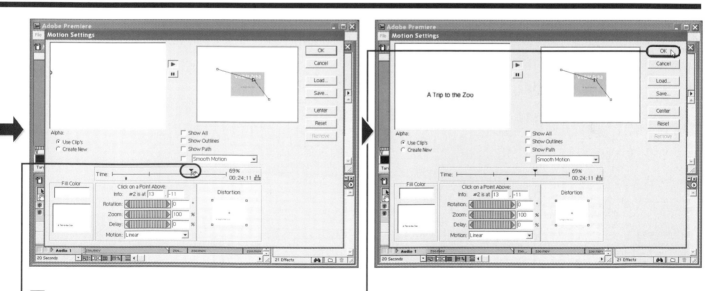

12 On the Motion Timeline,
drag the new keyframe right
to adjust the amount of time
the clip stops on the screen.

■ The longer the time
between that keyframe and
the previous keyframe, the
more time the title clip
appears to stop on the
screen.

■ The title clip stops on the
screen for the time between
the keyframes on the
timeline.

 Click **OK**.

■ Adobe saves the motion
settings for the clip.

*Note: You need to render the video
to view the title. See Chapter 14 for
information on previewing a video.*

SUPERIMPOSE A TITLE IN FINAL CUT PRO

You can add titles to your video in Final Cut Pro to introduce your video, label a scene, or even to provide movie credits. You can create titles to overlay on your video clips in Final Cut Pro, which has different types of titling. The easiest titles to apply are the Text titles you find on the Generators menu.

SUPERIMPOSE A TITLE IN FINAL CUT PRO

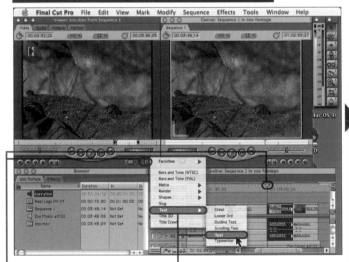

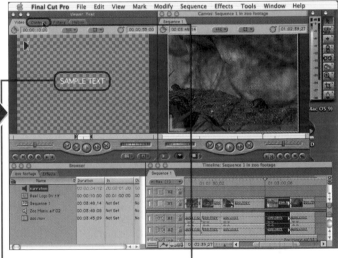

1 Click and drag the Playhead (▽) on the Timeline window to the position for the text.

2 Click the Generators button (▨▾).

■ A list of titling categories appears with Text, Title 3D, and Text Crawl providing titling options.

3 Click **Text**.

4 Click an option.

■ This example illustrates the Text option.

■ A sample title displays in the Viewer window.

5 Click the **Controls** tab.

254

What Text Title options do I have available to me?

Final Cut Pro provides six different Text Title options that you can apply in the same fashion described in the task steps. Although all options add text titles, they each create a different effect.

Title	Description
Crawl	A single line of text that scrolls horizontally across the screen.
Lower 3rd	A two-line title that displays in the lower 1/3 portion of the screen.
Outline Text	Creates outlined text that is centered on the screen. You can add a background image from any video clip.
Scrolling Text	Text that scrolls up from the bottom of the screen.
Text	Static text that displays on the screen.
Typewriter	Text displays on the screen one character at a time, as if typed by a typewriter.

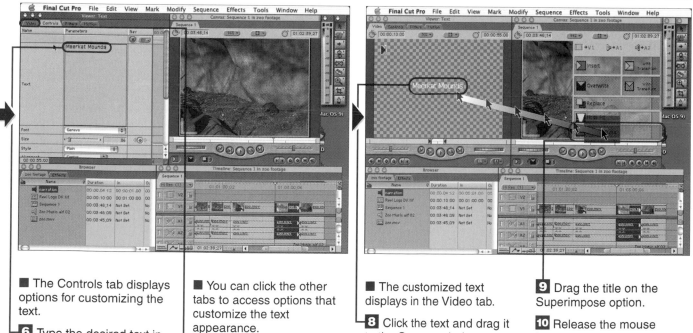

■ The Controls tab displays options for customizing the text.

6 Type the desired text in the Text field.

■ You can click the other tabs to access options that customize the text appearance.

7 Click the **Video** tab.

■ The customized text displays in the Video tab.

8 Click the text and drag it to the Canvas window.

■ A list of options displays in the Canvas window.

9 Drag the title on the Superimpose option.

10 Release the mouse button.

■ Final Cut Pro overlays the text on the selected video clip.

CREATE A 3D TITLE IN FINAL CUT PRO

You can create a 3D title to overlay your video clips in Final Cut Pro. 3D titles give your video a more professional look and you can customize them to fit the theme of your video. You add this effect by selecting the Title 3D option, which loads the Title 3D window.

CREATE A 3D TITLE IN FINAL CUT PRO

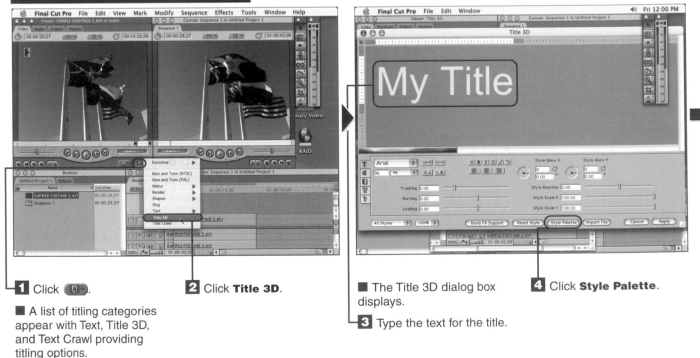

1 Click .

■ A list of titling categories appear with Text, Title 3D, and Text Crawl providing titling options.

2 Click **Title 3D**.

■ The Title 3D dialog box displays.

3 Type the text for the title.

4 Click **Style Palette**.

Can I alter the text formatting after I apply a style?

Yes, you can use any of the options on the T tab to alter your text.

Text Type and Size

Change the text type and size by clicking  next to the field and clicking a desired option.

Font Style

Click the Bold (**B**), Italics (**I**), and Underline (**U**) buttons to change the font style.

Alignment

Click these buttons to align text left (≡), center (≡), and right (≡).

Skew

Click and drag the Skew X dial (⟳) to skew the title horizontally. Click and drag the Skew Y dial (⟳) to skew the title vertically.

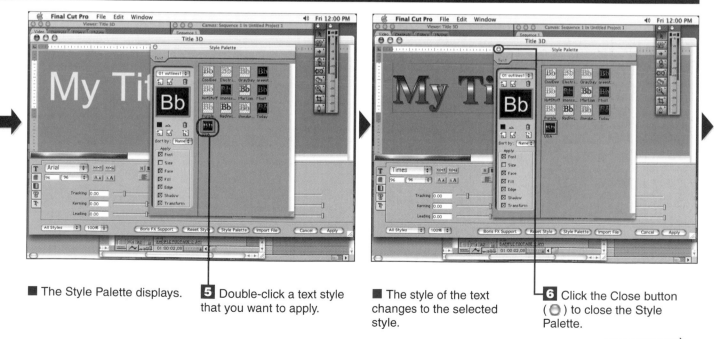

■ The Style Palette displays.

5 Double-click a text style that you want to apply.

■ The style of the text changes to the selected style.

6 Click the Close button (⊙) to close the Style Palette.

CONTINUED

CREATE A 3D TITLE IN FINAL CUT PRO

After you create a title, you need to place it on the timeline in the video track above the video clip you want to title. You must place the title in the V2 track.

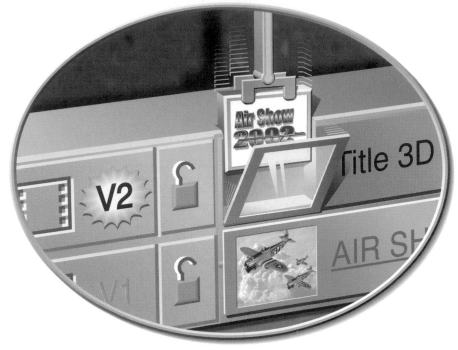

7 Click **Apply**.

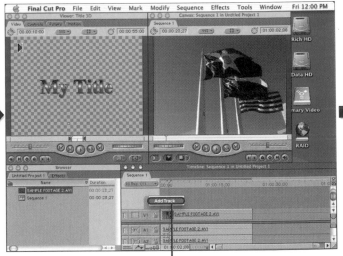

■ The title displays in the Viewer window.

8 Press Control and click the mouse on the timeline.

■ A menu displays.

9 Click **Add Track**.

How can I alter my title after adding it to the timeline?

1 Click the title clip on the timeline

2 Click the **Controls** tab on the Viewer window.

3 Click the Title 3D logo for Text Entry & Style.

■ The Title 3D window displays and you can change options by following the steps in this section.

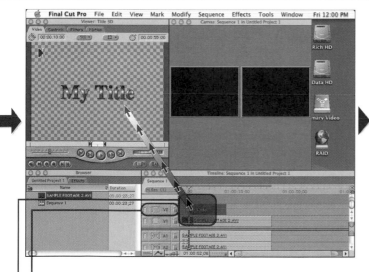

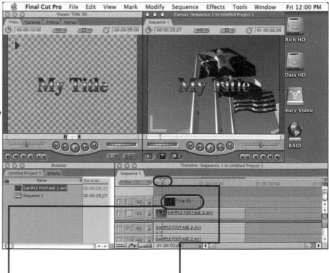

■ A V2 track displays on the timeline.

10 Click and drag the title from the Viewer window to the V2 track on the timeline.

Note: See Chapter 7 for more about the various parts of the Final Cut Pro window.

■ The title displays on the timeline.

■ You can click and drag ▽ at the title's location to view it in the Canvas window.

CHAPTER 14

Publishing Your Video

After you complete your edits to the video, you can export it so that others can view it. Before exporting, you need to render the entire video, a process where your software applies all special effects, transitions, and edits. You have several different export methods available to you depending on your planned video use. This chapter provides some good information about rendering and exporting your final video.

PREVIEW VIDEO IN ADOBE PREMIERE

You need to preview your entire video in Adobe Premiere before exporting it for others to view. With this process, you ensure that the video plays as you anticipate. When you select the Preview option, Premiere *renders*, or creates all special effects and transitions, for the entire video as specified on the timeline. Depending upon the size of the video, the rendering process may take some time.

You must also render your video in Final Cut Pro. See the section "Render Video in Final Cut Pro" for more information. You do not have to render your video in iMovie or Windows Movie Maker.

PREVIEW VIDEO IN ADOBE PREMIERE

1 Click **Project**.

2 Click **Project Settings**.

3 Click **Keyframe and Rendering**.

■ The Project Settings dialog box displays.

4 Click ▾.

5 Click **From Disk**.

6 Click **OK**.

Can I preview my video as it renders?

Yes, on the Project Settings dialog box you can click the **From Ram** option for the Preview field. If you select this option, Premiere displays each frame in the Monitor window as it renders the video.

A quicker method of previewing your video is to select the **To Screen** option for the Preview field. Although this option builds the preview quicker, it typically does not play back the effects and transitions at the appropriate speed.

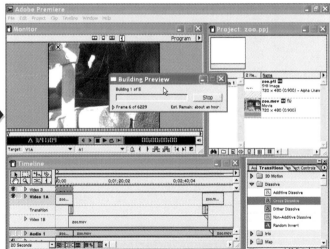

7 Click **Timeline**.

8 Click **Preview**.

■ The Building Preview dialog box displays as Premiere creates the video.

RENDER VIDEO IN FINAL CUT PRO

You need to render your video in Final Cut Pro to apply all of the special effects and transitions that you have added to your video. You can render your video at different quality levels. If you want to export your video for viewing, you should render at high quality.

You must also render your video in Adobe Premiere. See the section "Preview Video in Adobe Premiere" for more information. You do not have to render your video in iMovie or Windows Movie Maker.

RENDER VIDEO IN FINAL CUT PRO

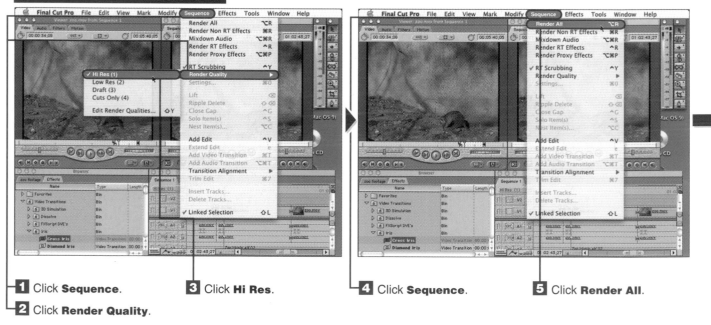

1 Click **Sequence**.

2 Click **Render Quality**.

3 Click **Hi Res**.

4 Click **Sequence**.

5 Click **Render All**.

Do I need to render at Hi Res if I am just testing my video?

No, in fact Final Cut Pro provides four different render settings that you can customize based upon your needs. To customize the rendering settings:

1 Follow steps **1** and **2** in this section.

2 Click **Edit Render Qualities**.

■ The Render Quality Editor dialog box displays.

3 Click a tab to select a render setting.

■ You can click the box next to each option (☐ changes to ☑) to select it.

4 Click **OK** to apply your changes.

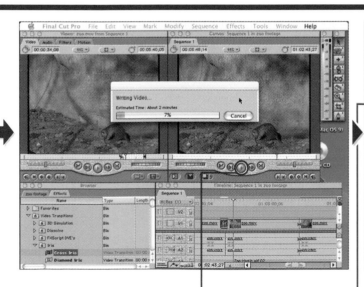

■ A dialog box displays as the video renders.

6 When the dialog box closes, click ⊙ to view the rendered video.

■ The video displays in the Canvas window.

■ Repeat steps **4** through **6** if you alter the video on the timeline.

E-MAIL VIDEO WITH WINDOWS MOVIE MAKER

You can e-mail your video directly from Windows Movie Maker using an established e-mail account on your computer. When you e-mail a movie to another person, they receive a message with your movie attached and directions on viewing it using Windows Media Player.

Please note that the e-mail option is only available in Windows Movie Maker.

E-MAIL VIDEO WITH WINDOWS MOVIE MAKER

1 Click **File**.

2 Click **Send Movie To**.

3 Click **E-mail**.

■ The Send Movie Via E-mail dialog box displays.

4 Click ⌄.

5 Click a quality level for your video.

■ If desired, type information about the video clip.

6 Click **OK**.

What quality should I select when sending my video via e-mail?

You can select any of the quality settings, but the higher the quality setting, the better the video. If you want to ensure that your recipient can view your video, select **High quality**. However, higher quality also means a larger file size and slower transfer through e-mail. E-mail servers have file size limits, so if your video file is too large, your recipient may not receive it. Selecting **Medium quality** provides a good quality video without creating an extremely large file. If you want to place your video on a Web server, you should consider saving it with the **Low quality** setting. This ensures a smaller video file, which users can easily download.

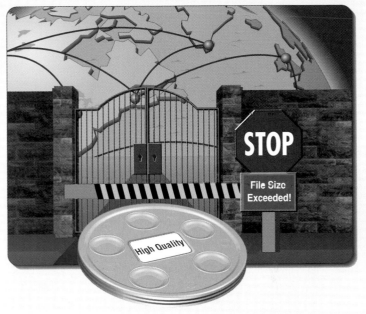

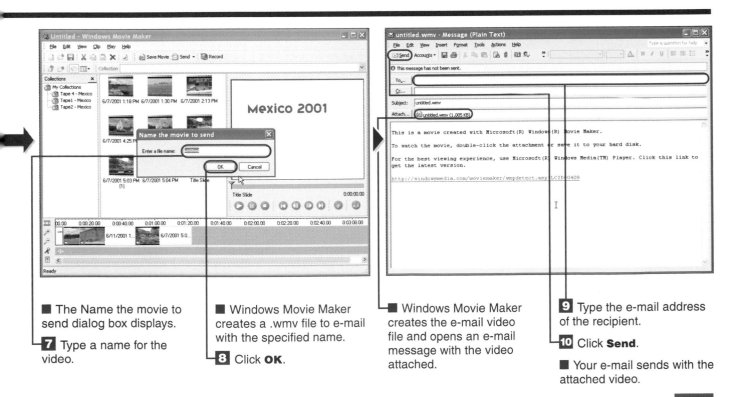

■ The Name the movie to send dialog box displays.

7 Type a name for the video.

■ Windows Movie Maker creates a .wmv file to e-mail with the specified name.

8 Click **OK**.

■ Windows Movie Maker creates the e-mail video file and opens an e-mail message with the video attached.

9 Type the e-mail address of the recipient.

10 Click **Send**.

■ Your e-mail sends with the attached video.

You can export your video for placement on a DVD. If you create a DVD, you want to export a high-quality version of the video.

Please note that the iDVD export option is only available in iMovie. The other video editing packages can also export for DVD; see the section "Export a High-Quality Video" for more information.

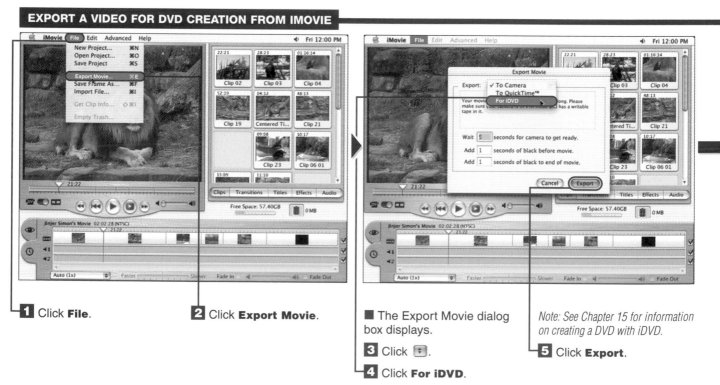

1 Click **File**.

2 Click **Export Movie**.

■ The Export Movie dialog box displays.

3 Click 🔅.

4 Click **For iDVD**.

Note: See Chapter 15 for information on creating a DVD with iDVD.

5 Click **Export**.

Do I have to use the For iDVD option in the Export Movie dialog box to create a DVD?

No. Keep in mind that DVDs allow you to store a high-quality, uncompressed version of your video. The **For iDVD** option creates a QuickTime .mov file of the highest quality. If you select **To QuickTime**, make sure you also select the Full Quality, Large format if you intend to create a DVD.

Export Movie

Export: ✓ To Camera
To QuickTime™
For iDVD

Your movie... long. Please make sure your camera... and has a writable tape in it.

Wait [5] seconds for camera to get ready.

Add [1] seconds of black before movie.

Add [1] seconds of black to end of movie.

Cancel   Export

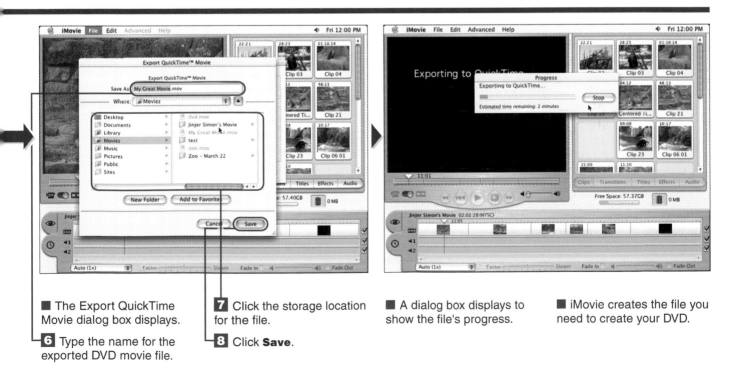

■ The Export QuickTime Movie dialog box displays.

6 Type the name for the exported DVD movie file.

7 Click the storage location for the file.

8 Click **Save**.

■ A dialog box displays to show the file's progress.

■ iMovie creates the file you need to create your DVD.

COPY VIDEO TO A DIGITAL VIDEOTAPE

You can copy your video back to a digital videotape. After you do this, you can play the tape on any digital videotape player. The easiest way to copy your tape involves connecting your digital video camera to the computer.

Although this task illustrates copying the video to a digital videotape using either Final Cut Pro or Premiere, you can also do this in iMovie. Movie Maker does not provide the option of copying video to a digital videotape.

COPY VIDEO TO A DIGITAL VIDEOTAPE

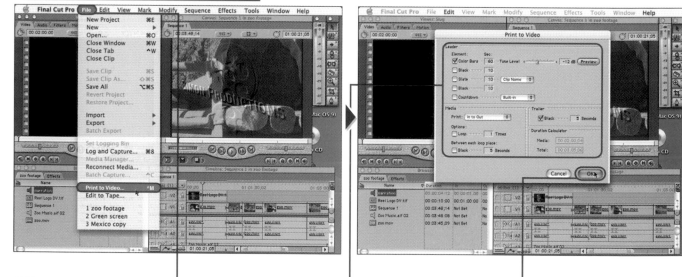

IN FINAL CUT PRO

1 Connect the video camera to the computer using the FireWire cable.

Note: See Chapter 8 for more on connecting your video camera to your computer.

2 Click **File**.

3 Click **Print to Video**.

■ The Print to Video dialog box displays.

4 Click the appropriate settings in the dialog box to specify how you want the video to copy to tape.

■ You can click the Leader options (☐ changes to ☑) to specify the video placed in front of the video footage and Trailer options for footage at the end.

5 Click **OK**.

■ Final Cut Pro copies the video to tape using the specified settings.

How do I copy video onto a digital videotape in iMovie?

After connecting your video camera to the computer using the FireWire cable:

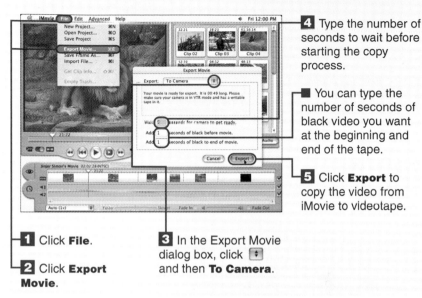

1 Click **File**.

2 Click **Export Movie**.

3 In the Export Movie dialog box, click ⬍ and then **To Camera**.

4 Type the number of seconds to wait before starting the copy process.

■ You can type the number of seconds of black video you want at the beginning and end of the tape.

5 Click **Export** to copy the video from iMovie to videotape.

IN PREMIERE

1 Connect the video camera to the computer using the FireWire cable.

Note: See Chapter 8 for more on connecting your video camera to your computer.

2 Click **File**.

3 Click **Export Timeline**.

4 Click **Print to Video**.

■ The Print to Video dialog box displays.

5 Click the appropriate settings to specify how you want the video to copy to tape (☐ changes to ☑).

■ You can type values for the Color bars and Play to specify the number of seconds in front of the video footage on the tape.

6 Click **OK**.

■ Premiere copies the video to tape using the specified settings.

EXPORT A HIGH-QUALITY VIDEO

You can create a DV-quality version of your final video. You do this to create a video that is the same quality as the original digital video footage. This allows you to import the file into other software packages with no loss of quality. For example, you use DV format in programs designed to create DVDs. For more information on DVD creation, see Chapter 15.

Although this section illustrates exporting with Adobe Premiere, you can also perform the same task in Final Cut Pro and iMovie. Windows Movie Maker does not create DV format video files.

EXPORT A HIGH-QUALITY VIDEO

1 Click **File**.

2 Click **Export Timeline**.

3 Click **Movie**.

■ The Export Movie dialog box displays.

4 Click ▼ and select the folder location for your video.

5 Replace **Untitled** by typing the name of your exported video.

Note: Do not change the extension on the filename.

6 Click **Settings**.

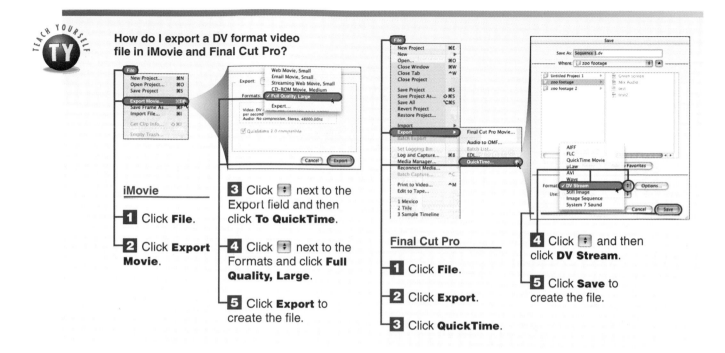

**How do I export a DV format video
file in iMovie and Final Cut Pro?**

iMovie

1 Click **File**.

2 Click **Export Movie**.

3 Click ⬍ next to the Export field and then click **To QuickTime**.

4 Click ⬍ next to the Formats and click **Full Quality, Large**.

5 Click **Export** to create the file.

Final Cut Pro

1 Click **File**.

2 Click **Export**.

3 Click **QuickTime**.

4 Click ⬍ and then click **DV Stream**.

5 Click **Save** to create the file.

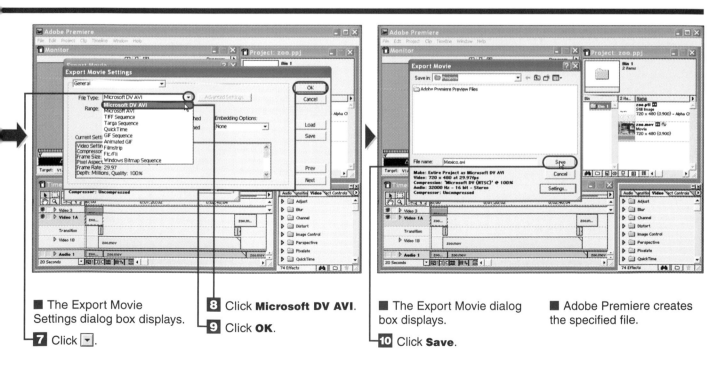

■ The Export Movie Settings dialog box displays.

7 Click ▾.

8 Click **Microsoft DV AVI**.

9 Click **OK**.

■ The Export Movie dialog box displays.

10 Click **Save**.

■ Adobe Premiere creates the specified file.

EXPORT A VIDEO CD FROM FINAL CUT PRO

You can export your video so that you can create a video CD. Because Final Cut Pro does not provide the ability to create video CDs, you need to load a program, such as Roxio Toast Titanium, for video CD creation. This software loads an option in Final Cut Pro for exporting the video so that you use it in your video CD creation.

To create a video CD with Roxio Toast Titanium using a Mac, see Chapter 15.

EXPORT A VIDEO CD FROM FINAL CUT PRO

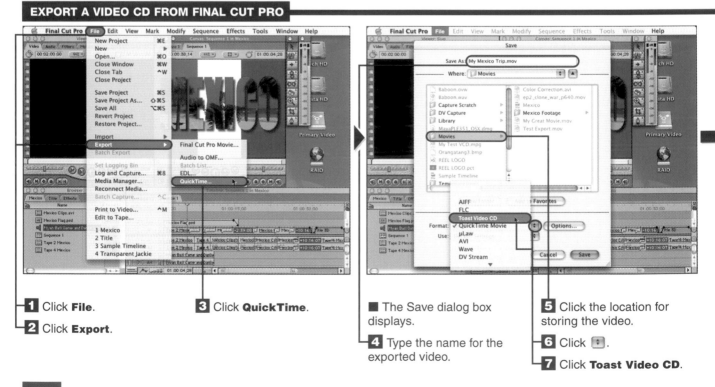

1 Click **File**.

2 Click **Export**.

3 Click **QuickTime**.

■ The Save dialog box displays.

4 Type the name for the exported video.

5 Click the location for storing the video.

6 Click 🔽.

7 Click **Toast Video CD**.

TEACH YOURSELF

Can I have the completed video export automatically open in Roxio Toast Titanium so I can create the video CD?

Yes. You do so by changing an option in the Toast Video CD Options dialog box:

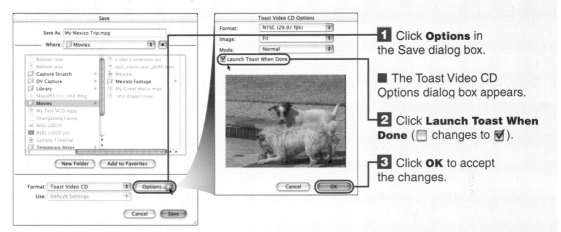

1 Click **Options** in the Save dialog box.

■ The Toast Video CD Options dialog box appears.

2 Click **Launch Toast When Done** (☐ changes to ☑).

3 Click **OK** to accept the changes.

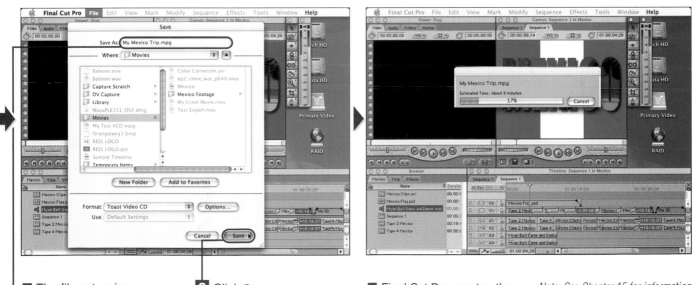

■ The file extension changes to .mpg.

8 Click **Save**.

■ Final Cut Pro creates the file needed to generate your video CD.

Note: See Chapter 15 for information on creating a video CD with Roxio Toast Titanium.

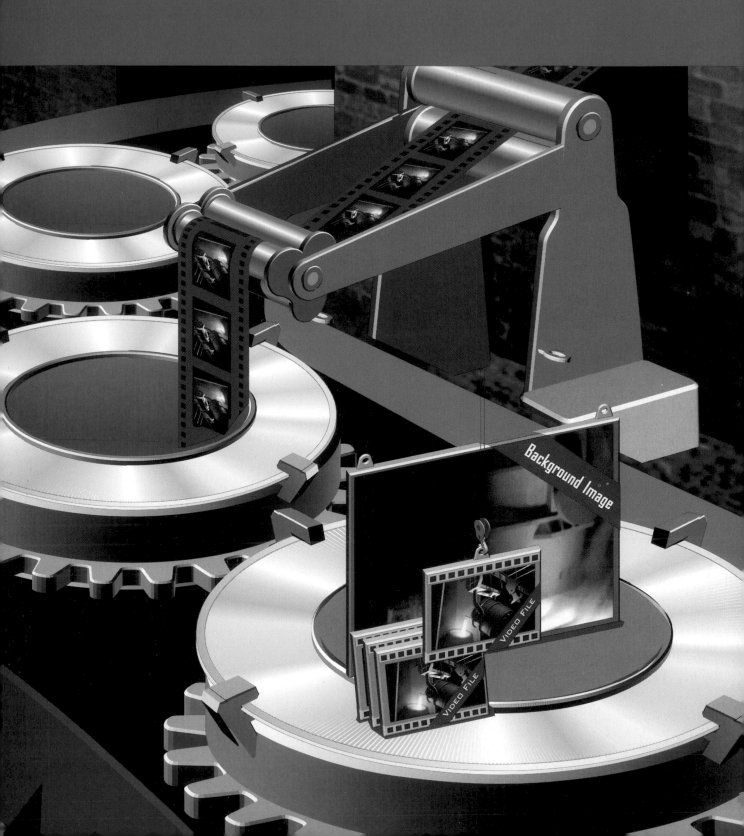

Creating a Video Disc

You can create a video disc by placing your exported video on either a Video CD or a DVD. To do so, you need a separate program designed for that task and a computer capable of burning DVDs or CDs. This chapter provides some good information about creating video discs on both the Macintosh OS X and the Microsoft Windows XP platforms.

CREATE A VIDEO CD WITH ROXIO TOAST TITANIUM ON MAC OS X

You can use Roxio Toast Titanium on your Macintosh OS X computer to create a CD to store your video files. You create the Video CD by importing MPEG files exported from Final Cut Pro or iMovie. You can then play the Video CD on any computer CD or DVD drive.

Although this section illustrates creating a video CD with Final Cut Pro, you can also create one using iMovie. See Chapter 1 for more on the other functions that a Video CD can serve. To export a video CD from Final Cut Pro, see Chapter 14.

CREATE A VIDEO CD WITH ROXIO TOAST TITANIUM ON MAC OS X

1 In the start window, click the Other button ([icon]).

2 Click **Video CD**.

3 Click **Select**.

■ The Video CD dialog box displays.

4 Click **One or more MPEG streams** (○ changes to ◉).

5 Click **OK**.

How do I create a Video CD file in iMovie?

To create a Video CD file in iMovie, you must have Roxio Toast Titanium loaded on your Macintosh computer. Once installed, you can follow these steps:

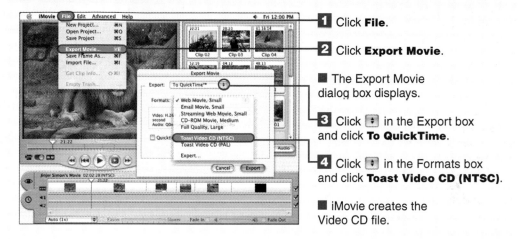

1 Click **File**.

2 Click **Export Movie**.

■ The Export Movie dialog box displays.

3 Click [✦] in the Export box and click **To QuickTime**.

4 Click [✦] in the Formats box and click **Toast Video CD (NTSC)**.

■ iMovie creates the Video CD file.

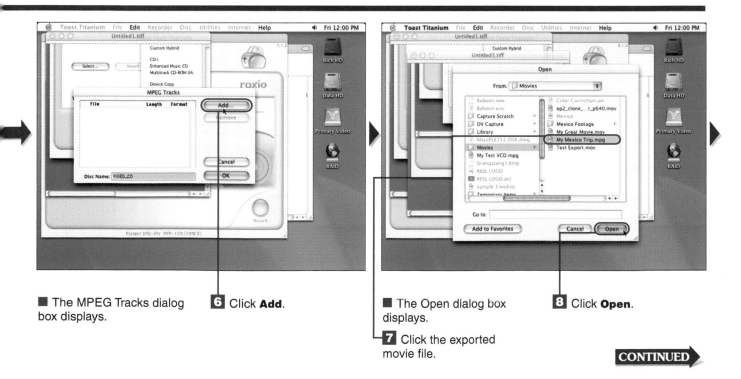

■ The MPEG Tracks dialog box displays.

6 Click **Add**.

■ The Open dialog box displays.

7 Click the exported movie file.

8 Click **Open**.

CONTINUED

CREATE A VIDEO CD WITH ROXIO TOAST TITANIUM ON MAC OS X

You can place multiple video files on the same Video CD. As you select each video file, the MPEG Tracks dialog box indicates the length of each video file.

CREATE A VIDEO CD WITH ROXIO TOAST TITANIUM ON MAC OS X (CONTINUED)

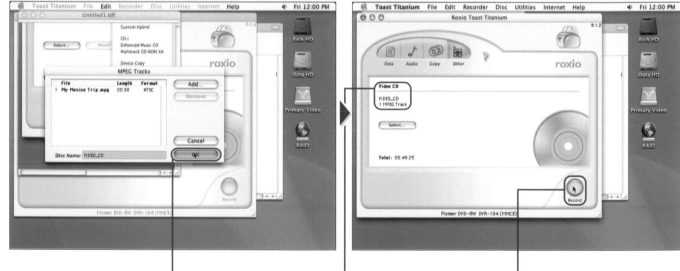

■ The MPEG Tracks dialog box displays a list of selected video files.

■ If desired, repeat steps **6** through **7** to add additional video files.

9 Click **OK**.

■ Roxio Toast Titanium indicates the number of video files, called tracks, selected for placement on the Video CD.

10 Place a CD in your CD-R drive.

11 Click **Record**.

What happens if I receive an error while burning the CD?

You may receive errors during the burning process due to problems with the speed of the CD-R. All CD-R drives and media have a maximum speed at which they can record. If your CD-R drive can record at 8x speed, but the CD-R media can only run at 2x speed, you need to select 2x speed in the Record dialog box to avoid errors.

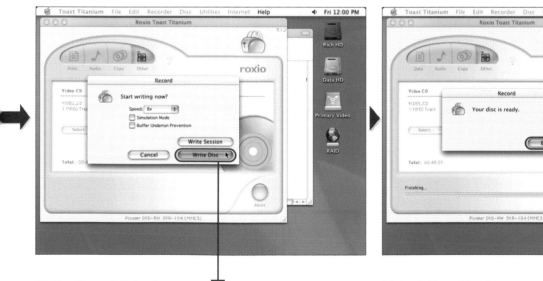

■ The Record dialog box displays.

12 Click **Write Disc**.

■ Roxio Toast Titanium burns the Video CD.

13 When the process is complete, click **Eject** to remove the CD.

CREATE A VIDEO CD WITH MGI VIDEOWAVE ON WINDOWS XP

You can use MGI VideoWave to create a Video CD using your exported video files in Windows XP. After you create a Video CD, you can play it in any computer CD or DVD drive. Also, most recent external DVD players that you connect to your television can play Video CDs.

MGI VideoWave uses a storyboard for the creation of the video for the Video CD. You can add multiple videos by placing them in the desired order on the storyboard.

CREATE A VIDEO CD WITH MGI VIDEOWAVE ON WINDOWS XP

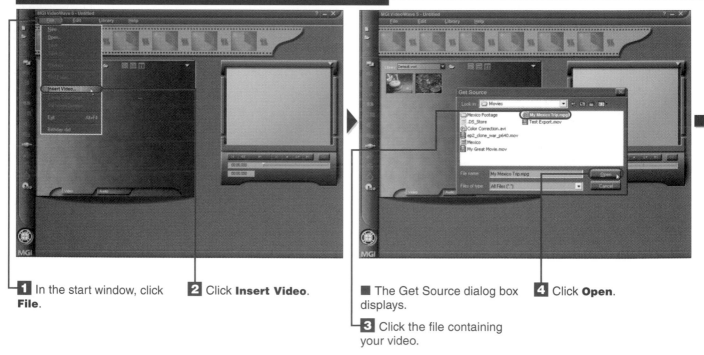

1 In the start window, click **File**.

2 Click **Insert Video**.

■ The Get Source dialog box displays.

3 Click the file containing your video.

4 Click **Open**.

Can I use MGI VideoWave to create a DVD?

Yes, this software allows you to create three different types of video discs.

DVD	High-quality video placed on a DVD disc. You can play this on computer DVD drives and standalone DVD players.
Mini-DVD	Places DVD content on a CD that most computer DVD players can read.
VCD	Creates a Video CD. MGI VideoWave places video content on a CD. You can play Video CDs on CD and DVD players in computers. They also work on most standalone DVD players.

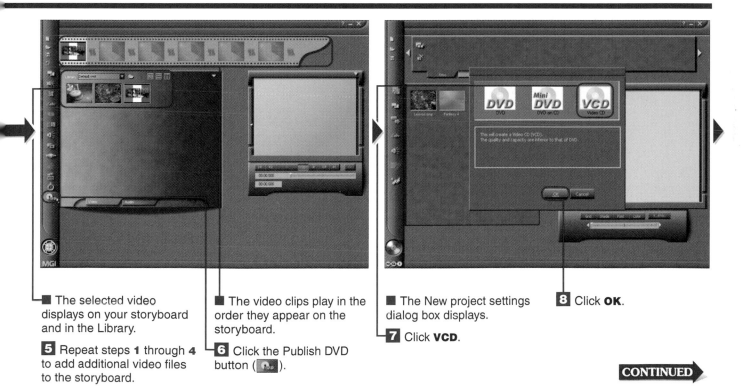

■ The selected video displays on your storyboard and in the Library.

5 Repeat steps **1** through **4** to add additional video files to the storyboard.

■ The video clips play in the order they appear on the storyboard.

6 Click the Publish DVD button ( ).

■ The New project settings dialog box displays.

7 Click **VCD**.

8 Click **OK**.

CONTINUED ▶

CREATE A VIDEO CD WITH MGI VIDEOWAVE ON WINDOWS XP

You create a Video CD by selecting your background image and then adding each video file to create a menu. The Viewscreen displays on the right side of the window. You drag the video files onto the Viewscreen to create a menu.

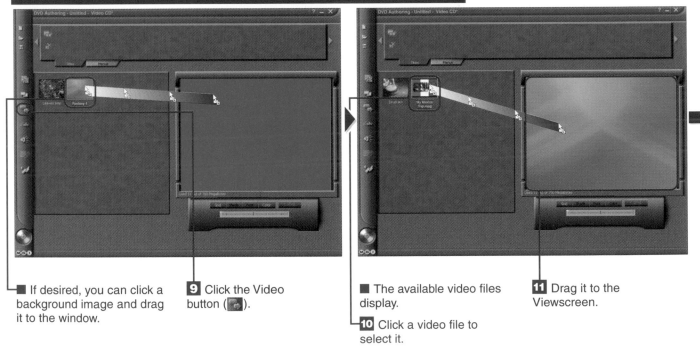

■ If desired, you can click a background image and drag it to the window.

9 Click the Video button ( ).

■ The available video files display.

10 Click a video file to select it.

11 Drag it to the Viewscreen.

**Why does the menu not display
when I play the Video CD?**

You can see the menus only if
you play your Video CD in a DVD
player. If you play the Video CD
in a CD player, you only see the
video without the menu.

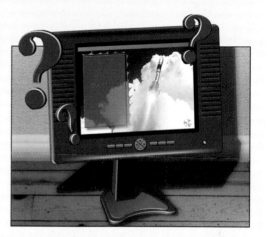

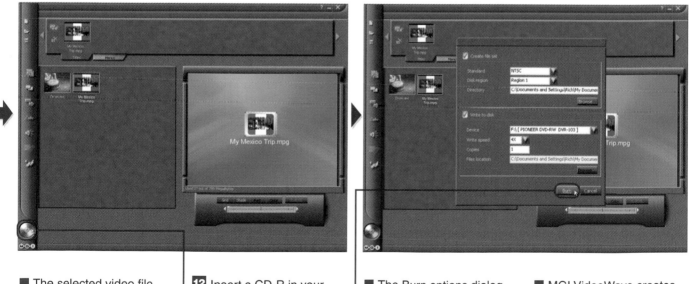

■ The selected video file
displays on the Viewscreen.

■ If you have additional
video, you can repeat steps
10 through **11**.

12 Insert a CD-R in your
drive.

13 Click the Burn
button ( ).

■ The Burn options dialog
box displays.

14 Click **Burn**.

■ MGI VideoWave creates
the Video CD.

CREATE A DVD WITH IDVD ON MAC OS X

You can use *iDVD*, a program provided with Mac OS X, to create DVDs. You create your DVD by selecting a theme and then adding your files to the menu. Most of the default templates provide an animated background if you select the Motion button.

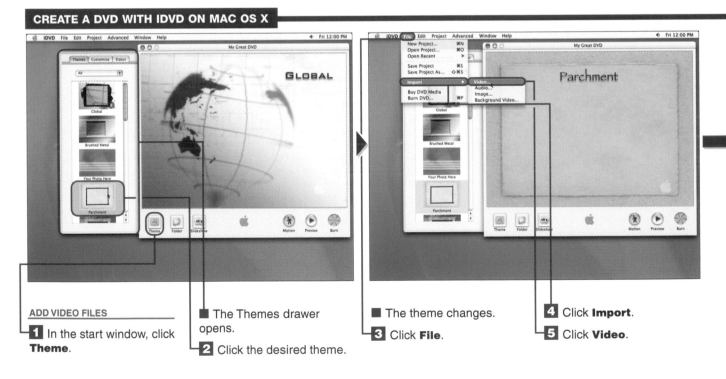

ADD VIDEO FILES

1 In the start window, click **Theme**.

■ The Themes drawer opens.

2 Click the desired theme.

■ The theme changes.

3 Click **File**.

4 Click **Import**.

5 Click **Video**.

How can I place more than 6 video files on the menu?

You can only have a total of six items on the menu with iDVD. If you want to add more than six video clips, you need to create a folder. To add a folder:

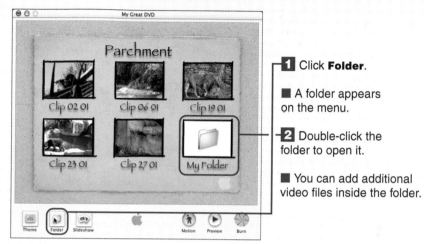

1 Click **Folder**.

■ A folder appears on the menu.

2 Double-click the folder to open it.

■ You can add additional video files inside the folder.

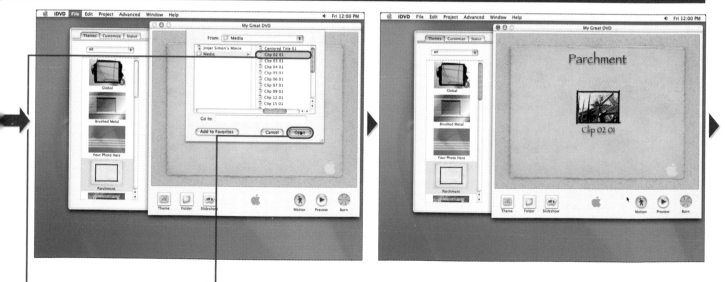

■ The Open dialog box displays.

6 Click a clip to import.

7 Click **Open**.

■ The selected video clip displays as a button on the menu.

■ You can repeat steps **3** through **7** to add additional video clips.

CONTINUED

CREATE A DVD WITH IDVD ON MAC OS X

You can customize both the menu title text and the button text. You can also specify whether the video on the button shows motion or just displays a specific video clip.

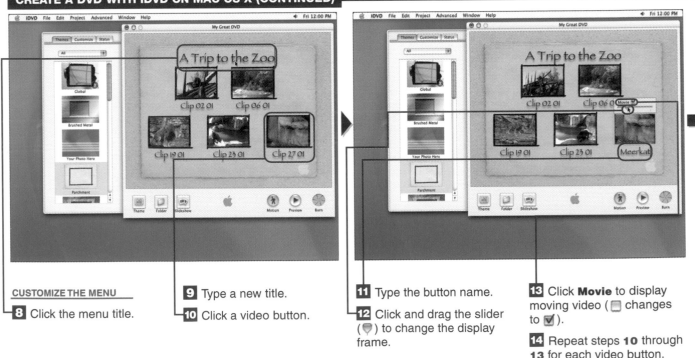

<u>CUSTOMIZE THE MENU</u>

8 Click the menu title.

9 Type a new title.

10 Click a video button.

11 Type the button name.

12 Click and drag the slider (🔵) to change the display frame.

13 Click **Movie** to display moving video (▣ changes to ☑).

14 Repeat steps **10** through **13** for each video button.

Can I change the shape of the buttons on the menu?

Yes. To customize the look of your menu:

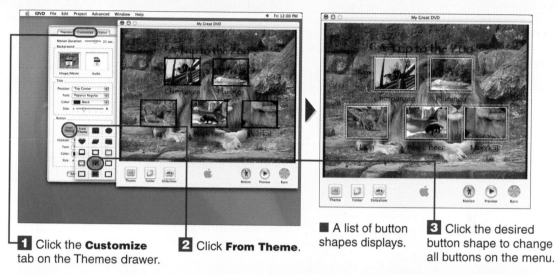

1 Click the **Customize** tab on the Themes drawer.

2 Click **From Theme**.

■ A list of button shapes displays.

3 Click the desired button shape to change all buttons on the menu.

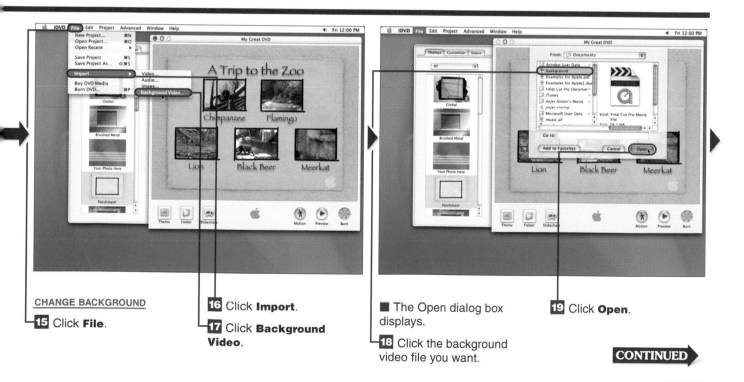

CHANGE BACKGROUND

15 Click **File**.

16 Click **Import**.

17 Click **Background Video**.

■ The Open dialog box displays.

18 Click the background video file you want.

19 Click **Open**.

CONTINUED ▶

CREATE A DVD WITH IDVD ON MAC OS X

You can preview your video within iDVD before burning the DVD. After you are happy with your menu layout, you can insert the DVD and burn the movie on it.

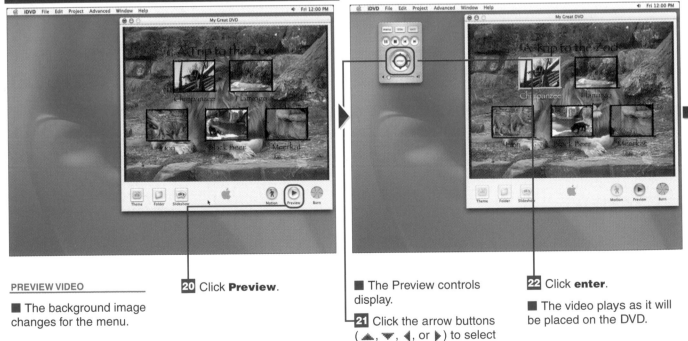

PREVIEW VIDEO

■ The background image changes for the menu.

20 Click **Preview**.

■ The Preview controls display.

21 Click the arrow buttons (▲, ▼, ◀, or ▶) to select a video button.

22 Click **enter**.

■ The video plays as it will be placed on the DVD.

What does the Motion button do?

iDVD gives you the option of displaying moving images on both the buttons and the background. If you click this button (), the motion of the background video clip displays, and each video button displays motion. You must select this button before clicking the Burn button ( ) if you want the motion to display on the burned CD. If you do not select the button, your DVD menu will have no motion.

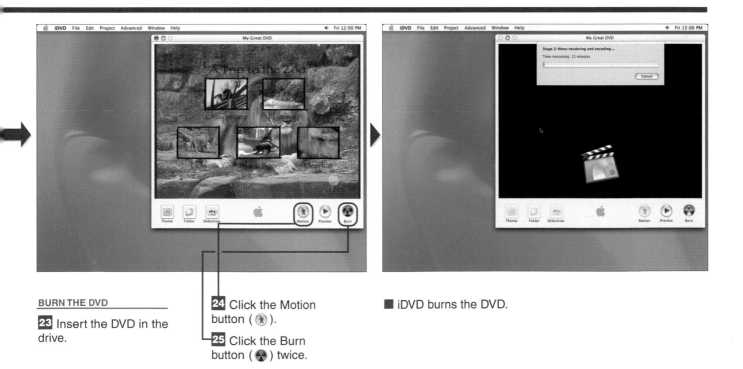

BURN THE DVD

23 Insert the DVD in the drive.

24 Click the Motion button ( ).

25 Click the Burn button ( ) twice.

■ iDVD burns the DVD.

INDEX

B

background sound, 51
backgrounds
    audio, 51
    visual. *See also* chroma keys; overlays
        lighting, 47
        remove, 218
        transparency, 234–235
backlights, 36, 44
batteries
    damage when recharging, 20
    illustration, 18
    Li-Ion (Lithium Ion), 20
    life expectancy, 21
    NiCad (Nickel Cadmium), 20
    NiMH (Nickel-Metal Hydride), 20
    quantity, 21
    recharge, 20–21
    rechargeable, 20
    size, 21
below eye-level height, 76
big close-up shot, 75
binary format, 5
bins, 124–125
bit depth, 153
blue cast, 39
blue screen. *See* chroma keys
Bluetooth technology, 31
Blur filter, 216
blurred images effect, 216
blurriness. *See* image stabilization; tripods
Border filter, 216
bounce light, 45
bright backgrounds, 47
brightness, 34
built-in microphone, 54
built-in sounds, 170
burn feature. *See* CDs/DVDs, burn
bust shot, 75

C

cables, FireWire, 99. *See also* input/output connectors
camcorders, analog, 100
camcorders, digital. *See also* digital cameras; Web cameras
    aperture
        and depth of field, 86–87
        description, 29
        settings, 34
    batteries
        damage when recharging, 20
        illustration, 18
        Li-Ion (Lithium Ion), 20
        life expectancy, 21
        NiCad (Nickel Cadmium), 20
        NiMH (Nickel-Metal Hydride), 20
        quantity, 21
        recharge, 21
        rechargeable, 20
        size, 21
    camera height, 76
    camera movement, intentional. *See* pan; zoom feature

camera movement, unintentional
    brace the camera, 83
    image stabilization, 28, 82
    monopods, 83
    shoot slowly, 83
    tripods, 83
CCDs (Charged Couple Devices), 24–25
codecs, 99
cost, 16
depth of field, 86–87
description, 13
Digital-8, 13
external power supply, 18
features, 17
frame composition
    center frames, 81
    headroom, 81
    pan, 78–79
    rule of thirds, 80
    safety margins, 81
    target zones, 80
    zoom, 84–85
hand movement, compensate for, 28
holding techniques, 82–83
image stabilization, 28
input/output connectors
    analog video, 26
    to another camcorder, 26
    to a computer. *See* FireWire
    headphones, 27
    illustration, 18
    uses for, 26–27
    to a VCR, 26
Internet access, 31
LCD screen, 19
lenses
    CCDs (Charged Couple Devices), 24–25
    change, 23
    converters, 23
    digital zoom, 23
    filters, 31
    illustration, 19
    optical zoom, 22
    plastic *vs.* glass, 22
    sizes, 22
lights, 36
microphone, 19
MiniDV, 13
operating controls, 18
optical stabilization, 28
overexposure indicator, 29
parts of, 18–19
picture button, 93
power supply, 18, 20–21
professional grade, 16–17
prosumer quality, 16
rain covers, 31
remote control, 30
shooting modes, 28
shop for, 16–17
shot types, 74–75
size, 17
sound levels, 60–61
still photos, 92–93
television-quality output, 17

INDEX

INDEX

INDEX

INDEX

INDEX